WOMEN AND PERSONAL PROPERTY IN THE VICTORIAN NOVEL

How key changes to the married women's property laws contributed to new ways of viewing women in society are revealed in Deborah Wynne's study of literary representations of women and portable property during the period 1850 to 1900. While critical explorations of Victorian women's connections to the material world have tended to focus on their relationships to commodity culture, Wynne argues that modern paradigms of consumerism cannot be applied across the board to the Victorian period. Until the passing of the 1882 Married Women's Property Act, many women lacked full property rights; evidence suggests that, for women, objects often functioned not as disposable consumer products but as cherished personal property.

Focusing particularly on representations of women and material culture in Charles Dickens, George Eliot and Henry James, Wynne shows how novelists engaged with the vexed question of women's relationships to property. Suggesting that many of the apparently insignificant items that 'clutter' the Victorian realist novel take on new meaning when viewed through the lens of women's access to material culture and the vagaries of property law, her study opens up new possibilities for interpreting female characters in Victorian fiction and reveals the complex work of 'thing culture' in literary texts.

Women and Personal Property in the Victorian Novel

DEBORAH WYNNE
University of Chester, UK

ASHGATE

Published by
Ashgate Publishing Limited
Wey Court East
Union Road
Farnham
Surrey, GU9 7PT
England
www.ashgate.com

Ashgate Publishing Company
Suite 420
101 Cherry Street
Burlington
VT 05401-4405
USA

British Library Cataloguing in Publication Data
Wynne, Deborah, 1963–
Women and personal property in the Victorian novel.
 1. English fiction – 19th century – History and criticism. 2. Law and literature – History – 19th century. 3. Property in literature. 4. Women's rights in literature. 5. Literature and society – History – 19th century. 6. Dickens, Charles, 1812–1870 – Criticism and interpretation. 7. Eliot, George, 1819–1880 – Criticism and interpretation. 8. James, Henry, 1843–1916 – Criticism and interpretation.
 I. Title
 823.8'09355–dc22

Library of Congress Cataloging-in-Publication Data
Wynne, Deborah, 1963–
 Women and personal property in the Victorian novel / by Deborah Wynne.
  p. cm.
 Includes bibliographical references and index.
 1. English fiction—19th century—History and criticism. 2. Women and literature—Great Britain—History—19th century. 3. Dickens, Charles, 1812–1870—Characters—Women. 4. Eliot, George, 1819–1880—Characters—Women. 5. James, Henry, 1843–1916—Characters—Women. 6. Women—Great Britain—Economic conditions—19th century. 7. Women in literature 8. Property in literature. 9. Material culture in literature. I. Title.

 PR878.W6W96 2010
 823'.8'09352042—dc22

                                                                      2010019051

ISBN 9780754667667 (hbk)
ISBN 9781409408970 (ebk)

Printed and bound in Great Britain by
MPG Books Group, UK

Contents

Acknowledgements

Perhaps a book about personal property should begin with an acknowledgement of the ways in which my main source of property, my labour, has been supported in terms of generous periods of research leave. The English Department at the University of Chester granted me two periods of leave, in which I began the book (in 2003–04) and worked towards its completion (in 2007–08). I would like to thank both Professor Chris Walsh, Dean of the Faculty of Humanities, and Dr Derek Alsop, Head of English, for ensuring that my project was supported. I was also fortunate enough to receive a Research Leave grant from the Arts and Humanities Research Council during the academic year 2008–09, which enabled me to finalize the book. I am very grateful for this perfectly timed opportunity. My colleagues in the English Department at Chester have been unstintingly generous and I have very much appreciated their sense of collegiality. I would also like to express my thanks to the librarians, Angela Walsh and Fiona McLean, both of whom have been extremely helpful.

I would like to thank everyone who has been generous with their time, listening to my ideas, advising me, reading draft chapters, and pointing out errors. Two people read virtually the whole of the book (and a number of chapters more than once). Anthea Trodd, whose scholarship has always been an inspiration, made many suggestions for improvement and I hope that she will accept my thanks for everything she has done to help me understand something of the intricacies of Victorian literature and culture. Chris Walsh first suggested I give Henry James another go; I am glad I did, although I still have a lot further to travel. I would like to express my thanks to Chris for his helpful comments on the various versions of chapters he read. Other colleagues, at the University of Chester and elsewhere, have kindly found time to read and comment on draft chapters. I would like to thank in particular John Bowen, Melissa Fegan, Emma Liggins, Lyn Pykett, Emma Rees and Alan Wall. The book's imperfections are, of course, entirely my responsibility. I would also like to note here my appreciation of the lunchtime discussions of the 'Victorianists': Melissa Fegan, Francesca Haig, Sarah Heaton, Emma Rees, Yvonne Siddle and Sally West, as well as my PhD students, Sue Elsley and Gina O'Brien Hill. All have discussed women and things with me and been generally inspirational.

Parts of this book have been presented at a number of venues, conferences, public lectures and staff research seminars, and I am very grateful to all of those people who invited me to speak and made useful comments and suggestions. An earlier version of Chapter 3 appeared in the online journal *19: Interdisciplinary Studies in the Long Nineteenth Century* (No 6, 2008) (www.19.bbk.ac.uk). I would like to thank Heather Tilley and Vicky Mills, the editor of the special issue on material culture, for permission to use this article. Chapter 4 includes revised material from a previously published essay. I would like to thank the Johns Hopkins University Press and the editor for permission to reprint material from 'The New Woman, Portable Property and *The Spoils of Poynton*' in the *Henry James Review* 31:2 (Spring 2010), 142–53.

I have very much appreciated the help and support of Ann Donahue, the commissioning editor at Ashgate, as well as Ashgate's two anonymous readers who have saved me from making some mistakes: I would like to record my thanks here.

My daughter Henrietta has been amazingly dutiful; not only did she reread *Clarissa* simply because I needed a few points clarifying about representations of women and property in eighteenth-century literature, but she has also never at any point looked bored when I talked (rather too much) about my research on the Victorian period. She has gently reminded me of times which were not Victorian, and cultures which were not British, and of the importance of visual as well as literary cultures. I am sorry that all of her wonderful and wide-ranging suggestions were impossible to include; the book remains stubbornly parochial (that is, Victorian and British in focus), despite her best efforts to broaden my horizons. I would like to thank her for her insights. Andrew, my partner, believed both that this book would get written when I presumed it never would and that I didn't need to be endlessly working on it. I would like to thank him for enticing me away from my desk.

Introduction

Property: Beyond the Commodity

Elizabeth Lynes, an eighteenth-century widow, owned real estate but failed to mention it in her will; instead, she listed numerous bequests of things, such as 'the great oval table and the little square table in the house along with the table in the summer house and six cane chairs'.[1] Clearly for Elizabeth Lynes property meant portable items, such as her tables and chairs. It is unthinkable that a woman listing her property in a will today would fail to mention her house; indeed, we now tend to use the term 'property' to refer to real estate rather than portable things, more often than not relegating the latter to the status of commodities, items subject to the vagaries of fashion. Indeed, modernity has come to be associated with the choosing of ephemeral objects which are only temporarily possessed. Thorstein Veblen in *The Theory of the Leisure Class*, first published in 1899, used the term 'conspicuous consumption' to refer to the habit of regularly dumping unfashionable items and buying new ones to replace them.[2] He argued that this restless relationship to commodities was a principal feature of life in a modern capitalist society. However useful the term 'conspicuous consumption' and related theories of commodity culture have been though, they do not always encompass the range and complexity of human–object relations. Usefully explaining some features of human behaviour, theories of commodity culture do not tell the whole story. Elizabeth Lynes's failure to think of herself as an owner of real estate was the result of her historical situation and we would be unwise to assume that the things listed in her will were merely commodities.[3] This book examines Victorian women's ownership of personal property (whether legally supported or illegitimate), focusing on novelists' representations of female modes of possession. It suggests that personal property should be treated less as an aspect of commodity culture and more as a complex relationship between humans and the material world.

Marx, in his theory of commodity exchange, was fully aware that not all objects could be classed as commodities. For him, an object cannot exist simultaneously as property and a commodity: indeed, commodities are defined by their movement within the market.[4] Commodities 'fall out of circulation' when they are owned.[5] When they are grounded, when they are needed for the

---

[1]   Maxine Berg, *Luxury and Pleasure in Eighteenth-Century Britain* (Oxford: Oxford University Press, 2005), p. 239.

[2]   Thorstein Veblen, *Theory of the Leisure Class* (London: Unwin, 1970), pp. 60–80.

[3]   See Berg, p. 236.

[4]   Karl Marx, *Capital* (ed.) David McLellan (Oxford: Oxford University Press, 1999), p. 53.

[5]   Ibid., *Capital*, p. 73.

individual's or group's immediate needs, they become property. The distinction Marx draws between commodities and property is important, yet few critics have considered the full implications of this.[6] Evidence suggests that many people in the nineteenth century focused on accruing portable property, keeping it and using it; they did not necessarily engage in the behaviour we now associate with conspicuous consumption. There was status to be conferred by the retention of things, and while this was an ideal, difficult times showed that even objects such as handkerchiefs and shirt buttons could be valuable, functioning flexibly, sometimes profitably in a world where the services of pawnbrokers and the ability to raise cash on possessions were vital aspects of the economy.[7] The ownership of portable property suggested stability and credit-worthiness, generating a sense of power within social and familial networks and fostering among owners a sense of identity and belonging in the world which Hannah Arendt has argued is central to the human condition.[8]

While there has been a proliferation of books on Victorian material culture in recent years, relatively few have focused on the complexly overlapping forces of the private and the public domains which characterize property ownership, or on how people used things once they had acquired them. Frank Trentmann, for example, has recently noted that the numerous studies focusing on 'purchase, acquisition, and shopping', rarely consider the issue of material use; for him, this suggests that 'historical material culture studies have been more about culture than about material'.[9] One of the most socially and politically important ways of relating to objects is ownership of them, yet an examination of the indexes of most books on Victorian material culture reveals how few critics have discussed the issue of personal property in significant detail. Even John Plotz's book, *Portable Property: Victorian Culture on the Move*, despite its title does not feature 'property' as an index item.[10] Why do so many critics of material culture overlook or elide the issue of ownership in relation to objects? One reason may be that property ownership now tends to refer to land and houses, or at least more economically significant items than spoons and chairs. This reluctance to think about things as property comes at a time when there is a strong interest in acquiring Victorian material objects, from photographs and ornaments to crockery and furniture, the myriad of

---

[6]   Peter Stallybrass in 'Marx's Coat' in Patricia Spyer (ed.), *Border Fetishisms: Material Objects in Unstable Places* (New York and London: Routledge, 1998) is an exception; he offers a fascinating analysis of Marx's property in the form of his coat.

[7]   See Stallybrass for a discussion of the importance of the pawnshop in the Victorian period. In Chapter 2 I discuss Dickens's attachment to shirt buttons.

[8]   See Hannah Arendt, *The Human Condition* (Chicago: University of Chicago Press, 1969). See also Frank Trentmann, 'Materiality in the Future of History: Things, Practices and Politics', *Journal of British Studies*, 48 (April 2009), pp. 286 and 288.

[9]   Trentmann, p. 291.

[10]   John Plotz, *Portable Property: Victorian Culture on the Move* (Princeton: Princeton University Press, 2008). His focus is on the portability of things, rather than their capacity to be owned. See particularly his Introduction, 'The Global, the Local, and the Portable', pp. 1–23.

mass-produced objects from the past which have survived the people who made and first owned them. Online retail outlets and auctions now facilitate the desire to own Victorian things, fragments of the past which have 'fallen out of circulation' only to recirculate in a different context.[11] This shopping for fragments of the past may help to explain the turn in academia towards material culture, which as Trentmann suggests, could be a response to a sense of guilt about being 'neglectful owners'; we have found new approaches to material culture studies as a way to express the 'more humble, caring attitude to things [that] will make for a more realistic, ecologically safer way of dealing with problems in human-nonhuman relations'.[12] Moreover, the very survival of the material world can act as a tribute to human responsibility. As Csikszentmihalyi and Rochberg-Halton have stated in *The Meaning of Things*, '[t]o preserve a breakable object from its destiny one must pay at least some attention to it. ... Thus a china cup preserved over a generation is a victory of human purpose over chaos'.[13] This aspect of the object world, the associations with identity, memory and affect, means that *things* cannot always be reduced to the category of the commodity; in some contexts even items of low monetary value, such as mass-produced teacups and chairs, need to be read in terms of property, for property embodies qualities we associate with human ideals of stability, an attribute which the commodity lacks. As Igor Kopytoff reminds us:

> Out of the total range of things available in a society, only some of them are considered appropriate for marking as commodities. Moreover, the same thing may be treated as a commodity at one time and not at another. And finally, the same thing may, at the same time, be seen as a commodity by one person and as something else by another.[14]

We need to be sensitive to these nuances when we consider objects in their historical and cultural contexts.

From early material culture studies from the 1970s and 1980s, such as Peter Conrad's *The Victorian Treasure-House* and Asa Briggs's *Victorian Things*, to more recent theoretically informed work, numerous books and articles have highlighted the significance of things in Victorian society and attempted to account for their prominent place in Victorian fictional narratives.[15] Two notable recent books on

[11]   See Cora Kaplan, *Victoriana: Histories, Fictions, Criticism* (Edinburgh: Edinburgh University Press, 2007) for an interesting discussion of the role of Victorian things, culture and literature in the twentieth and twenty-first centuries.

[12]   Trentmann, p. 292.

[13]   Mihaly Csikszentmihalyi and Eugene Rochberg-Halton, *The Meaning of Things: Domestic Symbols and the Self* (Cambridge: Cambridge University Press, 1981), p. 83.

[14]   Igor Kopytoff, 'The Cultural Biography of Things: Commoditization as Process' in Arjun Appadurai (ed.), *The Social Life of Things: Commodities in Cultural Perspective* (Cambridge: Cambridge University Press, 1986), p. 64.

[15]   Peter Conrad, *The Victorian Treasure-House* (London: Collins, 1973) and Asa Briggs, *Victorian Things* (London: B.T. Batsford, 1988).

this subject are Elaine Freedgood's *The Ideas in Things: Fugitive Meaning in the Victorian Novel* and Plotz's *Portable Property: Victorian Culture on the Move*. Both attempt to curb the over-simplified view that commodity culture 'explains' the representation of things in Victorian novels. Freedgood states that:

> our readings [of Victorian novels] are more often symptomatic of our own immersion in commodity culture than of the critical dictates or demands of realism itself. … We imagine that the realist novel 'thinks' about things the way that we do, or that we have learned commodity thinking from the novel and its representational traditions. We then fail to discern a culture that may have preceded commodity culture: what I call 'thing culture'.[16]

There has been a lot of 'commodity thinking' over recent decades, much of which has been influential on readings of Victorian literature. However, with the term 'thing culture', Freedgood modifies this way of thinking: for her, '[c]ommodity culture happened slowly' and people's relationships towards things evolved in complex ways.[17] She also states that during the Victorian period 'commodification was less secure, less consistently triumphant than we have imagined'.[18] Plotz also qualifies the emphasis on commodity culture, arguing that Victorian objects are 'dually endowed: they are at once products of the cash market and, potentially, the rare fruits of a highly sentimentalized realm of value'.[19] This growing scepticism towards the view that commodity culture constitutes the grand narrative of the Victorian period is most welcome. These studies have informed my own thinking; however, neither Freedgood nor Plotz pay much heed to the issue of property ownership. The study of ownership practices is the focus of *Women and Personal Property in the Victorian Novel*, which attempts to understand the political dimensions of material culture, what Trentmann has termed 'material politics', an attempt to find ways of 'providing a bridge between histories of politics and material culture'.[20]

The recent emergence of thing theory as a mode of enquiry has also played its part in moving us away from the reductive presumption that all things represented in literature are commodities.[21] Thing theorists bring literary objects into the foreground, exploring them in ways which resist traditional assumptions that things are there only as local colour or background detail. Indeed, thing theory has illuminated the way in which we discriminate against objects when we presume

---

[16]   Elaine Freedgood, *The Ideas in Things: Fugitive Meaning in the Victorian Novel* (Chicago: University of Chicago Press, 2006), p. 142.

[17]   Ibid., p. 8.

[18]   Ibid., p. 157.

[19]   Plotz, p. 2.

[20]   Trentmann, p. 286.

[21]   Brown, Bill, *A Sense of Things: The Object Matter of American Literature* (Chicago: University of Chicago Press, 2003).

that they are secondary, less important than human subjects, mere props in the stage business of human lives. Bill Brown has stated that:

> As they circulate through our lives, we look *through* objects (to see what they disclose about history, society, nature, or culture – above all, what they disclose about *us*), but we only catch a glimpse of things. We look through objects because there are codes by which our interpretive attention makes them meaningful, because there is a discourse of objectivity that allows us to use them as facts. A *thing*, in contrast, can hardly function as a window. … The story of objects asserting themselves as things, then, is the story of a changed relation to the human subject.[22]

While thing theory's approach to literary objects has influenced my approach to material culture studies, it has had a limited usefulness for this book, which considers things as they form a part of a property relationship. In other words, I emphasize the concept of ownership more than objects themselves. This is not to say that I see objects as unimportant; however, because property is a *relationship* it is impossible to separate things from the people who own them.[23] As Susan Pearce has argued, '[a]n ownerless object is a contradiction in terms, and objects which happen to stray often find masters, even objects which have sunk pretty far down in the rubbish category'.[24] Ownership has tended to be dismissed as unimportant by many thing theorists in their concern with the autonomy of objects; they look beyond their relationships to humans. I, on the other hand, emphasize the reciprocal relationships between humans and objects, seeing things as they exist as parties within a property relationship which is framed by the law and custom, but which also functions as a source of affect.

Thing theory has emerged from the groundbreaking work of writers such as Andrew H. Miller, whose theorization of commodity culture, *Novels Behind Glass: Commodity Culture and Victorian Narrative*, indicates numerous ways in which we can read material culture in the context of literary representation. Nevertheless, he does not fully explore the differences between nineteenth-century attitudes towards objects and modern consumer practices. He asserts that for the Victorians '[o]bjects are valuable not as they are used, but as they are exchanged; commodities realize their full economic and psychological value only at the moment one no longer possesses them'.[25] I want to argue the opposite: as far as most Victorians were concerned, objects were largely valuable when

---

[22]   Bill Brown, 'Thing Theory', *Critical Inquiry*, 28:1 (Autumn 2001): 4; emphasis in the original.

[23]   This notion of property as a relationship, rather than a thing, is discussed more extensively in Chapter 1.

[24]   Susan M. Pearce, *On Collecting: An Investigation into Collecting in the European Tradition* (London: Routledge, 1995), p. 170.

[25]   Andrew H. Miller, *Novels Behind Glass: Commodity Culture and Victorian Narrative* (Cambridge: Cambridge University Press, 1995), p. 34.

they stopped circulating as commodities and were retained and used as personal property. In the novels of the period, as subsequent chapters will demonstrate, the exchange of objects for money often constituted failure. This book focuses on the relationship between consumption and ownership practices (or Trentmann's concept of 'material politics') in the context of women, property and the law. The term 'property' today seems inappropriate in relation to 'trivial' and 'feminized' items such as teapots, ribbons and ornaments. This, as I will demonstrate, was not the case before the twentieth century, when all but the wealthiest focused on the potential in portable personal property as a source of status and a basis for well-being. Nevertheless, despite a modern unwillingness to see such things specifically as property, the important work done by critics such as Miller, Brown, Freedgood, Plotz and Trentmann offers ample evidence that the things represented in fiction are neither accidental nor superfluous.

My argument is based on the premise that all property relationships entail the performance of ownership; indeed, as we will see in Chapter 1, property ownership can be performative, for the speech act 'I own' actually constitutes ownership in certain circumstances. Indeed, female ownership is usually represented in literature in relation to certain performances and acts of assertion.[26] *Women and Personal Property in the Victorian Novel* is, then, concerned with how women used objects as property, reading women's attachments to objects as more significant than accounts of commodity culture and the female consumer suggest.[27] Modern paradigms of female consumerism, on one important level at least, are not applicable to a society where many women lacked full property rights. Until the passing of the Married Women's Property Act in 1870, wives were prohibited under common law from owning property. This context, if nothing else, should prompt us to hesitate before making presumptions about the modernity of Victorian attitudes towards the material world. It is also helpful to bear in mind that Victorian novelists represented women's practices of possession at a time when there were relatively few female owners of real property (that is, land and houses). Indeed, most wives were prohibited from owning property, a situation which should be emphasized, for before the 1870s marriage led to dispossession for most women. This legal disability framed wives' relationships to the material world. Under the common law, unreformed since the medieval period, women lost all legal rights on marriage, including the right to retain and control their property

---

[26] For a fascinating discussion of speech acts and performativity which draws productively on the work of J.L. Austin and Judith Butler, see Eve Kosofsky Sedgwick, *Touching Feeling: Affect, Pedagogy, Performativity* (Durham: Duke University Press, 2003).

[27] See in particular A.H. Miller; Christoph Lindner, *Fictions of Commodity Culture: From the Victorian to the Postmodern* (Aldershot: Ashgate, 2003); and Rachel Bowlby, *Just Looking: Consumer Culture in Dreiser, Gissing and Zola* (New York and London: Methuen, 1985).

because the law of 'coverture' meant that husbands 'covered' their wives' identity and publicly they existed as 'one'.[28]

Chapter 1 considers the law of coverture in detail, charting the reaction against patriarchal Roman law which took place from the 1850s onwards, when feminists demanded its abolition.[29] After years of debate in Parliament and in the press, the Married Women's Property Acts were passed in 1870, 1882 and 1893, eventually conferring full property rights on wives. Before the passing of the Acts, the denial of property ownership acted as a denial of legal identity for married women; nevertheless wives were able to find ways of overcoming their disability. Their tactics, and the representation of these in novels, along with a consideration of the objects which women used as their property, form the main focus of *Women and Personal Property in the Victorian Novel*. This book is threaded through by a series of related questions: How could a wife feel like the owner of something when she was denied legal rights to ownership? How far did the emergence of the feminist movement and the debates in Parliament influence the ways in which women and portable property were represented in the fiction of the period? Can the legal and social objectification of women be seen as relevant to the representations of female characters strongly identifying with, even forging reciprocal relationships with, the object world? I attempt to address these questions by closely examining a range of texts, as they represented women and things. My main focus, however, is the novels of the period. Novels do not simply reflect life; they do the important cultural work of exploring ideals, aspirations and anxieties. Literature thus exposes areas of experience which cannot be articulated so clearly in other forms of representation.

The prominent role of personal portable property in Victorian women's lives and in the literature and society of the period is the subject of this book; however, some readers may ask why I don't include the situation of Victorian men in my discussion, particularly when the most famous fictional promoter of portable property is Dickens's suburban clerk, Wemmick, in *Great Expectations* (1860).[30] There are two reasons for this. Firstly, most Victorian novels are peculiarly preoccupied with women's attachments to objects whether in the form of a love of expensive luxury items, an emotional relationship towards objects (such as memorials, love tokens or other sources of affect), or as semi-comic devotions towards 'insignificant' things such as teapots or bonnets. Secondly, the issue of women's ownership of property constituted a source of anxiety to a much

---

[28] For discussions of coverture see Lee Holcombe, *Wives and Property: Reform of the Married Women's Property Law in Nineteenth-Century England* (Toronto and Buffalo: University of Toronto Press, 1983), and Mary Lyndon Shanley, *Feminism, Marriage and the Law in Victorian England, 1850–1895* (London: I.B. Tauris, 1989).

[29] I am using the term 'feminist' somewhat anachronistically for it was first introduced in the 1890s. See Susan Kingsley Kent, *Sex and Suffrage in Britain, 1860–1914* (Princeton: Princeton University Press, 1987), p. 24.

[30] Wemmick will be discussed in more detail in Chapters 1 and 2.

greater degree than men's relationship to property. Male conflicts of ownership in Victorian novels tend to centre on money and real property, legal disputes based on inheritance or the misguided investment of capital and unwise speculation. In regard to male characters, property is usually related to business transactions, with fewer specific representations of men's emotional relationships towards personal property. Indeed, despite Wemmick's eccentric approach to the collecting of mourning jewellery, he does not share many female attitudes towards portable property, perhaps because he is also the owner of real estate at Walworth. This book focuses on women and their complicated relationships with things because so many Victorian novelists chose to represent these in powerful, sometimes disturbing and often contradictory ways, ways which have often been misread by critics imposing paradigms of twentieth- and twenty-first-century commodity culture on texts from the past.

Nevertheless, notions of gender difference cannot be overlooked for they were crucial in terms of the shifting legal frameworks of the property laws of the period. As Joan W. Scott has stated, '[p]olitical history has, in a sense, been enacted on the field of gender. It is a field that seems fixed yet whose meaning is contested and in flux'.[31] The issue of gender definition, along with the perceived threat of the unfixing of gender categories, was a troubling feature of the property debates in the period 1850 to 1900, when wives gradually gained legal recognition as autonomous individuals.[32] The Victorian novel's interest in, indeed focus on, female experience contributed to the cascade of definitions and counter-definitions of gender characteristics which grew out of the political and cultural shifts in nineteenth-century society. As Sharon Marcus has stated in *Between Women*, '[t]he nineteenth-century novel was one of the most important cultural sites for representing and shaping desire, affect, and ideas about gender and the family', and literature both represented and contributed to what she terms the 'Victorian gender system'.[33] I suggest that one of the ways in which this system was constructed was through human–object relationships. Indeed, property, as a concept and relationship, was central to Victorian society; Kathy Alexis Psomiades has argued that it even offered writers a 'language':

> The language of women and property fills Victorian novels and the writings of Victorian feminists alike not because these are the existing terms through which the culture thinks gender difference, but because these terms themselves are a

---

[31] Joan W. Scott, 'Gender: A Useful Category of Historical Analysis', *The American Historical Review*, 91:5 (December 1986): 1074.

[32] See Holcombe and Shanley for perceptive discussions of the passing of the Married Women's Property Acts.

[33] Sharon Marcus, *Between Women: Friendship, Desire and Marriage in Victorian England* (Princeton: Princeton University Press, 2007), pp. 8 and 27.

way of thinking through the increasing irrationality attached to the notion that men and women have different relations to property.[34]

However, the irrationality of patriarchal law ironically created opportunities for women, as well as restricting them. As this book demonstrates, Victorian women could sometimes ignore the legal strictures of coverture, even remain unaware of them, creating for themselves *feelings* of ownership which, while not supported by the law, were rarely challenged.

Yet occasionally wives could be made starkly aware of their non-existent rights. A well-known example concerns Millicent Garrett Fawcett, who only discovered that she did not legally own the purse she used when a pickpocket stole it and she heard in court that the thief was charged with 'stealing from the person of Millicent Fawcett a purse containing £1 18s. 6d., the property of Henry Fawcett [her husband]'.[35] No doubt she had up until then *believed* that she owned the purse and the money within it. Although Millicent Fawcett received a shock about her situation as a property owner, most of the time the law was unlikely to remind married women of their actual relations to personal property. As Anthony Trollope's narrator in *Framley Parsonage*, published in 1861, states when the bailiffs enter the Reverend Mark Robarts's home, 'O ladies, who have drawing-rooms in which the things are pretty, good, and dear to you, think of what it would be to have two bailiffs rummaging among them'.[36] In 1861, wives may have empathized with the sense of loss and violation represented in Trollope's novel without necessarily realizing that this loss, in one sense, had already been imposed on them by the law. This slippage between female experience and the law was not, as we will see in subsequent chapters, always evident to Victorians living through a period of major reforms of the marriage and property laws. Nevertheless, painful moments of realization of women's dispossessed state punctuate nineteenth-century novels.

This book is not, of course, the first to highlight the fact that female property ownership figures in fascinating and contradictory ways in the Victorian novel. Jeff Nunokawa in *The Afterlife of Property: Domestic Security and the Victorian Novel*, for example, suggests that Victorian novels present property both as something desirable and something which must be lost.[37] He argues persuasively that novelists represent women as antidotes to property ownership, forms of 'domestic treasure' which offer the illusion of stability: he states, 'women were

---

[34]   Kathy Alexis Psomiades, 'Heterosexual Exchange and Other Victorian Fictions: *The Eustace Diamonds* and Victorian Anthropology', *Novel*, 33:1 (Autumn 1999): 93–118, p. 99.

[35]   Quoted in Holcombe, p. 3.

[36]   Anthony Trollope, *Framley Parsonage* (Oxford: Oxford University Press, 1988), p. 527.

[37]   Jeff Nunokawa, *The Afterlife of Property: Domestic Security and the Victorian Novel* (Princeton: Princeton University Press, 1994), p. 8. See Walter Schmidgen in *Eighteenth-Century Fiction and the Law of Property* (Cambridge: Cambridge University Press, 2002) for a useful analysis of the role of property in the eighteenth-century novel.

enlisted as a form of estate that replaced insecure marketplace property'.[38] A similar point is made by Tim Dolin in *Mistress of the House: Women of Property in the Victorian Novel* when he argues that Victorian novelists presented 'the woman in the house ... as a powerful icon of stable property' and, for middle-class men, a 'substitute for landed property'.[39] Dolin's main concern is with the female owner of land, considering how she 'crosses over and occupies the conventional symbolic space of the woman-as-property'.[40] Nunokawa and Dolin offer insights into the ways in which Victorian society, perceiving the woman of property as a problem, attempted to reconfigure her as 'woman-as-property'. While my book draws upon their discussions, it also considers some of the wider definitions of property at work in the Victorian period, particularly the culture of personal property which has so often been misread for commodity culture.[41] Thus, the female owner of real estate, the main focus of Dolin's book, is not the focus of this book. My concern is with women's less substantial property, even down to personal items such as handkerchiefs, bags, pincushions and tablecloths, things which have not registered as important. Yet such things could be as important as real property to Victorian women, functioning as tangible aids to identity at a time when for men the identity of the property owner conferred voting rights. The 'property qualification', whereby only those men who owned property of a certain value (both as land and as money) were entitled to vote, meant that working-class men and all women were likely to have viewed the ownership of property as a necessary first step towards social recognition.[42]

This book shows the ways in which property relationships were framed by, and framed, gender relationships in the Victorian era. Existing in a precarious relationship to property, Victorian women employed numerous tactics to gain a hold on the object world. Chapter 1 discusses the ironic situation whereby many Victorian wives, constructing their worlds by means of objects, were not the legal owners of the things they considered to be their property. As Susan Pearce has argued, 'one major function of possessions is to manipulate the environment' in an attempt 'to construct a special private world which [the owner] can control directly in a wide range of ways'.[43] Victorian women's appropriation of things, even if this was only a magpie grouping of odds and ends which was not supported

---

[38]   Nunokawa, pp. 10, 15 and 98.

[39]   Tim Dolin, *Mistress of the House: Women of Property in the Victorian Novel* (Aldershot: Ashgate, 1997), p. 7.

[40]   Ibid., p. 8.

[41]   See Plotz for a useful discussion of the Victorian culture of portable property in relation to travel and the empire. However, he makes no mention of the ways in which gender framed the ownership of portable property, or indeed the issue of property rights which was a contentious one for much of the period.

[42]   See Asa Briggs, *Victorian People* (London: Penguin, 1965), p. 249 for details of the franchise and the imposition of a £10 'property qualification'.

[43]   Pearce, p. 174.

by the law, put them in the position of possessors, able to 'manipulate', 'construct' and 'control' not only their immediate environments, but also their sense of themselves as social beings. Chapter 2 discusses the novels of Charles Dickens and his representations of female owners and modes of possession, from the concept of collective ownership explored in *Bleak House* (1853) to the possessive and perverse individualism of Mrs Clennam and Miss Havisham in his later novels. Chapter 3 considers George Eliot's representations of women's relationships to the material world, particularly the problems and pleasures experienced by her renunciating heroines, Maggie Tulliver and Dorothea Brooke, as well as her female materialists, such as Rosamond Vincy and Gwendolen Harleth. Henry James's contemplations on female possessions form the basis of Chapter 4. His novels complicate representations of the woman of property, for he focuses on the tensions between the renunciating Victorian heroine and the *fin-de-siècle* New Woman.

These authors pay considerable attention to women's relationships with objects; they each respond to the issues raised by the marriage reform movement as well as thinking deeply about the concept of ownership. Additionally, they were each emotionally attached to their personal property, as their letters and journals reveal. Repeatedly they recount their fondness for, and fetishization of, a miscellany of objects, from watches and buttons to clothes and ornaments. Sometimes these cherished items functioned as 'biographical objects', objects which become intimately bound up in an individual's life so that they function as integral parts of a person's identity.[44] For Dickens, as we will see, his desk ornaments were particularly important to him, so much so that he carefully bequeathed them in his will. Eliot found the small home-made gifts donated by female admirers and friends a repeated source of pleasure, offering a sense of inclusion in a loving community of women. James was fascinated by a range of 'feminine' objects, from jewellery to items of clothing, some of which came temporarily into his possession and afforded him inspiration for his work. Dickens, Eliot and James were also ambiguous in their approaches to the concept of possession, this being seen both as a pleasurable human need for contact with the material world and potentially a source of moral decline.

Importantly, all three novelists depended for an income on their portable property, their labour in the form of literary property, and each found this vulnerable to piracy at some time during their careers. The tenuousness of writing as property before the development of international copyright law can be seen as analogous to the tenuousness of women's property on marriage before the 1882 Married Women's Property Act: both author and wife were largely dependent on

---

[44] The term 'biographical objects' (to signify both the life story of objects and the objects which become a part of an individual's identity) is discussed by Janet Hoskins in 'Agency, Biography and Objects' in *Handbook of Material Culture*, Christopher Tilley (ed.) (London: Sage, 2006), pp. 74–84. See also Kopytoff for a different interpretation of the biographical object. The concept of biographical objects will be discussed in more detail in the following chapters.

the goodwill of those who were free to appropriate their property. This is an issue which helps to contextualize each author's preoccupation with the female property owner. Clare Pettitt has argued that Dickens wanted his writings to be 'inalienable property' as well as 'for circulation'.[45] He could sell his writing, but could not control it or 'keep' it once it was circulating publicly. This is the tautology faced by all property owners: one cannot retain property *at the same time* as using the monetary value locked within it.[46] Dickens, aware of this double bind, often presents property as more of a problem than a pleasure. Indeed, the theft of his work by pirates at home and abroad was a continual source of annoyance.[47]

Eliot also depended on her own labour (which was usually the most economically important form of portable property people possessed) and, like Dickens, she found her name and her texts subject to theft. In the late 1850s, when she embarked upon her career as a writer of fiction, Marian Evans took ownership of the property 'George Eliot', a pseudonym which served as a device to protect her identity as a 'scandalous' woman who lived with a man to whom she was not married. Yet, in an extraordinary turn of events, Evans found her property stolen from her in 1858 by Joseph Liggins, who claimed to be the author of her work.[48] Yet Pettitt suggests that 'it was not in her role as artist that she felt most threatened by Liggins ... but rather in that of proprietor and stockholder'.[49] She was also concerned about controlling the boundaries of her 'property' when she asserted that she was:

> NOT the author of the Chronicles of Carlingford ... . A little reflection might, one would think, suggest that when a *name* is the highest-priced thing in literature, any one who has a name will not, except when there is some strong motive for mystification, throw away the advantages of that name. I wrote anonymously while I was an unknown author, but I shall never, I believe, write anonymously again.[50]

Eliot's writing, both in her fiction and her letters, reveals her concern about her property. This emerges occasionally in a tendency to blur emotion and business:

---

[45]   Clare Pettitt, *Patent Inventions: Intellectual Property and the Victorian Novel* (Oxford: Oxford University Press, 2004), p. 261. See also her interesting discussion of the links between literary piracy and coverture in relation to the work of Eliot and Gaskell.

[46]   While it is possible to argue that a landlord owns property and is able to access its monetary value in the form of rent, it is not possible for a landlord to have the *use* of a property for which his tenant pays him a rent.

[47]   See Paul Schlicke (ed.), *Oxford Reader's Companion to Dickens* (Oxford: Oxford University Press, 1999), pp. 119–22.

[48]   See Josephine McDonagh, *George Eliot* (Plymouth: Northcote House, 1997), pp. 29 and 99 note 11.

[49]   Pettitt, *Patent Inventions*, p. 150.

[50]   George Eliot to Sara Hennell, 23 April 1862, in *The George Eliot Letters*, vol. 4, Gordon S. Haight (ed.) (London: Oxford University Press, 1956–), p. 25.

for example, she writes to John Blackwood in 1862 to say 'It was pleasant to see your handwriting again, and I suppose as long as we are in the flesh a friend's handwriting in the form of a cheque will always be peculiarly touching'.[51] James, like his predecessors, chose to 'live by his pen', and also found his literary property subject to theft.[52] Leon Edel refers to one of a number of instances when James's work was pirated in America as an explanation for his interest in the work of the American Copyright League in New York. When the story 'A Bundle of Letters', originally published in the *Parisian*, was pirated in America, James wrote angrily to his parents about this blatant theft of his property.[53] As Edel notes, he 'had been pirated all too often'.[54]

Dickens and Eliot accrued their literary property during the mid-Victorian period. As we will see, this was a time when the issue of women's rights to retain property after marriage was heatedly debated, although neither Dickens nor Eliot lived to respond to the eventual conferring of full property rights on married women in 1882. Henry James, whose major work appeared after the deaths of Dickens and Eliot, was influenced by their scrutiny of the female owner and women's relationships to the material world. However, he was in a position to consider the issue of female property ownership in the aftermath of the Married Women's Property Act of 1882. As an American who made his home in Europe, he presented a rather different image of European society than that offered by the British novelists. These three major novelists offer a broad spectrum of representations of female ownership which ranges across the period of my study. Their novels demonstrate the ways in which Victorian women's complicated and shifting relationships to things registered in the literary imagination.

In 1880 James, on a visit to a wealthy acquaintance, wrote to his mother that he felt prompted 'to meditate … on the fleeting character of earthly possessions'.[55] This sort of meditation, as we will see, is central to the work of all three novelists. It is also a major question which has been raised by property theorists throughout history, for property is always tenuous, not only because the owner must die, but also because the law, the thief, the vagaries of the economy and the accidents of loss intervene between people and their relationships to the material world. The following chapter explores some of the ways in which this tenuousness has been discussed by property theorists, legal historians and cultural commentators, as well as by Victorian writers.

---

[51]   22 Oct 1862, *The George Eliot Letters*, vol. 4, p. 62.

[52]   See Leon Edel, *The Life of Henry James*, vol. 1 (London: Penguin, 1977), p. 676.

[53]   Ibid., p. 550.

[54]   Ibid., p. 681.

[55]   Letter to Mary James, 28 November 1880 reprinted in Leon Edel (ed.), *Henry James Letters*, vol. 2 (Cambridge: Harvard University Press, 1975), pp. 318–19.

Chapter 1
Women's Performative Properties

Property ownership fosters a sense of identity and rootedness in the world. As Arendt has argued, the ownership of things allows people the opportunity to 'retrieve their sameness, that is, their identity, by being related to the same chair and the same table'.[1] Yet property, while being a source of pleasure and stability, a basis for identity, is also liable to the dangers of alienation. It is as much about hopes and dreams as it is about legal rights; indeed, a lack of property rights does not automatically preclude a sense of ownership. Before the passing of the second Married Women's Property Acts in 1882, women's relationship towards property was usually based on an illusion of ownership, for most women lost all rights of possession on marriage. However, while wives' ownership of things was not supported by the common law, this book demonstrates that the law was often ignored, and illegitimate assertions of ownership (both witting and unwitting) were made. This chapter outlines some of the confusions and contradictions surrounding property ownership, focusing particularly on women's attachment to personal portable property, those 'feminine' things, including domestic objects, ornaments, jewellery and dress, which the majority of husbands were disinclined to appropriate (or perhaps too embarrassed to do so).

Yet Victorian women's attachment to portable property has often been misrecognized as an insatiable desire for commodities, a view which fails to address the fact that nineteenth-century women's relationships with the material world were particularly complex, indeed, precarious because of the arbitrariness of marriage custom and the law.[2] Because many women could only access feelings of ownership in relation to relatively inexpensive portable items (indeed, few women owned land at this period), they tended to treat objects as property rather than as disposable consumer goods. Although wives were unlikely to be the legal owners of 'their' personal property before the passing of the Married Women's Property Acts, they probably *believed* that they were and, as we will see, a belief in possession and a performance of ownership can in many instances actually constitute ownership. As Georg Simmel stated: '[t]he fact that one can "do what one wishes" with an object is not only a consequence of ownership but actually means that one owns it'.[3] Yet ponderous mechanisms of law have often failed to register the subtleties of property ownership.

---

[1]   Arendt, p. 137.

[2]   See for example Bowlby and Lindner for discussions of the female consumer.

[3]   Georg Simmel, *The Philosophy of Money*, trans. Tom Bottomore and Dan Frisby (Boston: Routledge and Kegan Paul, 1978), p. 322.

Commonly thought of as a part of the material world, property is actually a relationship, a site of affect, sentiment, dreams and passions which focuses on objects. As legal historians and theorists have emphasized, the general presumption that property consists of the *things* people own overlooks the fact that the law sees property in conceptual terms as rights and as a relationship between people and things.[4] This disjunction between everyday practices of property ownership and the frameworks of property law has engendered many misconceptions. As Kenneth R. Minogue has suggested, 'the attempt to grasp the concept of property is beset with mirage effects … . The best way to approach it is by indirection'.[5] Similarly, Frederick G. Whelan in his discussion of property as artifice has emphasized the arbitrary aspects of property law and the paradoxical situation whereby the law can even bring property into being. In his summary of the writings on property by Hume and Blackstone, Whelan shows how 'the property relation is one of legally defined rights, but that these rights pertain to legally defined things, indeed to things whose existence is in some cases constituted by the rules of property'.[6] Whelan adds that the so-called 'inviolability of property rights under the law of England is in reality a tautology, since property consists of rights defined and qualified by law'.[7] In other words, what the law decrees in relation to property rights always has the potential to be altered. This, as we will see, was the situation experienced by Victorian men who, before 1882 had an 'inviolable' right to appropriate their wives' property and earnings. Once the second Married Women's Property Act was passed in 1882, husbands lost that right. The ownership of property may confer power upon owners, yet the law has vacillated, even contradicted itself, in its approach to rights of possession.

Despite their many differences most commentators, whether property theorists, historians, lawyers, anthropologists or novelists, have made a link between the ownership of property and the possession of social power. The traditions, injustices, confusions and fantasies which have long underpinned Western notions of private property have also informed understandings of the relationship between people and things. However, while the law constructs one sort of property narrative, anthropologists and historians construct a rather different one which tends to be based on observed actual practices rather than theoretical situations. Victorian novelists on the other hand, living through a period of extensive reforms of the laws on marriage and property, produced property narratives which imaginatively recreate experiences of property ownership and dispossession which neither the

---

[4]   C.B. MacPherson (ed.), *Property: Mainstream and Critical Opinions* (Toronto: University of Toronto Press, 1978), p. 2.

[5]   Kenneth R. Minogue, 'The Concept of Property and Its Contemporary Significance' in J. Roland Pennock and John W. Chapman (eds), *Property* [NOMOS XXII] (New York: New York University Press, 1980), p. 5.

[6]   Frederick G. Whelan, 'Property as Artifice: Hume and Blackstone' in Pennock and Chapman, p. 121.

[7]   Ibid., p. 120.

law nor the historian can fully account for. In fact, property dreams and nightmares haunt most Victorian novels, making mirage and artifice appropriate terms to use in the context of their representations of property and property relations.

The relationship between property, power and identity became subject to scrutiny in the Victorian period with the 1850s debates on the reform of the marriage laws. The passing of the Married Women's Property Acts of 1870, 1882 and 1893 ended wives' traditional exclusion from property ownership. Between 1850 and 1900 many novelists emphasized the issue of property ownership by presenting property plots based on the destabilization of gender roles resulting from shifts in economic power. Victorian responses to the issue of wives' property rights and the fight for the social and legal recognition of women's personhood can be best understood in relation to the ways property has been theorized and imagined as a central component of human identity. The work of key property theorists, such as John Locke in his influential *Two Treatises of Government*, published in 1690, and David Hume in his *Treatise of Human Nature*, which appeared fifty years later, demonstrates why the issue of property has been crucial to the concept of personhood.

Property in 'fancy' and Theories of Ownership

Locke and Hume, despite their different opinions on its nature, realized that property is actually rooted in the imagination, or 'fancy', especially when it pertains to those objects which are not necessary for one's physical survival. Locke states in his *Two Treatises of Government* that '[g]old, silver, and diamonds are things that fancy or agreement hath put the value on, more than real use and the necessary support of life'.[8] In his *Treatise of Human Nature* Hume suggests something similar in relation to land when he argues that the boundaries of a person's possessions are often 'decided by no other faculty than the imagination', and he gives the example of a person arriving on a desert island who 'is deem'd its possessor from the very first moment, and acquires the property of the whole; because the object is there bounded and circumscrib'd in the fancy'.[9] He goes on to add that property is not 'real in the objects' we call our possessions, 'but is the off-spring of the sentiments'; in other words, the ways in which objects connect in 'the imagination' frames our notion of what we possess.[10] While Hume believes that 'Property must be stable, and fix'd by general rules', the actual legal frameworks which attempt to ensure stability and fixity originate in the 'fancy' or 'imagination' and 'sentiments' of individuals: to a certain extent, property is

---

[8] John Locke, *Two Treatises of Government* in *Political Writings*, David Wootton (ed.) (London: Penguin, 1993), p. 284.

[9] David Hume, *A Treatise of Human Nature*, Ernest C. Mosner (ed.) (London: Penguin, 1969), p. 558.

[10] Ibid., p. 560.

what we *think* we own.[11] Affect, then, lies at the basis of the state and its property laws; as Defoe exclaimed in 1709, 'We talk loudly of PROPERTY in *England*', and in Parliament property is 'the Language of the Place, 'tis the Darling of the *House – Their Laws* have been made to *preserve* it'.[12] The idea of property as a language is significant, as the work of Bourdieu and Barthes demonstrates, while Defoe's term 'Darling' also nicely indicates the affective nature of property, the emotional investment people make in things which does not always tally with the law intended to 'preserve' property.

Recent critics have largely agreed that Locke's *Two Treatises* has been highly influential in helping to define property relations and their centrality in British law.[13] Locke famously argued that property is 'natural', originating with the body and its ability to labour:

> [E]very man has a property in his own person. This nobody has any right to but himself. The labour of his body and the work of his hands, we may say, are properly his. Whatsoever, then, he removes out of the state that nature hath provided and left it in, he hath mixed his labour with, and joined to it something that is his own, and thereby makes it his property.[14]

This suggests that everybody who labours has a fundamental right to own property and that labour is a 'mixing' process, whereby our actions with objects somehow make people and things fuse together. However, the fact that Locke invested part of his income in the slave trade indicates that he did not envisage his theory as being applicable to everyone.[15] While the labour of slaves belonged to their masters, wives also possessed no property in their own labour, for before 1870, when wives were granted the right to retain their own earnings, it belonged exclusively to their husbands. The law's paradigms defining and regulating property are clearly based on a mixture of ideals and simplifications generated by desires which can be overturned when expediency demands. The ownership of slaves and women contradicts the notion put forward by Locke that property was a natural right based upon the ownership of one's own body, although Locke also denied the social qualities of private property by maintaining that it was not necessary to gain the consent or recognition of others in order to own things.[16] Such a view logically

---

[11] Hume, p. 549. See also Whelan, p. 113.

[12] Quoted in Kevin Hart, *Samuel Johnson and the Culture of Property* (Cambridge: Cambridge University Press, 1999), p. 171; emphasis in the original.

[13] See in particular, Minogue; Hart; Schmidgen; Whelan, p. 101; Paul Thomas, 'Property's Properties: From Hegel to Locke', *Representations*, 84 (Autumn 2003): 30–43; and Karl Olivecrona, 'Locke's Theory of Appropriation', *Philosophical Quarterly*, 24:96 (1974): 220–34.

[14] Locke, p. 274.

[15] See Maurice Cranston, *John Locke: A Biography* (London: Longman, 1957), p. 115.

[16] See Christopher J. Berry, 'Property and Possession: Two Replies to Locke – Hume and Hegel', in Pennock and Chapman, p. 89. See also Thomas, p. 42.

promotes the idea that the dispossessed, once they have 'mixed' their labour with some object, are right to appropriate it as their own. Locke, unaware of the radical potential of his property theory, would have undoubtedly denied this right to all persons.[17] Certainly, this is an idea held by many characters in Victorian novels, from the uneducated Mrs Tulliver in Eliot's *The Mill on the Floss* (1860) to the sophisticated aesthete, Mrs Gereth, in James's *The Spoils of Poynton* (1897). Both assert their claims to property on the basis of their labour. Mrs Tulliver's spinning and sewing of linen and Mrs Gereth's creation of an art collection lead them to presume, falsely, that their labour confers upon them a natural right to its results.

Hume, however, rejects Locke's view of property as 'natural', seeing it as a social concept, although he resembles Locke in that he expresses a utopian impulse in some of his definitions of how property relations work. He argues that 'married people in particular mutually lose their property, and are unacquainted with the *mine* and *thine*, which are so necessary, and yet cause such disturbance in human society'.[18] It was such idealistic views of marriage as a mutually beneficial institution which were seen as problematic by Victorian feminists. Frances Power Cobbe, for example, in an essay published in 1868, 'Criminals, Idiots, Women and Minors', amusingly imagined an alien arriving on earth to witness a marriage ceremony. The alien presumes when the groom states, 'With all my worldly goods I thee endow', that his wife will gain his property. The guide explains that it is actually '*her* goods and earnings, present and future, which belong to him at this moment'.[19] Hume also erroneously presumes from the fiction of the marriage ceremony that married couples are 'unacquainted' with the notion of the possession of their spouse's property because ideally it is 'shared'.[20]

The rhetoric and performances associated with property ownership (such as the marriage ceremony or the drawing up and reading of a will) were often misleading and could generate confusion, for the boundaries of property ownership have tended to be unclear and thus difficult to police. As Locke and Hume suggest, all property exists within the imagination before it exists in other forms and, as Whelan has noted, Hume presumed that property laws 'have been adopted principally because they reflect our imaginative dispositions'.[21] William Blackstone, an eighteenth-century lawyer whose summary of English law in his *Commentaries on the Laws of England* was enormously popular with nineteenth-century readers, reinforced this when he proclaimed that, 'There is nothing which so generally strikes the imagination, and engages the affections of mankind, as the right of property; or

---

[17]   For Locke's unwitting radicalism see Minogue, p. 17.

[18]   Hume, p. 549; emphasis in the original.

[19]   Reprinted in Susan Hamilton (ed.), *Criminals, Idiots, Women and Minors: Victorian Writing by Women on Women* (Ontario: Broadview Press, 1996), pp. 108–9.

[20]   See Sedgwick's chapter, 'Around the Performative: Periperformative Vicinities in Nineteenth-Century Narrative', pp. 67–92, for a useful discussion of the marriage ceremony (indeed, marriage itself) as a form of fiction.

[21]   Whelan, p. 113.

that sole and despotic dominion which one man claims and exercises over the external things of the world'.[22] Yet, despite Blackstone's position as a conservative defender of English law and upholder of tradition, he takes care to demonstrate that there is nothing 'natural' about property rights, although he conceded that they may seem 'natural' to those who own property. He states:

> And yet there are very few, but will give themselves the trouble to consider the original and foundation of this right. ... We think it enough that our title is derived by the grant of the former proprietor, by descent from our ancestors, or by the last will and testament of the dying owner; not caring to reflect that (accurately and strictly speaking) there is no foundation in nature or in natural law, why a set of words upon parchment should convey the dominion of land: why the son should have a right to exclude his fellow-creatures from a determinate spot of ground, because his father had done so before him: or why the occupier of a particular field or of a jewel, when lying on his deathbed, and, no longer able to maintain possession, should be entitled to tell the rest of the world which of them should enjoy it after him.[23]

There are no absolute property rights, Blackstone suggests, despite the commonly held assumption that English law protects the 'inviolable' rights of the property owner.

Yet while some property dreams and presumptions appear to be protected by law, others do not. As C.B. MacPherson states, 'What distinguishes property from mere momentary possession is that property is a claim that will be enforced by society or the state, by custom or convention or law'.[24] This was where the inequality between men and women lay: the law traditionally enforced men's rights to property, while women, particularly married women, could find the law to be their enemy rather than the protector of their rights. The exploitation of female vulnerability in relation to ownership rights has a long tradition, for historically many newly made widows, even from the aristocracy, found their property seized by men who took advantage of their socially and legally unprotected state. For example, Richard of Gloucester (later Richard III) appropriated the lands and valuable portable property of the Countess of Oxford on the death of her husband simply because he believed that men had greater rights to property than women.[25] This view continued to exist in the eighteenth century, when James Boswell in his *Life of Johnson* argued that male heirs should always be privileged over female ones (a view with which Johnson disagreed).[26] The patriarchal tradition

---

[22]   William Blackstone, *Blackstone's Commentaries on the Laws of England*, vol. 2, Wayne Morrison (ed.) (London and Sydney: Cavendish Publishing, 2001), p. 3.

[23]   Blackstone, vol. 2, p. 2.

[24]   MacPherson (ed.), *Property*, p. 3.

[25]   See Michael A. Hicks, *Richard III* (Stroud: Tempus, 2001), p. 83

[26]   James Boswell, *The Life of Johnson*, R.W. Chapman (ed.) (Oxford: Oxford University Press, 1998), p. 667.

of excluding females from power (and property, the main conduit to power) may have originated in a 'barbarous' past, yet even in the nineteenth century, when the massive shifts of industrialization, capitalism and urbanization had transformed the social and cultural life of Britain, the law continued to support men's property rights until 1882, despite the fact that many wills demonstrated that the majority of testators divided their property equally between sons and daughters.[27] Because common law was largely relevant to a feudal society, the British legal system failed to meet the needs of bourgeois families, particularly middle-class women. It is not, therefore, surprising that the tendency towards reform promoted by the Law Amendment Society and supported by feminist activists was increasingly insistent from the 1850s onwards.[28]

The utopian view expressed in the law and articulated by Hume that husbands and wives were 'one' and that the latter's needs were 'covered' by the former's protection was found to be increasingly untenable, for urbanization, increased educational opportunities and exposure to new mass media such as novels and magazines generated changes in attitudes towards marriage and the family.[29] While the idea of husband and wife being 'one' persisted as an ideal, the complexity of economics (global, national and local), family ties and working practices, along with the widespread acceptance of the notion of marriage based on love as a norm, meant that a pragmatic approach was needed, both in terms of the law and consensus.

Married Women's Property and the Law

Lee Holcombe has shown that 'since property and status went hand in hand in English law, wives were reduced to a special status, subordinate to and dependent upon their husbands'.[30] A wife became on marriage a *feme covert*, all her actions were 'covered' by her husband who became responsible for them, a situation which, as Mary Lyndon Shanley notes, meant that 'a wife was regarded in many ways as the property of her husband'.[31] Husbands also controlled their wives' property and earnings. Ben Griffin has stated that on marriage:

> all of a women's personal property passed to her husband when she married, as did any property she subsequently acquired, and the husband gained an interest in any freehold land. The only way around this rule of the common law – the legal

---

[27] R.J. Morris, *Men, Women and Property in England, 1780–1870* (Cambridge: Cambridge University Press, 2005), p. 135.

[28] Holcombe, pp. 48–87.

[29] Leonore Davidoff and Catherine Hall, *Family Fortunes: Men and Women of the English Middle Class, 1780–1850* (London: Hutchinson, 1987), p. 157.

[30] Holcombe, p. 25.

[31] Shanley, p. 8.

doctrine of coverture – was to be found in the courts of equity, where property could be placed in the hands of trustees for the separate use of a woman.[32]

If a married woman 'owned' property of any value, such as land or investments, it tended to be secured in a trust drawn up in equity and controlled (usually) by male trustees. This meant that wives with valuable property, as Poovey has argued, were related to it in ways that were 'both indirect and limited'.[33] Even if a wife was fortunate enough to have a marriage settlement, she was not usually free to sell her property or raise credit on it. This limitation was in place because the law 'did not function to extend women's rights but to protect the property rights of a man, initially the father, but, according to the terms of the trust, whatever man was designated trustee'.[34] In practice, then, the law of equity presumed that a woman who married potentially became the site of a property dispute or conflict of interests between men, where fathers attempted to protect what they considered to be 'their' family's property from the control of daughters' husbands. As Caroline Cornwallis stated in a *Westminster Review* article of 1856, 'so hazardous is it thought by fathers in general to leave their daughter's property in the hands of the husband … that none who can afford to pay legal expenses, trust their property on so frail a foundation as the intended husband's prudence and integrity'.[35] The presumptions about marriage and property enshrined in law supposed that husbands automatically looked after their wives' interests, although the wealthy were sceptical about this and took steps to limit husbands' powers. Yet the majority of people were subject to the common law, and thus unable to curb husbands' powers. The high-profile case of Caroline Norton in the early Victorian period helped to expose the vulnerability of wives for she, despite the fact that she was born into the upper class, was unable to prevent her tyrannical husband from appropriating her property and earnings.[36]

Before the passing of the Married Women's Property Acts, there were distinct tensions between the law, gender relations and everyday practices of property ownership. The common law made no provision for the wife who was more responsible and reasonable than her husband: women were treated as minors and thus liable to (and ironically enabled to) behave irresponsibly. Women could commit certain crimes with impunity, their husbands being deemed responsible for their actions.[37] As Davidoff and Hall have demonstrated, women's situation in

---

[32]   Ben Griffin, 'Class, Gender, and Liberalism in Parliament, 1868–1882: The Case of the Married Women's Property Acts', *The Historical Journal*, 46:1 (2003): 62.

[33]   Mary Poovey, *Uneven Developments: The Ideological Work of Gender in Mid-Victorian England* (London: Virago, 1989), p. 71.

[34]   Poovey, *Uneven Developments*, p. 72.

[35]   Quoted in Philippa Levine, *Victorian Feminism, 1850–1900* (London: Hutchinson, 1987), p. 141.

[36]   For a discussion of Caroline Norton's situation and her attack on the marriage laws, see Shanley, pp. 17 and 33.

[37]   Holcombe, p. 30.

relation to property ownership had worsened since the seventeenth century: 'With the ending of customary rights of dower, a development recognized by law in 1833, marriage virtually turned legal control of a woman's property permanently over to her husband'.[38] Paraphernalia, which consisted of the 'clothing and personal ornaments that a woman possessed at the time of her marriage or that her husband gave her during marriage', was only precariously in wives' control, for a husband was entitled to raise money on this property and his creditors could seize it.[39] There also appeared to be a prevailing view that women were naturally irresponsible. Sir John Simeon, for example, an opponent of reform of the married women's property laws, argued that a wife who was 'inclined to spend largely upon her dress, and upon dissipation and amusements' would have greater scope to misbehave if she was to be given property rights.[40]

However, there were deeper fears than those centred on the frivolity of wives. As Shanley states, opponents to changes in the married women's property laws argued that marriage itself was under threat, for if a wife gained a legal identity she would metaphorically separate herself from her husband, and their interests may not then be identical.[41] Griffin has also emphasized the fact that men's rights tended to dominate the parliamentary debates on wives and property. The continuation of coverture was based on the idea that 'male authority in the household was an essential component of masculine identity and was essential to preserving the home as a refuge from the public sphere'.[42] Many were anxious about the consequences of women's agency, fearing that autonomous, independent wives would pose a threat to the home and the institution of marriage.[43] This linkage of property and personhood can be related to Hegel's proposition that property ownership is an act of will and thus essential for personhood.[44] In his *Elements of the Philosophy of Right*, Hegel argued that 'not until he has property does the person exist as reason'.[45] If wives were autonomous property owners they would 'exist as reason' and enter society to assert their individuality, an idea which threatened the conservative view of marriage as a union of unequal partners, with wives as dependent on husbands and legally disabled for their own protection. Feminists, however, suggested that marriage could be seen as a form of prostitution, and that one of the ironies of the law's protection of women from the world of finance was that under

---

[38]   Davidoff and Hall, p. 276.

[39]   Holcombe, p. 22.

[40]   Cited in Griffin, p. 74.

[41]   Shanley, p. 46.

[42]   Griffin, p. 86.

[43]   See Shanley, p. 46 for the arguments put forward by opponents for reform of the marriage laws.

[44]   See Margaret Jane Radin, *Reinterpreting Property* (Chicago and London: University of Chicago Press, 1993), p. 195 for a discussion of Hegel's theory of personhood.

[45]   G.W.F. Hegel, *Elements of the Philosophy of Right*, Allen W. Wood (ed.), H.B. Nisbet (trans.) (Cambridge: Cambridge University Press, 1991), p.73.

existing conventions the 'marriage market' encouraged middle- and upper-class women to calculate on gaining a suitable establishment through an advantageous marriage.[46] Another feminist argument was that the MPs who opposed marriage reform ensured that their own daughters' and sisters' fortunes were protected by the 'separate estates' drawn up in expensive marriage settlements under equity.[47] In other words, the daughters of the wealthy did have some (albeit limited) rights of property ownership and the very men in parliament who arranged for the legal protection of their property were denying the same rights to less wealthy women whose actions were governed by the common law.

Beginning with the presentation of Barbara Leigh Smith's pamphlet, *A Brief Summary in Plain Language of the Most Important Laws Concerning Women*, to the Law Amendment Society, the political campaign to reform the marriage laws collected signatures for various petitions in support of the Married Women's Property Bill.[48] The Married Women's Property Committee was established in 1868 and continued to work until the 1882 Act was passed, the 1870 Act being wholly inadequate in protecting women's rights to retain the property they brought to a marriage.[49] The 1870 Act succeeded in affording some protection to working women in terms of protecting their earnings; however, the Act did not provide wider rights to property. The law continued to be based on the notion that women were irresponsible beings, but there were concessions for working-class women who were presumed to need to be protected from abusive and violent husbands who did not scruple to steal their wives' earnings and property to spend on alcohol. There was a belief that middle-class and upper-class women did not need the law to be changed because their husbands were 'gentlemen' and thus unlikely to be violent and abusive. Some of the debates even suggested changing the law for working-class women only.[50] Certainly, few middle-class wives earned money from employment conducted outside the home. Griffin has demonstrated that reform was largely brought about by 'the men in parliament constructing melodramatic narratives in which they were the selfless heroes protecting women against brutal, drunken husbands'.[51] In other words, issues of class dominated what feminists hoped would be a debate about gender inequality.[52]

After two decades debating the issue, Parliament eventually passed the first Act in 1870. However, as Griffin indicates, the 1870 Act was inadequate, leaving

---

[46]   See Shanley, p. 60.

[47]   Holcombe, p. 38 and Shanley, p. 74.

[48]   See Carol Bauer and Laurence Ritt (eds), *Free and Ennobled: Source Readings in the Development of Victorian Feminism* (Oxford and New York: Pergamon Press, 1979), p. 172.

[49]   Poovey, *Uneven Developments*, pp.72–4; Shanley, pp. 47 and 68–76; and Susan Hamilton, *Frances Power Cobbe and Victorian Feminism* (Basingstoke: Palgrave, 2006), p. 66.

[50]   Griffin, pp. 66–70.

[51]   Ibid., p. 83.

[52]   See Shanley, p. 67.

too many loopholes in the law which meant that it was being administered inconsistently, with some wives being able to secure their property against a husband's appropriation, while others were unable to because some magistrates continued to insist that wives could not legally sue their husbands. This sort of inconsistency led to the changes made in the 1882 Act. Another reason put forward in the support of this second Act was that 'creditors were lobbying intensively for changes in the law, as it was proving difficult to recover debts from married women'.[53] Griffin sums up the effects of the 1882 act as 'extend[ing] the rules of equity to all married women's property, and [it] was therefore a triumph for the argument that the protection offered to the rich should be offered to the poor'.[54] The 1882 Act was heralded by *The Women's Suffrage Journal* as 'the Magna Charta' of women's freedom.[55] However, there was a further Act in 1893 which made wives fully liable for their own debts.[56]

Yet, it is possible that the changes in the law had little effect on the perceptions of women who had always presumed that they owned their things. Victorian novels published before 1882 abound with representations of women who, believing themselves to be property owners, *act* as property owners by writing wills and appropriating the things they desire regardless of the fact that they had no legal rights to property. These characters forcefully demonstrate that property exists most powerfully in the imagination or fancy. As Holcombe has pointed out, there are some legal inaccuracies in Dickens's novels: Mrs Quilp in *The Old Curiosity Shop* (1841) cannot inherit her husband's property because he has committed suicide, while Mrs Weller in *The Pickwick Papers* (1837) had no legal right to make a will, as she does in the novel.[57] Yet Dickens's novels reflect practices which actually took place, the law failing to intervene. Indeed, the limits of the law are suggested in *Oliver Twist* (1838); when Mr Bumble is told that 'the law supposes that your wife acts under your direction', he replies, 'If the law supposes that ... the law is an ass – a idiot'.[58] He is indicating that 'the law' makes presumptions which are not necessarily accurate, that it is 'duped' about the real relations it is designed to frame and control. Suicides can be hidden from the law, not every will can be policed, women can insist that a ring or a table is their own and fight off those who try to appropriate it. The law can be taken advantage of: if enough people refuse to believe in it, then it cannot effectively be enforced. Women's contempt for patriarchal law has, unsurprisingly, a long history. For example, in the fifteenth century an official of the City of Florence was ordered to enforce the sumptuary

---

[53]   Griffin, p. 80.

[54]   Ibid., p. 81.

[55]   Quoted in Shanley, p. 124.

[56]   Margot C. Finn, *The Character of Credit: Personal Debt in English Culture, 1740–1914* (Cambridge: Cambridge University Press, 2003), p. 266.

[57]   Holcombe, p. 14.

[58]   Dickens, Charles, *Oliver Twist*, Kathleen Tillotson (ed.) (Clarendon: Oxford University Press, 1988), p. 335.

laws which prevented many women publicly wearing elaborate ornamentation. In his report to his superior he stated:

> In obedience to the orders you gave me, I went out to look for forbidden ornaments on the women and was met with arguments such as are not to be found in any book of laws. There was one woman with the edge of her hood fringed out in lace and twined round her head. My assistant said to her, 'What is your name? You have a hood with lace fringes'. But the woman removed the lace fringe which was attached to the hood with a pin, and said it was merely a wreath. Further along we met a woman with many buttons in front of her dress; and my assistant said to her, 'You are not allowed to wear buttons'. But she replied 'These are not buttons. They are studs. Look, they have no loops, and there are no buttonholes'. Then my assistant, supposing he had caught a culprit at last, went up to another woman and said to her, 'You are wearing ermine'. And he took out his book to write down her name. 'You cannot take down my name', the woman protested. 'This is not ermine. It is the fur of a suckling'. 'What do you mean by suckling?' 'A kind of animal'.[59]

Such tactics of evasion have long been employed to trick officialdom and combat absurd rules and, as I will demonstrate, the common law rules on marriage and property were no exception. These laws may have been problematic, even 'idiotic', causing grief for many women; however, they were sometimes easy to break and evade.

Victorian women may have consoled themselves with the realization that the property laws could only rarely be enforced. The wife who treated the clock on the mantelpiece as though it were her own was not realistically going to be reprimanded or apprehended if she sold or pawned it, unless her husband called upon the law to support his claims. Ironically, before 1870, she could steal it from her husband with impunity, for only husbands had a legal existence. Custom, the origin of the law, also potentially had the power to override the law. The statement 'I own' is a performative which can work powerfully to reinforce Locke's theory of the origin of property: that having contact with a thing or using that thing is the same as possessing it. Hume also made this clear when he defined possession as a relationship with an object 'not only when we immediately touch it, but also when we are so situated in respect to it, as to have it in our power to use it: and may move, alter, or destroy it, according to our present pleasure or advantage'.[60] Pearce has argued in *On Collecting*, that the power of ownership allows one 'to construct the relationship between "I" and "me" which creates individual identity, between the individual and others, and between the individual and the finite world of time and space'.[61] Clearly, possession confers power and impediments to possession

---

[59]   Quoted in Christopher Hibbert, *The House of Medici: Its Rise and Fall* (London: Allen Lane, Penguin, 1975), p. 22. I am grateful to Henrietta Wynne-Atkinson for drawing my attention to this quotation.

[60]   Hume, p. 557.

[61]   Pearce, p. 177.

inflict on individuals impoverishment, both in terms of social status and sense of personhood. This impediment was imposed on married women before 1870 and was one of the main targets of Victorian feminists' attack upon the law. However, not all women felt this impediment, or took it seriously.

Yet it was not only feminists who highlighted the complexities of property and the law in relation to women and marriage. Indeed, as we will see, a range of novelists found dramatic potential in the figure of the female property owner, both as a victim of the marriage laws who loses control of her personal property because of the privileging of a husband's rights, as does Mrs Tulliver in George Eliot's *The Mill on the Floss*, and as a schemer who uses marriage as a route towards property and power, as do Lady Audley in Braddon's sensational *Lady Audley's Secret* (1862), and Lizzie Eustace in Trollope's *The Eustace Diamonds* (1873). For Lizzie, physical possession of an object, in this case the diamond necklace belonging to the Eustace family, becomes in her eyes her own legal possession as long as certain performances are publicly enacted to demonstrate the physical proximity of the thing and her person. As the next section will demonstrate, Trollope's novel offers an important representation of the theatricality of property ownership among the upper classes, highlighting the ways in which ownership involves rituals of display and concealment as Lizzie attempts to disrupt the property traditions of the class she has married into.

'What lady will ever scruple to avoid her taxes?': *The Eustace Diamonds*

Shortly after the passing of the first Married Women's Property Act, *The Eustace Diamonds* was serialized in *The Fortnightly Review* from 1871 to 1873. Trollope actually began writing his novel of female duplicity and desire in December 1869, completing it in August 1870, the same month in which Parliament passed the bill. The novel centres on the ambitious Lizzie Greystock, who marries Sir Florian Eustace for his money. Her husband's death after a year of marriage offers her an opportunity to appropriate the Eustace family's diamonds, which happen to be in her possession when Sir Florian dies. The novel focuses on her attempts to assert herself as the legal possessor of the gems. Trollope, however, rather than presenting an oppositional voice to the feminist reform movement, actually focuses on how the laws could be bypassed and undermined by a determined wife or widow. Indeed, the novel exposes the laws on property as arbitrary. Lizzie's theft of the diamonds is ironically made easier by the law itself because the lawyers, unclear about the nature of heirlooms, are reluctant to test her case in court. Lizzie also attempts to 'steal' Frank Greystock, the fiancé of her rival Lucy Morris, the virtuous bourgeois governess. Indeed, the 'clever, sharp and greedy' Lizzie (a direct descendent of Thackeray's Becky Sharp)[62] is a woman in whose hands no property would be safe, for even before she came of age, she was dealing with pawnbrokers, raising

---

[62]   This point is also made by A.H. Miller, p. 160.

cash on her jewellery and getting into debt; in fact, Trollope suggests that Sir Florian's disillusion began with his knowledge of his wife's debts.[63]

The novel also questions the ancient notion of women as chattels, where no distinction is made between property in objects and property in women. This topic has been widely discussed by feminist critics, most notably by Gayle Rubin in her essay 'The Traffic in Women: Notes on the "Political Economy" of Sex', in which she argues that patriarchy depends upon women being treated as men's property, exchangeable between men to reinforce their family bonds and networks.[64] However, Psomiades has challenged this view, particularly the argument put forward by critics of *The Eustace Diamonds*, who see Trollope representing Lizzie Eustace and Lucy Morris in terms of property; Lizzie in particular has been viewed as both objectified and commodified.[65] Psomiades, however, suggests that Trollope represents both women as having 'economic agency, Lizzie as the possessor of property and Lucy as a wage earner'.[66] Andrew Miller also sees Lizzie as an agent, determined to keep the diamonds 'as a perverse and oddly modern form of pride, pride at work in a culture that defines identity through possession'.[67] Her agency is evident when Lizzie attempts to appropriate Frank as her own property; in a reversal of Rubin's argument, Psomiades emphasizes the power of women who own property, whether in the forms of land and monetary wealth or in the form of their own labour. As Miller states, *The Eustace Diamonds* represents people as objects and social life as 'a series of exchanges – thefts, losses, gifts, inheritances'.[68]

Trollope's representation of Lizzie as a woman of property is an unusual one, for although she is a young widow and a mother who owns a considerable property, she is seen by many as 'a little minx' (ED 2, 357). She has an income of £4,000 a year, the use of an estate in Scotland during her life, and is in possession of a necklace worth £10,000 which she hopes to sell. Mr Camperdown, the Eustace family's attorney, instigates legal action against Lizzie for the return of the necklace, which the Eustaces erroneously believe to be a family heirloom. It does not actually

---

[63]   Anthony Trollope, *The Eustace Diamonds*, W.J. McCormack (ed.) (Oxford: Oxford University Press, 1992), vol. 1, p. 9. Subsequent references will be cited in the text following the abbreviation 'ED', the volume number and page reference.

[64]   Gayle Rubin, 'The Traffic in Women: Notes on the "Political Economy" of Sex' in *Toward an Anthropology of Women*, Rayna R. Reiter (ed.) (New York: Monthly Review Press, 1975), pp. 157–210.

[65]   See in particular Lindner's chapter, 'Trollope's Material Girl: Gender and Capitalism in *The Eustace Diamonds*', pp. 65–92. Sara L. Maurer in 'The Nation's Wife: England's Vicarious Enjoyment in Anthony Trollope's Palliser Novels' in *Troubled Legacies: Narrative and Inheritance*, Allan Hepburn (ed.) (Toronto and London: University of Toronto Press, 2007), pp. 53–86, offers an interesting revision to the view that Trollope represents women in terms of property.

[66]   Psomiades, p. 98.

[67]   A.H. Miller, p. 165.

[68]   Ibid., p. 170.

belong to the family because of a clumsily drafted will. Mr Camperdown (like the more sinister Mr Tulkinghorn in *Bleak House* who, as we will see in the next chapter, persecutes Lady Dedlock because of her social rise) is indignant because Lizzie 'brought no money into the family' (ED 1, 37). He believes that she should not be 'allowed to filch' the necklace 'as other widows filch china cups, and a silver teaspoon or two! It's quite a common thing', he states, 'but I've never heard of such a haul as this' (ED 1, 40). His tolerance of widows who steal those things which were not part of their paraphernalia, but they were fond of during their marriage, only extends to women who take a few relatively inexpensive items. Trollope suggests that this common practice is condoned by the law because it does not seriously detract from the value of the family estate. Lizzie's more audacious attempt to 'filch' the Eustace family's diamonds, the value of which would provide an estate for a younger son (ED 1, 249), sets her apart, not only from the widows who adhere to a more genteel code of 'thieving', but also from those idealized female characters in Victorian realist novels who find renunciation easier than appropriation. Lizzie Eustace is thus an anti-heroine, more suited to the world of the sensation novel than the 'high-realist' milieu of the Palliser series.[69] Trollope's brief reference to 'filching' widows suggests a generally tolerant attitude to those women who cannot bear to be parted from the portable items they used and loved; as long, that is, as those items have a relatively low market value.

Lizzie cannot (or will not) make a distinction between different items of portable property. For her, portability, the fact she can carry her property with her and wear it, makes it alienable property. She states: 'If a thing is a man's own he can give it away; – not a house, or a farm, or a wood, or anything like that; but a thing he can carry about with him, – of course he can give it away' (ED 1, 57). In other words, she believes that all portable property is alienable, while real estate is not. Her understanding of the laws of property is naïve, as Trollope indicates when he refers to her 'heavy load of ignorance' about money (ED 1, 15). Yet, as we will see later in this chapter, the distinction between alienable and inalienable property is particularly prone to confusion on the part of owners and Lizzie's view of portable property could actually be, under certain circumstances, supported by the law. As Alan Roth has demonstrated in his discussion of the novel, Mr Dove's research into actual cases involving disputed heirlooms reveals that judges supported widows' claims to retain items of portable property if they were seen to use them during the time of their marriage.[70] By wearing the diamonds during and after her marriage and keeping them about her person, Lizzie actually strengthens

---

[69]   D.A. Miller, *The Novel and the Police* (Berkeley and London: University of California Press, 1988), p. 11. See also Mary Poovey, who has recently stated that Trollope's novels have been considered by many modern literary critics 'as the most referential of all Victorian fiction', *Genres of the Credit Economy: Mediating Value in Eighteenth- and Nineteenth-Century Britain* (Chicago and London: University of Chicago Press, 2008), p. 384.

[70]   Alan Roth, 'He Thought He Was Right (But Wasn't): Property Law in Anthony Trollope's *The Eustace Diamonds*', *Stanford Law Review*, 44 (1992): 889.

her position as the owner of the necklace. She understands that property ownership can only be realized as a performance or series of performances, through which she asserts her claims to possession.

Yet the strength of Lizzie's claim, based on her public performances with the Eustace diamonds, is not recognized by Trollope. As Roth has shown, Mr Dove's research is fundamentally flawed.[71] Roth states:

> Lizzie's claim to the necklace as paraphernalia was not as doubtful as Mr Dove opined. The strength of her claim rested on the fact that the necklace was in her constant … possession from the moment Sir Florian gave them to her until he died. Trollope did not say how often she wore them, but even a few times during her brief marriage might be enough to confer paraphernalia rights.[72]

Roth also demonstrates that, for the law, performatives offer proofs of gift-giving, ownership and exchanges of property, and he cites the case of *Grant v. Grant*, where the judge declared that 'if the donor [of a gift] makes an express declaration that "I do now give it", I am of the opinion that is sufficient'.[73] Lizzie's claim to the necklace is based on her assertion that her husband made such a statement. However, because no one witnessed this, she could not successfully base her claim on this ground alone. Yet, as Roth has argued, her actual wearing of the necklace in public constitutes a performance of ownership which could have become legal ownership under the law of paraphernalia, particularly if 'she wore them frequently and as a matter of her own volition rather than her husband's'.[74] Given the fluidity of the law in practice (rather than the rigidity of the law in theory), it was in wives' interests to display and use those objects they liked as much as possible in public, for they could subsequently base a claim for ownership on their displays.

In *The Eustace Diamonds* Trollope supplements his representations of Lizzie's property performances with the property displays of another female materialist, Mrs Carbuncle. She and her niece Lucinda are, with Lizzie, described as 'worldly, hard, and given entirely to evil things' (ED 2, 270). Mrs Carbuncle, in debt and living precariously in high society, understands the power of property well, for she expends considerable energy extorting from her acquaintances wedding presents for her niece, who has been coerced into an engagement with the boorish Sir Griffin. Mrs Carbuncle collects expensive presents as 'tribute', as part of the maintenance of a suitable display of wealth to fool her creditors and facilitate her niece's social advance through marriage:

---

[71]   Roth claims that Mr Dove's opinions were based on those of Trollope's barrister friend, Charles Merewether (p. 881 note 19); he also suggests that Trollope does not present a good case because he does not want Lizzie to get away with her 'theft'.

[72]   Ibid., p. 891.

[73]   Ibid., p. 893.

[74]   Ibid., p. 894.

In spite of pecuniary difficulties the trousseau was to be a wonder; and even Lizzie was astonished at the jewellery which that indefatigable woman had collected together for a preliminary show in Hertford Street. She had spent hours at Howell and James's, and had made marvellous bargains there and elsewhere. Things were sent for selection, of which the greater portion were to be returned, but all were kept for the show … to add to the quasi-public exhibition of presents on the Monday. The money expended had gone very far. The most had been made of failing credit. (ED 2, 266–7)

Like Lizzie, Mrs Carbuncle realizes that property (even if one does not own it) must be displayed to be effective. It is significant that Lucinda's rebellion against the mercenary marriage her aunt has imposed upon her takes the form of violence against the portable property she receives in the form of the presents and trousseau: 'the bride absolutely ran a muck among the finery, scattering laces here and there, pitching the glove-boxes under the bed, chucking the golden-heeled boots into the fireplace, and exhibiting quite a tempest of fury against one of the finest shows of petticoats ever arranged' (ED 2, 267). Trollope's critique of women's relationships to property and society's treatment of them *as* property is ultimately limited by his condemnation, on moral grounds, of Lizzie and Mrs Carbuncle (Lucinda is ultimately redeemed by the mental breakdown she suffers on her wedding day). Yet it is interesting that both of his 'worldly, hard' women seek the solace of coverture offered by husbands. Mrs Carbuncle, impoverished and unhappily married, wants her niece to be suitably 'covered' by a husband's wealth, while Lizzie desperately seeks a husband, 'a man bound to defend her, – a man at any rate bound to put himself forward on her behalf and do whatever might be done in her defence' (ED 2, 259). So desperate is she that she even considers as a husband Major Mackintosh, the policeman who discovers her act of perjury, who is 'not exactly a Corsair, as he was a great authority over the London police, – but a powerful, fine fellow' (ED 2, 264). Lizzie finally marries Mr Emilius who 'agree[s] to no settlements prejudicial to that marital supremacy which should be attached to the husband' (ED 2, 369). Lizzie Emilius's second loveless marriage results in her loss of control of the fortune which came to her from her first mercenary marriage. For Trollope, female wickedness resides not so much in a rebellion against feminine submission to the traditions of marriage and coverture, but in a too calculating approach towards them.

Coverture: the Law and its Breakages

As we have seen, before the passing of the Married Women's Property Acts the property laws could in certain circumstances be manipulated in wives' and widows' favour: yet the law was actually designed to protect men's interests, which is why the rules of coverture had persisted unchanged during centuries of patriarchal control. The source of Victorian feminists' protest against the marriage laws, coverture was based on the presumption that married women were incapable of behaving responsibly or independently. However, for some women, such as Margaret Oliphant, coverture was not to be taken literally. In an 1856 article, 'The Laws Concerning Women', Oliphant stated that 'It is a mere trick of words to say that the woman loses her existence and is absorbed in her husband'.[75] Clearly, those who sought the reform of the marriage laws did not necessarily speak for all women, and coverture was not always an unwelcome aspect of married life for women. As Margot Finn argues, recent feminist critics' emphasis on coverture as an impediment to women's economic freedom and the reason for their restriction to the private sphere is too reductive, for it fails to take into account the tactics used by married women to gain some level of agency in the marketplace.[76] For example, feminist historian Amy Louise Erikson has argued that, '[m]ost women, even those with a marriage settlement, were largely at the mercy of their husband's good will, both during and after marriage'.[77] Finn suggests, however, that there were many 'informal settlements' made in women's favour on marriage, and she focuses on a significant 'disjuncture between legal theory and social practice'.[78] These contradictions have sometimes been ignored by feminist historians who, 'focusing on the "disabling" effects of coverture, have tended to overlook the ways in which English women, at times assisted by English men, succeeded in suppressing, subverting, eroding and evading the strictures of the common law'.[79] Women's agency in relation to money and property has been seen as more extensive than has hitherto been suggested. Jill Phillips Ingram, for example, in her discussion of Renaissance women's writing on property, argues that '[t]o highlight women's troubles concerning property rights is not to assert their general economic disenfranchisement across the board: we should not overstate the case'.[80] Nancy Henry, discussing women of the Victorian period, has also argued that historians hostile to capitalism 'have blinded us to some important dimensions of the Victorians' interactions in the financial world, particularly, for example, the ways in which investing women benefited from and contributed to the Victorian culture of investment'.[81] Finn concludes her argument on the flexible approaches

---

[75]   Margaret Oliphant, 'The Laws Concerning Women', *Blackwood's*, vol. 76 (1856): 379–87, cited in Elizabeth K. Helsinger, Robin L. Sheets and William Veeder (eds), *The Woman Question: Society and Literature in Britain and America, 1837–1883*, vol. 2 (Manchester: Manchester University Press, 1983), p. 6.

[76]   Margot Finn, 'Women, Consumption and Coverture in England, c.1760–1860', *The Historical Journal*, 39:3 (Sept. 1996): 704–5.

[77]   Amy Louise Erikson, *Women and Property in Early Modern England* (London: Routledge, 1993), p. 151.

[78]   Finn, 'Women, Consumption and Coverture', pp. 706 and 717.

[79]   Ibid., p. 720.

[80]   Jill Phillips Ingram, *Idioms of Self-Interest: Credit, Identity, and Property in English Renaissance Literature* (London: Routledge, 2006), p. 97.

[81]   Nancy Henry, '"Ladies Do It?": Victorian Women Investors in Fact and Fiction', in Francis O'Gorman (ed.), *Victorian Literature and Finance* (Oxford: Oxford University Press, 2007), pp. 114–15.

to coverture used by married couples with the point that 'the law of coverture is best described as existing in a state of suspended animation',[82] and that 'the legal disabilities of married women were less sweeping and less straightforward that the strictures of coverture might suggest'.[83] Indeed, the situation was rarely clear-cut or simple for there were many ways in which women could evade or confuse both husbands and law.

A pertinent example of what Finn calls the 'Janus-face' of coverture is evident in Flaubert's *Madame Bovary* (1857).[84] Although his novel represents a woman's experience of marriage in mid nineteenth-century France, it is relevant to a study of the English situation, not only because it was influential on later Victorian writers' depictions of marriage, but also because Flaubert highlights the notion of coverture in imaginative terms as a literal need for a covering, a form of protection. When Emma Bovary, unhappily married and insufficiently 'covered' by her husband, is unable to pay her debts, 'her eyes wandered to the mantelpiece adorned with Chinese hand-screens, to the big curtains, to the armchairs, to all those things that had sweetened the bitterness of her life' (MB 324).[85] Her creditors' forcible repossession of the things she had accumulated to 'sweeten' existence precipitates Emma's suicide. Her obsession with objects has been read as a classic case of commodity fetishism, an example of a mindless and excessive consumerism. Yet, it is highly significant that Emma Bovary's debts are made in trying to satisfy her desire for coverings, for screens and protective wrappings, 'curtains, a carpet, material for covering chairs, several dresses and various toilet articles' (MB 295). Despite her willingness to undress during her liaisons with Rodolphe and Léon (or perhaps even because of it?), she seems desperate to accumulate portable property as a protective cover. However, a number of critics have shown a desire to strip these off, some even relishing her exposure. Walter D. Redfern offers an extreme example of this impulse, suggesting that 'the only time we can spontaneously respect this irritating woman is when she is finally stripped of her possessions by the bailiff, and can at last stand clear in her impoverishment reduced to her mere self without its paraphernalia'.[86]

'Paraphernalia' is a very significant word for Redfern to choose, for as we have seen this was the only property that English law allowed widows to retain. Significantly, the Select Committee on the Married Women's Property Bill dismissed paraphernalia as 'a small exception' to the rules of coverture, for it consisted of 'little things'.[87] Yet even a wife's paraphernalia, this miniature form

---

[82]   Finn, 'Women, Consumption and Coverture', p. 707.

[83]   Ibid., pp. 713–14.

[84]   Ibid., p. 709.

[85]   Gustave Flaubert, *Madame Bovary*, Gerard Hopkins (trans.) (Oxford: Oxford University Press, 1999), p. 324.

[86]   Walter D. Redfern, 'People and Things in Flaubert', *The French Review* (Winter, 1971): 82.

[87]   Cited in R.J. Morris, p. 388.

of property, was not fully under her own control, for husbands had certain rights of ownership over it. Redfern's desire to strip Emma Bovary of all that she tenuously possesses is a denial of her humanity, if we accept the idea that property ownership is intimately related to personhood. *Madame Bovary* has attracted other hostile readings from critics who see Emma's so-called 'bovaryst' desire for so-called trivial things as something reprehensible.[88] Yet Emma's marriage affords her no adequate 'covering' and if we read her desire for things as that of the desire to protect herself with property, then her actions are logical, rather than a nonsensical drive to amass trivial things.

Because of the ambiguity of coverture and the difficulty of defining and retaining paraphernalia, as well as the fact that their ownership of land and investments was usually placed out of their control, Victorian wives before the passing of the Married Women's Property Acts probably felt a desire to *own* something. For many theorists from Locke onwards, this need is a basic aspect of the human condition. As Arendt has argued, things 'give rise to the familiarity of the world, its customs and habits of intercourse between men and things'.[89] In other words, to be a social being, to be placed within the world, one needs to own and thus have control over things, and this is why portable property has traditionally been so important to women. As we have seen, female owners of real property were once rare, and their powers of ownership often severely restricted by marriage settlements and trust funds; however, their possession of portable property was not viewed as central to the debates on the reform of the marriage laws because it posed much less of a threat to the male order of possessive individualism. Women's control of substantial property in land and investments challenged traditional gender roles, whereas women's ownership of relatively inexpensive movable goods presented much less of a threat. Although women may have illegitimately pawned or sold small items, such as ornaments, which were technically the property of their husbands, this was not generally seen as quite so serious a financial transaction as a woman investing or selling real property. Sir John Butler, speaking in Parliament in 1857, suggested that chaos would ensue if a wife had control over real property, for it might be invested:

> without consulting her husband, in some worthless railway shares or in some unsound speculation, and her husband might find that the whole of that property, to which he had looked, perhaps, for the maintenance of himself during his lifetime, and for the benefit of his children afterwards, had been swept away.[90]

---

[88] See Tony Tanner, *Adultery and the Novel: Contract and Transgression* (Baltimore and London: The Johns Hopkins University Press, 1979), pp. 297–8; and Frederic Jameson, *The Political Unconscious: Narrative as a Socially Symbolic Act* (London and New York: Routledge, 2007), p. 146.

[89] Arendt, p. 94.

[90] Quoted in Poovey, *Uneven Developments*, p. 74.

The law was effective in preventing wives from selling the land settled on them in equity, but there was little likelihood of legal intervention when a wife pawned a necklace she thought that she owned.

While women's feelings of ownership may have been illusory from a legal perspective, the chances were that most women *felt* and *believed* that they owned their personal portable items. Denied full access to the ownership of real property, women made do with securing their identity on such personal, portable things. Yet, as Shanley has demonstrated, portable property was seen increasingly as an important source of wealth throughout the nineteenth century. She suggests that the greater security women had over their portable property 'lay not in feminist ideas but in the shift of wealth from land to movable property and the uncertainties of nineteenth-century economic life'.[91] In other words, while women had tended to own 'second best' property in the past, during the economic vicissitudes of the Victorian period portable property was increasingly recognized as a flexible alternative to real estate and the sluggishness of the parliamentary debaters in recognizing this shift away from land towards things and money meant that women's ownership of movables was not subjected to the same level of legal scrutiny as was their ownership of land.

Portable Property: the 'fall out of circulation'

The law has long made a distinction between personal (or movable) and real (or landed) property; however, as J.H. Baker has indicated, this distinction has not always been as straightforward as it at first seems. He gives the example of a meeting of English judges in 1647 who considered whether the dung spread on land was classified as a chattel (and thus subject to the laws on portable property) or part of the land itself. They concluded that 'dung spread on the ground was part of the realty whereas a heap of dung was a chattel'.[92] Yet movable items, such as house keys and title deeds were considered legally to be 'realty', a part of real estate. The law treated each type of property separately because, as Baker states, there was 'a marked difference in value and permanence between land, which was a capital asset producing a continuous livelihood or income, and most ordinary chattels, such as grain or cattle, which were consumable'.[93] However, the growth of industrialism conferred a greater importance on movable wealth. When, late in the century, Lady Bracknell in Oscar Wilde's *The Importance of Being Earnest* (1895) asks Jack about the basis of his wealth, he replies that it is 'in investments', to which Lady Bracknell replies, 'That is satisfactory. … [L]and has ceased to be a profit or a pleasure. It gives one position, and prevents one from keeping it up.

---

[91] Shanley, p. 16.

[92] J.H. Baker, *An Introduction to English Legal History*, 4th ed. (Oxford: Oxford University Press, 2007), p. 380.

[93] Baker, p. 379.

That's all that can be said about land'.[94] The humour resides in the fact that for centuries land had been the basis of wealth and prestige, and one would expect a traditionalist such as Lady Bracknell to favour this form of wealth. However, both she and Jack know that money is far more important in the modern urban context of high capitalism.

Of course, it was not only women who valued portable property. Its advantages were evident to everyone who needed to raise money in an emergency. John Locke himself, implicated in a conspiracy against James II, was forced to flee Britain. He wrote to Edward Clarke to send his property:

> Pray talk with Dr Thomas about the best way of securing the books and goods in my chamber at Christ Church if there should be any danger. There is a pair of candlesticks, too, and a silver standish of mine in Mr Percivall's hands. When a safe and sure way of returning money to me is found I would have them also turned into money and returned to me.[95]

Locke also refers to other items he owned, such as a ruby ring, linen, shirts, a clock and stockings, all of which he wants to be sold and the wealth stored within them transformed into the most liquid form of property: money. The liquidity of portable property, whether in the form of investments, movable items (such as Locke's candlesticks and ruby ring) or in cash itself, helped to power a world based on the transactions of financial markets.

The movement, or exchange, of things into the 'universal equivalent' called money was examined by Marx as the basis of modern capitalism. The circulation of commodities, 'the products of social labour', is particularly the target of his scorn for it engenders a reversal of the human–object hierarchy by 'develop[ing] a whole network of social relations spontaneous in their growth and entirely beyond the control of the actors'.[96] The workers who create commodities are unable to control them, and those who invest in their circulation in the marketplace are equally dominated by the things themselves. Marx goes on to explain how the world of circulating commodities works:

> Every commodity, when it first steps into circulation, and undergoes its first change of form, does so *only to fall out of circulation again* and to be replaced by other commodities. Money, on the contrary, as the medium of circulation, keeps continually within the sphere of circulation, and moves about in it'.[97]

While money cannot escape the bondage of its continual movement between owners, commodities fall out of the system and are swiftly replaced by others. Marx

---

[94]   Oscar Wilde, *The Importance of Being Earnest* in *The Norton Anthology of English Literature*, S. Greenblatt et al. (eds), 8th ed. (New York: Norton, 2006), p. 1708.

[95]   Cited in Cranston, p. 230.

[96]   Marx, *Capital*, p. 72.

[97]   Ibid., p. 76; emphasis added.

says very little about this 'fall', the moment when commodities eventually come to rest within human lives: food is consumed and transformed into living flesh, clothes are worn, while some things find a resting place as a piece of cherished portable property. In circulation things remain commodities; however, once they have 'fallen' their commodity status is lost. Marx gives no name for the 'fallen' commodity for it enters a private realm where its meanings are by no means fixed.

Marx's own experience of commodities and their 'fall' into his own life was often problematic. Like Locke, he was made painfully aware of the need to convert objects into money at short notice. Peter Stallybrass has discussed Marx's experience of dire poverty when he lived in exile in London. Like many working-class people of the Victorian period, he relied on the services of pawnshops in order to survive. As Stallybrass states, the poor stored the little wealth they possessed 'not as *money* in *banks* but as *things* in the *house*. Well-being could be measured by the coming and going of those things. To be out of pocket was to be forced to strip the body. To be in pocket was to reclothe the body'.[98] This situation was shared by many middle-class women, outwardly comfortably off, but often unable to raise capital, even on a small scale. Lacking property rights, unable to enter into a contract or access money independently, married women from middle-class homes sometimes depended on the value *in* things in the way that working-class people did and, like them, were able to use portable property to raise money in emergencies. Like their working-class counterparts, they were often placed in extremely vulnerable positions as far as their emotional investments in things were concerned: 'Memories were thus inscribed for the poor within objects that were haunted by loss'.[99] The trauma of loss, of appearing in the world without a decent covering (Marx himself was sometimes unable to visit the British Library in winter because he was forced to pawn his overcoat), was the humiliation inflicted on the poor by capitalism and on women by patriarchy.[100]

The concept of portable property was, then, important in an era where money exchanges dominated the marketplace. As Blackstone wrote in 1766, 'Our courts now regard a man's personalty in a light nearly, if not quite, equal to his realty'.[101] The value locked in land was often slow to be released, sometimes involving lengthy legal procedures or negotiations with buyers; however, with the rise of the bourgeoisie in the eighteenth and nineteenth centuries there was a marked shift away from fixing wealth in landed property to investing in the more flexible forms of portable property. While real estate is, in Edmund Burke's term, 'sluggish, inert and timid',[102] movable property was seen by many middle-class people as

---

[98] Stallybrass, p. 202; emphasis in the original.

[99] Ibid., p. 196.

[100] Ibid., p. 187.

[101] Blackstone, vol. 2, p. 313.

[102] Edmund Burke, *Reflections on the Revolution in France and on the Proceedings in Certain Societies in London Relative to that Event. In a Letter to Have been Sent to a Gentleman in Paris* (London: J. Dodsley, 1790), pp. 74–5.

'a good way to store wealth' for, as well as being liquid and thus easily taken to the marketplace and sold, possessions 'could also be pawned to assist a family over periods of sickness or joblessness'.[103] The bourgeois family developed in the context of portable property, which often formed the basis of its wealth. MacPherson, in his discussion of possessive individualism, defines bourgeois society as 'a society in which the relations between men are dominated by the market' and it is the ownership of commodities and 'the success with which they utilize that ownership to their own profit' which underpins the development of modern society.[104]

In legal terms, there has been a major distinction made between movable and immovable property, a distinction which Henry Maine in *Ancient Law* describes as the 'only natural classification of the objects of enjoyment'.[105] As we have seen with Locke's theory of property, the idea of what is 'natural' has often dominated perceptions of ownership. In English law real property (that is, land and buildings) was traditionally treated as superior to personal property (movable goods). As Whelan has stated, the laws concerning real property tend to be based on common law, which is unwritten and 'inferred from custom and from the records of court decisions', while the laws concerning personal (or movable) property are written in statutory law and based on acts of parliament.[106] Whelan also notes that 'Much of the current law respecting personal or movable property ... has its origin in statutes, a fact that reflects the relatively greater importance of this kind of property in modern times, characterized as they have been by the growth of commerce'.[107] On a personal level, portable property also helped to shape domestic life, as well as functioning as a convenient store of wealth.

R.J. Morris emphasizes this in *Men, Women and Property in England, 1780–1870*, demonstrating the ways in which portable property 'created the opportunities and stage sets upon which the values of politeness, domesticity and piety were acted out. [It] brought utility and status'.[108] In his examination of wills made by middle-class people in Leeds in the 1820s and 1830s, he found evidence that the family home was often viewed as of less importance than the transfer of objects between family and friends:

> This lack of concern [for the family house] was another mark of the social boundary of the middle classes. There was none of the continuity of possession for house and estate characteristic of the aristocratic landed family. Nor was

---

[103] James C. Riley, 'A Widening Market in Consumer Goods' in Evan Cameron (ed.), *Early Modern Europe: An Oxford History* (Oxford: Oxford University Press, 2001), p. 257.

[104] C.B. MacPherson, *The Political Theory of Possessive Individualism: Hobbes to Locke* (Oxford: Oxford University Press, 1962), p. 162.

[105] Henry Maine, *Ancient Law: Its Connection with the Early History of Society and its Relation to Modern Ideas* (London: John Murray, 1920), pp. 283–4.

[106] Whelan, p. 115.

[107] Ibid., p. 116.

[108] R.J. Morris, p. 49.

there any sense of attachment, moral, emotional and economic, between family and land evident in many studies of peasant inheritance. On death, the family house and the business became assets which were open to acquire new meanings or simply be turned into cash by way of the market.[109]

Instead of prioritizing real estate, many of the middling classes were what Morris terms 'things' people, those who had a high regard for their personal portable property and designed their wills in order to distribute such objects to those most likely to understand and appreciate the bequest.[110] His research reveals that most 'things' people were women.[111] While men tended to make relatively straightforward wills involving greater levels of real estate in relation to portable property, and adhering to the custom of providing primarily for their widows and children, women were much more likely to write distinctive, complicated wills that 'mark[ed] out their social and emotional world. Compared to males their marked world was much broader. It contained a wider range of family, and more friends, including servants'.[112] Women from wealthier families were usually put in the position of 'passive' property owners as far as real estate and investments were concerned; however, they often enjoyed a much greater sense of autonomy in relation to their portable property. For example, the widow of a stonemason, Elizabeth Craven, who died in February 1830 was, according to Morris, a 'things' woman, and her will illustrates the sense of control she enjoyed as an owner of portable property. Her (erratically punctuated) will contained the following bequests:

Nephew, John Craven Ryley
Mahogany desk, or bureau, feather bed, flock mattress, pier glass and
    small oak stand
Nephew, Thomas Ryley
Oak chest of drawers, eight days clock, two silver table spoons
Nephew, William Ryley
My silver pint, mahogany card table, oak dining table, round oak table, seven
silver tea spoons, my silver sugar tongs
Elizabeth Hutton, wife of John Hutton, Leeds.
My mahogany elbow chair, my red and white china and the sum of £50
    in money.
John Mawson of Leeds, gentleman
My silver gill and cream jug.[113]

Here we can see that even small items of cutlery and furniture have been carefully passed to relatives and friends for their enjoyment and use as well as memorials of the dead. Women often formulated complex bequests in order to enhance

---

[109]   Ibid., p. 124.

[110]   Ibid., p. 128.

[111]   Ibid., p. 129.

[112]   Ibid., p. 240.

[113]   Reprinted in R.J. Morris, p. 248.

emotional bonds, reward services and acts of kindness, and to try to control the afterlife of cherished objects.[114]

Portable things were, then, important stores of monetary value. At a time when the burgeoning commodity culture of the period created increased access to objects (both visually, via media representations, and in terms of ownership), the novel presents many portable things bluntly in terms of property. One of the most well-known fictional advocates of the advantages of portable property is the office clerk Wemmick in *Great Expectations* who, when Pip asks him about the collection of mourning jewellery he wears explains that they are, 'all gifts … I always take 'em. They're curiosities. And they're property. They may not be worth much, but, after all, they're property and portable. It don't signify to you with your brilliant lookout, but as to myself, my guiding-star always is, "Get hold of portable property"'.[115] Later he states that 'Every man's business … is portable property' (GE 409). However, the lower middle-class Wemmick has the advantage over married women of the period for he also owns and has full control of real estate in Walworth, his 'Castle', having 'got hold of it, a bit at a time. It's a freehold, by George!' (GE 208). For Wemmick, it is the durability of things, their ability to outlast their owner, which makes them valuable. This distinction between the mutability of men and the durability of things is evident when he complains to Pip about 'the sacrifice of so much portable property' to the Crown when Magwitch is condemned to die (GE 451). When Pip reproaches Wemmick for not focusing on 'the poor owner of the property' (GE 451), Wemmick replies: 'I do not think he could have been saved. Whereas, the portable property certainly could have been saved. That's the difference between the property and the owner, don't you see' (GE 452).

Wemmick is acutely aware of the difference between people and things: the felons who bequeath him jewellery die, while the jewellery itself continues to exist. This distinction informs the tradition of property transmission; as Minogue has stated, it was 'the material link … between the living, the dead and those yet to be born'.[116] Arendt sees this distinction between human mutability and the ability of things to survive as the basis of the human condition:

> The reality and reliability of the human world rest primarily on the fact that we are surrounded by things more permanent than the activity by which they were produced, and potentially even more permanent than the lives of the authors. Human life, so far as it is world building, is engaged in a constant process of reification, and the degree of worldliness of produced things, which all together form the human artifice, depends upon their greater or lesser permanence in the world itself.[117]

---

[114]   Ibid., pp. 95–6.

[115]   Charles Dickens, *Great Expectations*, David Trotter and Charlotte Mitchell (eds) (London: Penguin, 1996), p. 201. Subsequent references will be cited in the text following the abbreviation, 'GE'.

[116]   Minogue, p. 8.

[117]   Arendt, pp. 95–6.

For Wemmick, in receipt of portable property from those condemned to die, the things are quite obviously more permanent than the owners. He is also aware of the uses to which their things can be put and, as someone who sees his survival as potentially precarious, his collection of curiosities exists always on the verge of alienability. Yet the portable property in his collection does not function for him as part of a process of affective world building, for he has no emotional bond or long-term commitment to the things he accumulates. He appears to accept the alienability of things without any qualms; whether he would feel so casual about the alienability of his real property is another question. Many Victorian women, on the other hand, were unable to make similar investments in real property, tending instead to stabilize their sense of identity by means of portable things. However, the danger inherent in making an emotional and personal investment in things is that portable property has traditionally been much more liable to alienation than real estate.

Alienable/Inalienable Property

While liberal theorists equate freedom with the ability to alienate one's property, Marx and others have focused on the problems inherent in alienation. The anthropologist Annette B. Weiner and the philosopher Margaret Jane Radin have examined the concept of the alienability in some detail. Both arrive at similar conclusions: that the loss of certain types of property can result in a loss of personhood or the undermining of a group's identity (whether it be a nation's or a family's). Such property, they argue, is too precious and important to be alienated and to avoid this happening, individuals and groups work to ensure its inalienability. Their arguments are relevant to a consideration of Victorian women and their portable property, for both suggest universality in human relationships to things and thus help to illuminate the various attitudes which underpin the representation of objects and portable property in Victorian novels.

Weiner's book *Inalienable Possessions: The Paradox of Keeping-While-Giving*, a study of property ownership in Oceanic societies, is based on the idea that 'all exchange is predicated on the universal paradox – how to keep-while-giving'.[118] Drawing upon and challenging Mauss's book *The Gift*, in which he expounds his theory of reciprocity and exchange in terms of gift giving and receiving, Weiner identifies a category of possessions she terms 'inalienable', those objects which can only be given to others temporarily before they must be returned. She defines an inalienable possession as one which has 'its exclusive and cumulative identity with a particular series of owners through time … transcendent treasures to be guarded against all the exigencies that might force their loss'.[119] There is plenty of evidence to show that for European women, the 'inalienable' possession was an ideal form of property, for it would be protected from appropriation by others,

---

[118] Annette B. Weiner, *Inalienable Possessions: The Paradox of Keeping-While-Giving* (Berkeley: University of California Press, 1992), p. 4.

[119] Ibid., p. 33.

including husbands. However, Weiner emphasizes the paradoxical nature of inalienable possessions because they can slip out of the owner's grasp by being 'exchanged, lost in warfare, destroyed by rivals, sold'.[120] This, of course, means that there is actually no such thing as an inalienable possession, just an imaginary, theoretical possibility of pure and unthreatened ownership. The *OED* defines 'inalienable' as not capable of being transferred to another because the law forbids it. Weiner's own use of the word is a shorthand for an ideal form of possession – a thing which cannot be appropriated by 'outsiders'. Yet it is clear from the examples that she gives that this ideal is an impossibility in practical terms, particularly in the context of Western capitalism. For example, she states of eighteenth-century European aristocrats that, 'By giving up their inalienable landed property and possessions ... in order to afford the newest luxuries and fashions, the nobility was in danger of diminishing, or even losing, the strength of their political authority'.[121] Yet if their property was really 'inalienable', they would have been forbidden by law from selling it. The liberal basis of the English law of property meant that this restriction on alienation was rare. In other words, while an inalienable possession is an ideal, it is actually impossible for one individual to *own* it. This is evident from those cases where the law supported inalienability. If it was possible to sell inalienable property, then son-less characters such as Mr and Mrs Bennet in *Pride and Prejudice* need not have worried about Mr Collins as the heir to the entailed estate, and Sir Hugo Mallinger in *Daniel Deronda* could have simply cut out Grandcourt and bequeathed his property to his daughters. Neither Mr Bennet nor Sir Hugo 'own' their estates, for it really belongs to the family which transcends and controls each individual member in terms of the distribution of property. The issue of alienability, as we have seen, is central to Trollope's *The Eustace Diamonds*, for it exposes the problems of ensuring inalienability; a badly drafted will means that the Eustace family loses possession of what was meant to be an inalienable heirloom. A carefully drafted will would have ensured that no individual family member could have actually owned it.

The social system based on inalienable property is almost obsolete in the West (apart from inalienable property in the form of 'heritage' objects, such as the Crown Jewels or Stonehenge belonging to Great Britain), despite Weiner's claims that 'the presence of inalienable possessions was not displaced by capitalism nor was the power of these possessions ignored by financiers'.[122] She erroneously gives as examples of inalienable possessions things which have been alienated and are perfectly capable of being alienated again, such as the paintings and art objects which rich industrialists collect.[123] In fact, despite their uniqueness and associations with specific cultures and traditions, such objects are all too prone to

---

[120] Ibid., p. 37.

[121] Ibid., p. 33.

[122] Ibid., p. 35.

[123] Ibid.

being circulated in open markets. Turning to the realm of literary representation, one only has to consider Mrs Gereth's fruitless attempts to ensure the inalienability of her collection in Henry James's *The Spoils of Poynton*, a novel discussed in detail in Chapter 4, to realize the ease with which apparently inalienable objects can slip from an 'owner's' grasp.

Yet Weiner's concept of inalienable possessions, while a fantasy for those living in the period of high capitalism, is a useful one to use when considering women's portable property. The ambition of the female property owners who fill Victorian novels is to keep during life and to bequeath to chosen heirs after death. As we will see in Chapter 3, the Dodson sisters in *The Mill on the Floss*, by 'naming' their possessions, attempt to use 'inalienable' property to maintain the Dodson identity long after they have lost the Dodson name on marriage. The issue of naming in the context of ownership is an important one. Janet Hoskins, drawing upon the work of the anthropologist Violette Morin, identifies the concept of a 'biographical object' as a thing which is 'formative of its owner's identity ... . People who surround themselves with biographical objects do so to develop their personalities and reflect on them'. She adds that biographical objects are used 'as part of the narrative process of self-definition'.[124] Thus, owners 'invest aspects of their own biographies in things'.[125] We will see this in Chapter 2, where Dickens, himself prone towards an emotional investment in biographical objects, represents numerous characters in terms of their 'signature' objects. Yet naming a thing and investing oneself in it do not guarantee ownership. As Eliot shows, the exigencies of coverture and capitalism meant that women's presumptions about the inalienability of their possessions were not supported by the law and thus ownership needed to be asserted via illegitimate tactics.

Writing from the perspective of a philosopher of the law, Margaret Jane Radin in her book of essays *Reinterpreting Property*, published in 1993, a year after *Inalienable Possessions*, comes to a similar conclusion: that some possessions are so important to personhood that they should not be alienated. Drawing on the notion (originally proposed by Maine in *Ancient Law*) that the West has moved from a society based on status to one regulated by contract, Radin asks whether some objects should not be classed as property at all. Analyzing the ways in which personhood has been framed in the West, she identifies a 'thin theory of the person' which envisions people as free and mobile, able to alienate all of their possessions, including themselves.[126] In other words, the extreme libertarian model of property ownership is that one is free to sell oneself into slavery because one owns oneself. The opposite view to this she terms the 'thick theory of the person' which places a high value on 'rootedness' and the importance of the relationships people forge with things; this idea of personhood is based on the argument that the temporal or

---

[124] Hoskins, p. 78.

[125] Ibid., p. 74.

[126] Radin, p. 26.

spatial continuity of these relationships should not be disrupted.[127] The problem with both of these extremes, Radin argues, is that the libertarian view sees people in terms of mobile commodities, while the opposite view promotes the idea of stasis and fixed hierarchies.[128] Summing up these extremes, she states that '[t]he mythology of property expresses rootedness, and the mythology of contract expresses mutability'.[129] Radin (like Weiner) leans towards the status side of the equation, arguing against the freedom to view oneself and others as commodities and all property as equally alienable.

In a chapter on the rhetoric of alienation, Radin plays with the double meaning of the word, noting that alienation is both equated with the freedom necessary to a functioning capitalist economy, where '[e]verything must be both ownable and saleable' and also signifies 'a pathology to be avoided'.[130] Radin identifies a fundamental contradiction surrounding modern conceptions of property:

> The ideology of property as it has come down to us affirms what I would call a personal-continuity thesis: that property is necessary to give people 'roots', stable surroundings, a context of control over the environment, a context of stable expectations that fosters autonomy and personality.[131]

Yet this thesis exists in opposition to the impulse of market forces which values things according to their exchange capacity (what Radin calls her 'object–fungibility thesis'). Radin addresses this contradiction in the following terms:

> But if property is a property of persons, then alienation of property breeds alienation of persons. If the person-object bond is broken, the stable context destroyed or prevented from forming, the basis of plans and memories ignored or smashed, then the autonomy of freedom of contract can be merely a sign of the estrangement of persons.[132]

She sees one way out of this dilemma by making a distinction between 'personal' property (by which she does not mean portable property but 'biographical' objects, things which function as sources of identity and affect or personhood) and 'fungible' property (money and shares are the examples she gives of non-affective property). This distinction needs to be made, she argues, because '[w]edding rings are not the same kind of property as widgets'.[133]

Both Weiner and Radin show that because some property is not readily exchangeable, no market value should be placed upon it. They emphasize the fact

---

[127] Ibid., p. 31.
[128] Ibid.
[129] Ibid., p. 24.
[130] Ibid., p. 192.
[131] Ibid., p. 197.
[132] Ibid.
[133] Ibid.

that the pain involved in the forcible removal of what Radin terms 'personal' property and Weiner terms 'inalienable' property cannot be equated to a monetary value. In other words, financial compensation for the loss of such goods is inadequate to cover the loss to personal or group identity. This conception of property helps to explain the impassioned calls by Victorian feminists for the reform of the married women's property laws, for women's vulnerability lay in their inability to secure those things they considered essential to their identity. The notion of women being able to retain certain types of property because they constituted their personhood was at the heart of the drive to improve women's standing and status in Victorian society; property rights and personhood are linked in such a way that the removal of one quality jeopardizes the other.

Yet, the liberal tendency to promote the alienability of all possessions could occasionally work in women's favour because the exchangeability of property in the marketplace confers power and status. Portable property as a repository of wealth could, if necessary, be exchanged for money and, as Victorian women were undoubtedly aware, only money could buy certain freedoms.[134] Those women whose lives were framed by a capitalist system may have hoped to keep their possessions, but also knew that selling (rather than giving) was a valuable freedom. While inalienable possessions are an ideal in certain contexts, it is actually the *alienability* of property which makes it valuable because it makes it ownable. Victorian women's attachment to portable property was based on a powerful concept of ownership which had more than economic consequences: owning things worked on a psychic level, too. The processes of fetishization were always at work in a society which valorized objects and used them symbolically.

The 'alien world of objects': Fetishism and Fallen Women

Karl Marx was all too aware of the imaginary nature of property and the law. The source of the problem, according to Marx, was that capitalist society encourages 'the personification of objects and the reification of people'.[135] Indeed, the object-world can be as menacing in Marx's writings as it is in Dickens's novels. Both writers seem compelled to use active verbs when describing objects. In *Capital*, for example, the commodity is 'a very queer thing', which 'steps forth', 'stands on its head' and has 'grotesque ideas'; it operates as 'the fantastic form of a relation between things' which Marx sees as the basis of commodity fetishism.[136] He argues that this leaves the worker locked in a conflict with things:

> The worker is related to the *product of his labour* as to an *alien* object. For on this premise it is clear that the more the worker spends himself, the more powerful

---

[134] See Henry for a discussion of Victorian women's investment practices.

[135] Marx, *Capital*, p. 390.

[136] Ibid., pp. 42–3.

the alien objective world becomes which he creates over against himself, the poorer he himself – his inner world – becomes, the less belongs to him as his own.[137]

Marx uses the term 'fetishism' (originally coined in 1757 to describe the worship of objects) to emphasize the alien qualities of commodities.[138] Yet, as we have seen, he also refers to the commodity's 'fall' into another identity in relation to its owner. The worker, then, is alienated by the processes of mass production, but this does not preclude meaningful relationships with objects, even mass-produced ones. In other words, it is the context of a human–object relation which influences its meaning. We will return to Marx shortly. In the meantime, it is important to bear in mind that fetishism is a concept which has been employed in a variety of ways to suit a number of different purposes.

For example, another major theorist of fetishism, Freud, is interested in its ability to provide a channel for the libidinal economy. However, he focuses on an object so alien, it never existed in the first place: the maternal penis. It works as 'a token of triumph over the threat of castration and a protection against it'.[139] As many critics have noted, Freud's model of fetishism precludes the possibility of the female fetishist, for women share the mother's 'castrated' state. While feminists have tended to emphasize the limitations of Freud's theory, many have found psychoanalytic readings of fetishism useful as a way of describing some women's experiences.[140] Emily Apter, for example, in her book *Feminizing the Fetish* takes a less gendered view of 'partial object substitutionism in sexuality'[141] than Freud's, moving beyond 'received interpretation[s] of fetishism ... as a negative effect of commodification' to argue that there exists a 'critical fetishism, an aesthetic of fetishization that reflexively exposes the commodity as an impostor value'.[142] Commodity fetishism, as Apter rightly indicates, fails to account for a wide range of human–object relationships and numerous feminist critics have agreed, arguing that for women fetishism can work as a positive strategy.

Indeed, without the possession of full social rights, Victorian women were metaphorically castrated when they married. In the context of wives' lack of legal

---

[137] Karl Marx, *The Economic and Philosophic Manuscripts of 1844*, Martin Milligan (trans.) (Moscow: Foreign Languages Publishing House, 1961), pp. 69–70; emphasis in the original.

[138] See William Pietz, 'Fetishism and Materialism: The Limits of Theory in Marx', in Emily Apter and William Pietz (eds), *Fetishism as Cultural Discourse* (Ithaca and London: Cornell University Press, 1993), pp. 119–51; pp. 130–31.

[139] Sigmund Freud, 'Fetishism', in *On Sexuality*, Angela Richards (ed.), James Strachey (trans.), vol. 7, The Pelican Freud Library (London: Penguin, 1977), p. 353.

[140] See Teresa de Lauretis, *Technologies of Gender: Essays on Theory, Film and Fiction* (Bloomington and Indianapolis: Indiana University Press, 1987), p. 20.

[141] Emily Apter, *Feminizing the Fetish: Psychoanalysis and Narrative Obsession in Turn-of-the-Century France* (Ithaca and London: Cornell University Press, 1991), p. x.

[142] Ibid., p. 12.

(and thus public) existence, women's fetishism has a specific and understandable logic. Yet the logic of the fetish is not usually evident; as Laura Mulvey states of the Freudian fetish, it acts as a 'phantasmatic inscription. It ascribes excessive value to objects considered to be valueless by the social consensus'.[143] Thus relatively 'valueless' objects (that is, in terms of monetary or exchange value) which recent critics have read as merely commodities, may have functioned as positive fetishes and as forms of property. We have seen that before the passing of the Married Women's Property Acts wives needed to ignore or refuse the law if they were to believe themselves to be the possessors of objects: possession itself was thus a phantasm, a situation identical to the fetishist's ability to entertain two mutually exclusive ideas at the same time. This is a process of 'disavowal' which, as Freud states, is what happens when the fetishist retains his belief in the mother's penis at the same time as he gives up this belief. While most Victorian women knew that husbands possessed legal rights over their wives' property, they also probably refused to believe that they owned nothing, for to acknowledge that one owns nothing is a state of abjection. This 'refusal, or blockage, of the mind' both defines fetishism and, more importantly, offers a strategy for survival.[144] Fetishism works so well because, as Freud observes, the fetishist has the advantage of the 'meaning of the fetish ... not [being] known to other people' and it can thus be enjoyed without punishment.[145] It is the relative invisibility of the small items of portable property that women use – invisible, that is, to the law and to men (both tending to define 'property' in much bigger terms) – which allows the fetishized object to pass unnoticed. Clearly, a Victorian woman who tried to fetishize a valuable piece of jewellery in this way was likely to fail in the retention of her fetish.

Yet fetishism has not always been recognized as a valuable strategy. It is helpful to turn again to *Madame Bovary*, with its powerful depiction of a female fetishist, a literary representation of fetishism in action. Critics have been all too ready to focus on the heroine's 'bovarysm'. Tony Tanner, for example, sees her fetishism in terms of a cop out because 'fetishized objects are relatively safe, easily available, undemanding in reciprocity or commitment and thus allowing the person whose feelings have been aroused to remain in a passive, spectator/ consumer relationship to the other'.[146] Drawing upon the Marxist notion that mass production under capitalism engenders the anti-social forces of commodification and reification, Tanner develops this view by saying that the fetishization of objects is a 'deliberate way of *not* seeing' the other.[147] However, as Marx suggests when he refers to the commodity's 'fall out of circulation', not all objects are always (forever) commodities. Here, it is important not to oversimplify the complexity of human–object relations, so crucial to identity formation. Tanner's view of Emma

---

[143] Laura Mulvey, *Fetishism and Curiosity* (London: British Film Institute, 1996), p. 2.

[144] Mulvey, p. 2.

[145] Freud, 'Fetishism', p. 354.

[146] Tanner, p. 288.

[147] Ibid., p. 290; emphasis in the original.

Bovary's fetishism depends upon his judgment about what constitutes a useful, necessary, or valuable object when he argues that her tragedy is exemplified in her need for 'useless' objects. When Lheureux lures Emma into debt, Tanner states that the shopkeeper-cum-money-lender:

> Propos[es], quite implicitly ... that Emma can fill the gaps of desire with materials and things. He is in fact the most dangerous seduction for Emma, for he works by trying to transform the vagueness and indistinctness of erotic-emotional desire into a specific greed for an infinity of unnecessary commodities. (MB 297)

The key word here is 'unnecessary'. While Lheureux's commodities seem superfluous to Tanner, they are clearly necessary for Emma. Tanner's view of what he terms her 'pointless accumulation of useless material and costumery' suggests that women's things are 'useless' and trivial, symptomatic of their infantilization, thus making them easy 'prey' to the capitalist.[148] Emma's relationship to the object world, because it is grounded in the social world, is necessarily a gendered one and Tanner explicitly links her tendency towards the accumulation of objects with her adultery:

> In adultery Emma does not become another person, another role, another pose, etc., she becomes a *chose*, a thing devoid of indwelling determinants and thus *pliant* to the handling, shaping forces and figures around her. She enters the realm of interchangeable objects, which is the dehumanized, reified realm of the society and its prevailing currencies, financial and emotional.[149]

What Tanner fails to register is that far from feeling dehumanized by her investment in objects, Emma may find her only sense of agency in her ability to possess objects. By enjoying a feeling of ownership, Emma surrounds herself with things as reminders (or to use Freud's term 'memorials') that she is not a thing (despite other people persisting in seeing her as one). Material objects then, far from obliterating an awareness of difference, may actually engender one: Emma knows she is not a thing because she possesses power over things. When that power is exposed as illusory, she consumes arsenic, as though her last action is to convert herself into a thing (a corpse) as a way of avoiding passivity, or even making a final comment on the act of consumption itself. In this way she finally resists everyone (including some literary critics) who has tried to convert her into a thing.

Madame Bovary and Lizzie Eustace are to varying degrees depicted as 'fallen' women, and Victorian novelists found the representation of desire for property a good way of signalling other, less easily representable, forms of female desire. The desire to own things, then, often becomes a mask for sexual desire. Another important representation of female fallenness and fetishism from the mid-Victorian period is Lucy Audley, the former governess and abandoned wife who marries

---

[148]   Ibid., p. 298.

[149]   Ibid., p. 367; emphasis in the original.

bigamously into the landed gentry in Braddon's *Lady Audley's Secret*. Lucy, like Lizzie Eustace, gains access to luxurious things on her marriage. However, the unreality of Lucy's property is repeatedly emphasized by means of its association with magic, fairytales and childhood. The narrator states that 'Lady Audley seemed as happy as a child surrounded by new and costly toys';[150] she is transformed from a working woman into 'a social fairy weaving potent spells' (LAS 222), inhabiting rooms which resemble a 'little Aladdin's palace' (LAS 296). All of this has been gained by means of her 'fairy dower' (LAS 297, 310); that is, her beauty. Yet Lucy, like Lizzie Eustace, having suffered poverty, tends now to reduce everything to a monetary value. This is a quality she shares with the working-class Luke (who, on discovering that she had a child before her marriage to Sir Michael, succeeds in blackmailing her). When he sees Lucy's open jewel box he desires to 'handle the delicate jewels; to pull them about, and find out their mercantile value' (LAS 30). The penetration of women's jewel boxes and cabinets by men is, as we will see in subsequent chapters, a recurring image of the vulnerable and sexualized female property owner. Lucy, like Luke, prices everything and is always aware of the tenuousness of her possession of them. When her husband's nephew, Robert, finally confronts her, she gazes on 'every precious toy that was scattered about in the reckless profusion of magnificence', aware of 'how much the things had cost, and how painfully probable it was that the luxurious apartment would pass out of her possession' (LAS 373).

Lucy, like Emma Bovary, relies upon her body as a way of bargaining for the 'precious toys' which sweeten her existence. Believing her beauty to be 'a boundless possession' (LAS 296), 'a little royalty' (LAS 382), she presumes that she can reinvest it when she is ejected from her home at Audley Court. However, her eventual banishment to a lunatic asylum removes her from the world of financial exchange and the possibility of reinvesting her beauty in another man. Braddon signals Lucy's inability to prostitute herself, to put her ownership of her own body to use, in the description of her bed in the asylum: 'a bed so wondrously made, as to appear to have no opening whatever in its coverings, unless the counterpane had been split asunder as with a penknife' (LAS 388). The violence of the imagery, along with the premature death of Lucy, reflects Flaubert's representation of the end of Emma's career as a woman who uses sex and her possessions to colour her life. Indeed, Braddon was very familiar with Flaubert's novel for she used *Madame Bovary* as the basis of her own novel, *The Doctor's Wife* (1864).

The sensational qualities of *Madame Bovary* and *Lady Audley's Secret* are based on the links drawn between women, sexuality and the possession of desirable objects. For many Marxist critics, the degenerative processes of bourgeois life under capitalism are most evident in women's desires for 'useless' objects.[151]

---

[150] Mary E. Braddon, *Lady Audley's Secret*, David Skilton (ed.) (Oxford: Oxford University Press, 1991), p. 52. Subsequent references will be cited in the text following the abbreviation 'LAS'.

[151] See Tanner and Jameson.

While not trying to suggest that the capitalist tendency towards reification and commodification is without its problems, or that women's desires for things serve them well in all social contexts, I do want to consider the association between women and 'useless trinkets' in relation to Victorian women's practices of property ownership as a potentially positive one. Far from being privatized, women's desires to own objects could function as a route into the social and the political. What Tanner calls an accumulation of 'useless trinkets' may actually have functioned as a basis for the construction of a social identity. If we accept this, then clearly the objects women desire to possess are not 'useless'.

Dismissals of such problems as 'trivial' have their basis in privilege. Stallybrass has identified a similar sense of superiority in relation to those critics of fetishism who either smile on or condemn the fetishization of objects. Stallybrass has discussed the traditional views of the (male) European (from the Renaissance onwards) who defines himself as 'a subject unhampered by a fixation upon objects', aware only of the market value of exchangeable commodities, rather than having an emotional need for them.[152] For Stallybrass this is actually a form of impoverishment and the basis of the commodity fetishism outlined by Marx in *Capital*.[153] For the European (unaware of his own fetishization of that *thing* called money) sees 'primitive' people, such as 'natives', women and the working classes not as subjects but as naively subject to the lure of object fetishism. However, Stallybrass, like Marx, sees the European male's commodity fixation as an example of bad fetishism. Women, working-class people and so-called primitive people who fetishize things because of the 'possibility that history, memory, and desire might be materialized in objects that are touched and loved and worn', offer examples of good fetishism, for the objects they possess have a meaning beyond mere exchange value.[154] This, for Stallybrass (and, of course, for Marx) is a valid human–object relationship, yet it is often misunderstood, seen as worthless or even demonized by those who see objects only in terms of their monetary value.

The 'naïve' consumer, fetishist or reader, if we accept Stallybrass's argument, is actually less gullible than those who are the unwitting victims of commodity fetishism, for they know that the objects they feel attached to exist beyond mere exchange value, that part of those objects is simply not reducible to money. As Radin has stated, 'objects held by persons for purposes of wealth gain through market trading are to be thought of differently from objects held as integral to personal continuity'.[155] Thus while Emma Bovary is for most critics the apotheosis of naivety (hence the development of the term 'bovaryst' to signify the ingenuous consumer), both in her reading habits and in her desire to accumulate domestic and personal things, her ways of reading and her possessions are survival strategies intended to shore up her defences in a world determined to objectify her.

---

[152]   Stallybrass, p. 186.

[153]   See also Radin, pp. 214–15

[154]   Stallybrass, p. 186.

[155]   Radin, p. 198.

Harry Shaw defends her reading practices as not so naïve after all, and this can be equally well applied to her accumulation of objects: 'Emma's gesture [as a reader/ fantasist] is not to be despised, for it is a version of one of the most important possibilities literature opens up to us, the possibility of a utopian revolt against the insufficiencies of the present'.[156] Whether we read women's desire for the consolations of the object world as a 'utopian revolt' or a need to 'take cover' against the hostile forces of patriarchy, both views shift the naïve female reader/ consumer into the realms of political engagement.

In a society, then, where a valued social identity depends upon the ownership of property, the fetish-substitute for women takes the form of any object which can be possessed as property; however, such objects were unlikely to be directly named as 'property'. Women's fetishism, unlike the fetishism Freud discusses, appears to be a social strategy as much as a psychological strategy, for the possession of small objects which can be valued (in both senses of the word), which one can display, preserve, repair and be proud of offers a variation of the identity formation associated with the ownership of real property, where identity is intimately bound up in a piece of land and the house which stands upon it. As Lori Merish has argued in *Sentimental Materialism*, the ownership of domestic and personal things works to 'contain feelings of dependency, and promote feelings of agency'.[157] That many Victorian women could only access feelings of ownership and status via the miniature and the portable has led to a misrecognition of them as avid consumers, mindlessly accumulating trivial things. Yet, Susan Stewart's discussion of the miniature (here, in relation to the dolls' house) has indicated its capability of achieving transcendence:

> The reduction in scale which the miniature presents skews the time and space relations of the everyday lifeworld, and as an object consumed, the miniature finds its 'use value' transformed into the infinite time of reverie. This capacity of the miniature to create an 'other' time, [is] a type of transcendent time which negates change and the flux of lived reality … .[158]

As we will see, this intimate relationship with 'miniature' property, portable objects rather than real estate, as well as allowing the fetish to work positively, also helps women avoid the dangers of commodity fetishism, the 'bad' fetishism which Marx mocks in *Capital*. Thus, as Laura Mulvey argues in *Fetishism and Curiosity*, women can create '*an armour of fetishistic defence against the taboos of the feminine that patriarchy depends on*'.[159] The fetish can function not

---

[156] Harry E. Shaw, *Narrating Reality: Austen, Scott, Eliot* (Ithaca and London: Cornell University Press, 1999), pp. 61–2.

[157] Lori Merish, *Sentimental Materialism: Gender, Commodity Culture and Nineteenth-Century American Literature* (Durham and London: Duke University Press, 2000), p. 5.

[158] Susan Stewart, *On Longing: Narratives of the Miniature, the Gigantic, the Souvenir, the Collection* (Durham and London: Duke University Press, 1993), p. 65.

[159] Mulvey, p. 14; emphasis in the original.

only as a covering, but as a form of defence. As we will see in the next chapter, Dickens's 'fallen' woman in *Bleak House*, Lady Dedlock, also needs a cover, both in terms of a respectable identity as a wife to Sir Leicester Dedlock, but also in the form of a memorial, in this instance a handkerchief, which reminds her of her illegitimate daughter, Esther. The next chapter will further explore the concepts of the memorial in the context of Dickens's work, and the ways in which female property is presented as both an ideal and a problem.

Chapter 2
Circulation and Stasis:
Feminine Property in the Novels
of Charles Dickens

Dickens is perhaps the Victorian writer we are most likely to associate with the exuberant representations of things, particularly those items termed portable property. Wemmick, the collector of curiosities in *Great Expectations* and a well-known advocate of the advantages of owning portable property, accepts all gifts from clients, however absurd or trifling, on the basis that 'they're property and portable'.[1] Dickens's novels are themselves collections of curiosities and the vast array of objects he represents has long attracted critical attention. For example, in 1858 Walter Bagehot considered Dickens's genius to lie in 'his sensitivity to external objects', his novels offering 'pages containing telling *minutiae* which other people would have thought enough for a volume'.[2] For Dorothy Van Ghent, writing in the mid twentieth century, Dickens's objects both warn against and compensate for the fragmentation associated with modernity: 'in a world visibly disintegrated into things, one way to find [coherence] is to mention everything. Hence [Dickens's] indefatigable attention to detail'.[3] More recently, Elaine Freedgood has referred to Dickens's 'nearly crazed' tendency to provide 'lists, catalogs, reports, inventories, and descriptions [which] are so excessive as to be hilarious. ... In the myriad of things that stack up in piles of overstocked paragraphs, Dickens seems to be trying to name *all* things ...'.[4]

One of the most detailed of Dickens's lists (and certainly a good example of his interest in property and 'sensitivity to external objects') exists in the form of his last will and testament, which opens with bequests to women: to Ellen Ternan (considered by many to have been Dickens's mistress) he bequeaths £1,000; to his servant, Anne Cornelius and her daughter he leaves £19 19s each; to his unmarried daughter, Mary, he bequeaths £1,000 and an annuity of £300; and to his sister-in-law, Georgina Hogarth, he not only leaves £8,000, but states that she will have most of 'my personal jewellery ... and all the little familiar objects from my writing-table

---

[1]   Charles Dickens, *Great Expectations*, David Trotter (ed.) (London: Penguin, 1996), p. 201.

[2]   [Walter Bagehot,] 'Charles Dickens', *National Review* (October 1858), reprinted in, *Charles Dickens: The Critical Heritage*, Philip Collins (ed.) (London: Routledge and Kegan Paul, 1986), p. 393.

[3]   Dorothy Van Ghent, 'The Dickens World: A View from Todgers's' in *Dickens: A Collection of Critical Essays*, Martin Price (ed.) (New Jersey: Prentice-Hall, 1987), p. 29.

[4]   Freedgood, p. 103.

and my room, and she will know what to do with those things'.[5] This includes the miscellany of diminutive objects Dickens needed to have before him on his desk, which included a bronze figurine of two toads fighting a duel; a statue of a man overwhelmed by pet dogs; another of a Turkish man smoking a pipe; a porcelain figure of a monkey; and an image of a rabbit placed on a gilt leaf.[6] This desk-world of miniature figures formed a fantastic still life of accessories which functioned as aids to the writing process. Georgina Hogarth knew 'what to do' with them (whether she was instructed by Dickens or acted on her own initiative): she preserved them, and many can now be seen at the Dickens House Museum in London.[7]

There follows in the will a bequest to his eldest son, Charles, who receives his library, *All The Year Round*, money and a few items of jewellery, 'shirt studs, shirt pins, and sleeve buttons'.[8] Dickens's watch, with its chains and seals, went to his friend John Forster.[9] All of these bequests come before any mention of his copyrights, while his wishes regarding his real estate appear almost as an afterthought: he demands that it be 'converted into personalty upon my decease'.[10] Gad's Hill Place, the home of Mary and Georgina since 1857, does not seem to have had emotional resonance for Dickens, unlike his desk ornaments, sleeve buttons or watch. The will ends with a final list ('hilarious' despite the context): a request that no one who attends his funeral should wear 'scarf, cloak, black bow, long hat-band, or other such revolting absurdity'.[11]

Dickens was clearly a 'things' man, to borrow R.J. Morris's term 'things' people for those who take the trouble to mention small items of personal property in their wills. In this he was unusual for, as we saw in the previous chapter, most wills written in the nineteenth century which specified numerous bequests of personal property were written by women.[12] The miscellaneous figurines on Dickens's desk, small objects dismissed by the world at large as economically insignificant repositories of affect, were meaningful to him, as his will indicates. This type of sentimental personal property also appears in his novels as an indicator of an alternative value system to the patriarchal institutions he so abhors: the prison, workhouse, court, counting-house and Parliament. The 'telling minutiae' (to use Bagehot's term) of the fictional things Dickens represents, diminutive, and

---

5   'Charles Dickens's Last Will and Codicil, 12 May 1869 and 2 June 1870', in Charles Dickens, *The Pilgrim Edition of the Letters of Charles Dickens*, vol. 12, Graham Storey (ed.) (Oxford: Clarendon Press, 1982–), p. 730.

6   Peter Ackroyd, *Dickens* (London: Minerva, 1991), p. 530, and Claire Pettitt, 'On Stuff', *19: Interdisciplinary Studies in the Long Nineteenth Century*, http://www.19. bbk.ac.uk (Spring, 2008), p. 1.

7   http://www.dickensmuseum.com.

8   'Dickens's Last Will', pp. 730–31.

9   Ibid., p. 731.

10   Ibid.

11   Ibid., p. 732.

12   R.J. Morris, p. 128.

thus 'feminine', nevertheless exist within, and are regulated by, more powerful institutions.[13] Yet, in Dickens's work they can often undermine from within, neutralizing the Podsnap tendency towards the 'hideous solidity' of Victorian material culture, where '[e]verything was made to look as heavy as it could and to take up as much room as possible'.[14] Dickens's interest in feminine diminutive things culminates in his final novel *The Mystery of Edwin Drood* (1870), where the schoolgirl heroine Rosa and her friends enjoy a makeshift dormitory supper during which 'a dressed tongue had been carved with a pair of scissors, and handed round with the curling tongs. Portions of marmalade had likewise been distributed on a service of plates constructed of curlpaper'.[15] Lacking plate and cutlery, the girls use as makeshifts their portable property: the tools of feminine adornment. This interest in the childish, toy-like qualities of girls' property emerges again later in the novel when Rosa runs away to London to escape the sexual attentions of John Jasper: 'She hurried a few quite useless articles into a very little bag' (MED 226), so little that Mr Grewgious asks, 'Is that a bag? ... and is it your property, my dear?' (MED 229). Dickens's tone, both affectionate and patronizing, is a reminder that the diminutive and the feminine have traditionally been dismissed as insignificant and are thus vulnerable to comic treatment.[16]

Yet despite his jokes about women's diminutive things, Dickens cannot hide the fact that the possession of them takes place within larger disciplinary systems. Even his own Devonshire Terrace home indicates that the domestic was not always a congenial context for possession, for the attic rooms used as bedrooms by his daughters, Mamie and Katey, were regularly policed by Dickens himself. While he understood their need to inhabit a space of their own, furnished and decorated to their taste, he insisted on making regular inspections, even going so far as to examine the interiors of their drawers and cupboards. As Gladys Storey (a friend of Katey's) explained, 'Remonstrances [for untidiness] were frequently consigned to notepaper, folded neatly and left by him on their pincushion, which they called "pincushion notes"'.[17] His daughters, allowed their own separate realm

---

[13] See the chapter on *Bleak House* in D.A. Miller, *The Novel and the Police* (Berkeley: University of California Press, 1988) for a discussion of disciplinary structures in Dickens's novel.

[14] Charles Dickens, *Our Mutual Friend*, Michael Cotsell (ed.) (Oxford: Oxford University Press, 1989), p. 131. Subsequent page references will be cited in the text following the abbreviation 'OMF'.

[15] Charles Dickens, *The Mystery of Edwin Drood*, Margaret Cardwell (ed.) (Oxford: Oxford University Press, 1982), p. 142. Subsequent page references will be cited in the text following the abbreviation 'MED'.

[16] See Patricia Ingham, *Dickens, Women and Language* (New York and London: Harvester Wheatsheaf, 1992), p. 19 for a discussion of Dickens's use of the adjective 'little' in relation to women.

[17] Gladys Storey, *Dickens and Daughter* (1939), quoted in Michael Slater, *Dickens and Women* (London: J.M. Dent, 1983), p. 180.

within the household, were not left completely free from their father's control.[18] The significance of the pincushion (an item which Esther and Ada are delighted to find on *their* dressing table when they arrive at Bleak House[19]) suggests, of course, women's use of pins, which in turn connotes the pin money which had for centuries been an important source of income for many women. According to the *OED*, the term 'pin money' originated in the fourteenth century, when women were given money once a year by husbands or fathers in order to buy pins, a luxury item at this period. Pin money, then, has for centuries signified both women's financial dependency on men and the small items of personal property they desire. Dickens's 'pincushion notes' succinctly suggest the generosity of the father (in allowing his daughters space, pins and pincushions) and the price he exacts in return (in this case, his surveillance of the objects he provides).

Dickens's pincushion notes represent his notion of what constitutes proper paternal care, a care which he believed should reach into every corner of his household. Yet he nevertheless expressed uneasiness in his novels about the power of fathers (or father figures) to affect the lives of their families, and the unacceptable conditions they sometimes impose upon property ownership. Even his heroes, whom one would normally expect to be beneficiaries of patrimony, are often as disadvantaged as his heroines. His novels suggest that for men the acquisition of property from fathers or father substitutes is a flawed process, perpetuating the son's bondage to his father. Indeed, sons usually need to reject or lose their legacies if they are to survive to the end of the narrative.[20] From Richard Carstone's fatal encounter with the Jarndyce and Jarndyce Chancery case to later heroes, such as Arthur Clennam, Charles Darnay, Pip, and John Harmon, property proves to be oppressive and legacies come with unacceptable conditions attached. Men's energies, Dickens suggests, tend to be sapped by patrimony because the father's legacy is prone to dominate the inheritor. Even the unenergetic dilettante Mortimer Lightwood in *Our Mutual Friend* (1865) comes to realize that his inheritance of his 'own small income ... has been an effective Something, in the way of preventing [him] from turning to at Anything' (OMF 812). The power inherent in property to debilitate its owners is, according to Pierre Bourdieu, part of the tradition of patrimony whereby the inheritance and the heir must be locked together to perpetuate the family identity. He states that this transfer of power between men depends upon a:

> *reciprocal appropriation* between the material, cultural, and symbolic patrimony and the biological individuals shaped by and for the appropriation ... . The tendency of the patrimony (and hence of the entire social structure) to persevere

---

[18]   See Thad Logan, *The Victorian Parlour* (Cambridge: Cambridge University Press, 2001), pp. 34–5 for a discussion of the home as both prison and site of self-expression for Victorian women.

[19]   Charles Dickens, *Bleak House*, Nicola Bradbury (ed.) (London: Penguin, 2003), p. 87. Subsequent pages references will be cited in the text following the abbreviation 'BH'.

[20]   As Nunokawa argues, Dickens's novels offer 'a fantasy of economic stability ... in which the loss of money clears the way for secure domestic fortune', p. 50.

in itself can only be realized if the inheritance inherits the heir, if the patrimony manages to appropriate itself possessors both disposed and apt to enter into a relation of reciprocal appropriation.[21]

Yet for Dickens the idea that the male heir and the father's property enter into a reciprocal relationship is an unacceptable one, for he sees patrilineal forms of property transmission as a denial of freedom for sons, even a denial of life itself. As Anny Sadrin has noted in *Parentage and Inheritance in the Novels of Charles Dickens*, his work increasingly focuses on 'the problems raised in the sons' lives by the burden of inheriting, ... the increasing reluctance to accept what is assigned'.[22] Patrimony thus places sons in subordinate positions to fathers, who are usually represented in Dickens's novels as inadequate or hostile.[23] Indeed, as Lynn Cain argues, the novels express 'deep underlying anxiety about the role of men in a changing culture', an anxiety which manifests itself in a need both to represent fathers as redundant as well as to idealize the concept of paternal care.[24]

To a similar extent women's power to bequeath to daughters, or surrogate daughters, is also presented as a source of anxiety, and the legacy Estella inherits from Miss Havisham, as we will see below, is perhaps the most extreme example of a problematic female inheritance. Dickens rarely seems comfortable with female characters who can wield power by means of their wealth. The anxieties associated with women and property transmission are allayed completely however in *The Mystery of Edwin Drood*, where the dead mother's property never reaches her daughter. Rosa's mother's ring, a bequest from mother to daughter, actually remains in the possession of men: her father takes it from his dead wife's hand and (dying himself soon after) passes it into Mr Grewgious's keeping; it is then passed on to Edwin. According to Rosa's father's will, he can only give it to Rosa if their betrothal 'com[es] to maturity'; when it does not, it is returned to Mr Grewgious's care (MED 124–5). Edwin, returning the ring to him, imagines it stored 'like old letters or old vows' which fade in importance 'until, being valuable, they were sold into circulation again to repeat their former round' (MED 151). The surrogate father, Mr Grewgious, however, acts as though he is really the ring's owner: 'I have had it so long, and have prized it so much!' (MED 126). The woman who is intended to possess this ring, Rosa, never even knows of its existence. She is kept out of its

---

[21]   Pierre Bourdieu, 'The Invention of the Artist's Life', Erec R. Koch (trans.), *Yale French Studies*, 73 (1987), p. 80; emphasis in the original.

[22]   Anny Sadrin, *Parentage and Inheritance in the Novels of Charles Dickens* (Cambridge: Cambridge University Press, 1994), p. 13.

[23]   See Dianne F. Sadoff, *Monsters of Affection: Dickens, Eliot and Brontë on Fatherhood* (Baltimore: The Johns Hopkins University Press, 1982), pp. 10–64, and Carolyn Dever, *Death and the Mother from Dickens to Freud: Victorian Fiction and the Anxiety of Origins* (Cambridge: Cambridge University Press, 1998), p. 95.

[24]   See Lynn Cain, *Dickens, Family, Authorship: Psychoanalytic Perspectives on Kinship and Creativity* (Aldershot: Ashgate, 2008), p. 133, and Sadrin, p. 149 on the contradictory impulses in Dickens's novels which both condemn and valorize paternity.

circuit between the three men and will play no part in its projected circulation on the open market. Her exclusion from her mother's property seems to be, for Dickens, the only way for her to avoid the mercenary associations of property ownership.

This deep ambivalence in the representation of women as property owners is at work in most of Dickens's novels. On the one hand women's relationships to sentimental personal property are often presented as an ideal form of possession (for example, Esther's possession of Allan Woodcourt's bouquet is unproblematic because it transcends the market economy based on the ideology of possessive individualism); yet on the other hand, when women do take control of significant amounts of property and its transmission, as Miss Havisham does, the destructive qualities of their legacies are usually emphasized. When forceful women of property, owners of real estate, create for themselves a space which is inaccessible to male control, such as Betsey Trotwood, Mrs Clennam or Miss Havisham, it is shown to be vulnerable to loss or destruction, as though Dickens half believed what English law presumed: that women had a tendency to be ineffective managers of their own property.[25] Dickens's novels express disturbance at the notion of women's freedom to own real estate, for this confers a social power which for him is potentially de-sexing.[26] However, women's attachment to smaller items of affective property, such as bouquets or handkerchiefs, is presented as free from the corrosive forces of acquisitiveness. Such things share the qualities he associated with his sleeve buttons, watch and desk ornaments: they act as memorials, objects with intimate associations on which no sullying cash value could be placed. Dickens's female characters are, perhaps, the most intriguing female property owners in the novels of the period. Yet despite their oddities, they highlight aspects of ownership and exchange which are far removed from the custom of primogeniture.

Although *Bleak House* (1853) and *Great Expectations* represent opposite forms of female ownership and property transmission, both novels depict alternatives to primogenture. *Bleak House* is radical in its critique of a legal system based on possessive individualism, symbolized by the Jarndyce and Jarndyce Chancery dispute. The novel proposes an alternative system which disrupts traditional notions of private property by representing collective property relations within a female community. In this earlier novel Dickens explores the concept of labour as property and, unusually, depicts female labour as a form of capital to be invested. He also represents forms of affective property (such as the keepsake) and 'reciprocal' property (things which are living, such as the pet bird, or seem to be living, such as the doll). These types of property work in opposition to the deadly effects of property in the Chancery dispute. Yet in *Little Dorrit* (1857) and *Great Expectations*, Dickens depicts the female property owner as perversely preventing the circulation of property within families. In these later novels, Dickens exhibits

---

[25]   Even Betsey Trotwood, who is presented so positively in *David Copperfield*, seems especially vulnerable as far as the management of her property is concerned.

[26]   See Slater, p. 354, for a discussion of Dickens's responses to 'powerful' women.

an ambivalent representation of female ownership which may have originated in his ambivalent responses to the emerging feminist movement.

Dickens and Feminism

From the 1850s onwards, Dickens's novels were written against a background of intense feminist activity as campaigners such as Barbara Leigh Smith, John Stuart Mill, Frances Power Cobbe and Caroline Cornwallis exposed to public scrutiny the fact that women in Britain lacked adequate legal safeguards. At the heart of the feminist campaign was the issue of married women's property rights. Despite some misgivings, Dickens was broadly sympathetic towards the idea of property rights for women, publicly intervening in 1868 (the year when the Married Women's Property Committee was established) in the debates on the first married women's property bill. He asked Joseph C. Parkinson, a contributor to *All The Year Round*, to write an article on the bill:

> There is a bill before Parliament (but I forget whose it is) for enabling a married woman to possess her own earnings. I should like to champion the sex – reasonably – and to dwell upon the hardship inflicted by the present law on a woman who finds herself bound to a drunken profligate, and spendthrift husband – who is willing to support him – does so – but has her little savings bullied out of her, continually. The case is this: – The bill will not pass, we know very well; but would it not be wise and just to take any such opportunity of setting right some little item in the wrong that springs up under our laws of marriage and divorce? Grant what we are told by bishops, priests, and deacons about sanctity of marriage, indissolubility of marriage tie etc. etc, Grant that such things *must be*, for the general good. Cannot we – and ought not we – in such a case as this, to help the weak and injured party? Reverse the case, and take a working man with a drunken woman saddled on him as long as he lives, who strips his house continually to buy drink. If he must not be able to divorce himself – for 'the general good' should, in return, punish the woman.[27]

This letter resulted in Parkinson's 'Slaves of the Ring' (4 July 1868) which presents examples of wives and husbands bound as 'slaves' to the marriage laws, unable to divorce their dissolute spouses. Yet, as his focus on women's modest earnings and 'little savings' indicates, Dickens saw the married women's property bill largely as a measure designed to help working wives, rather than a development towards equal rights for all women.

Like many Victorian men who supported the bill, Dickens saw the issue in terms of the protection of vulnerable working women from unreasonable lower-class men.[28] Parliamentary debates on married women's property rights,

---

[27] 4 June 1868, in *Pilgrim Edition of the Letters of Charles Dickens*, vol. 12, p. 127; emphasis in the original.

[28] See Griffin, pp. 66–70 and 83.

as Griffin has demonstrated, focused on 'melodramatic narratives' of villainous working-class men appropriating the property of hardworking virtuous women (in other words, narratives which were characterized by class and gender stereotyping); these tended to overshadow the feminist demand for equality and the conferring of property rights on all wives regardless of class.[29] Unsurprisingly, Dickens wanted to include a similar topical 'melodramatic narrative' in *All The Year Round*, and Parkinson's 'Slaves of the Ring' opens with a case study based on a typical Dickensian heroine, a 'pretty, shy-faced, dove-eyed, modest little daughter', whose property and earnings are forcibly and legally appropriated by her 'pimply, bloated, watery-eyed, tremulous-handed, dishonest, maudlin, odious drunkard' of a husband.[30] This narrative of ideal femininity under attack from brutish masculinity was typical of the rhetoric used by proponents of reform, a rhetoric which in the end proved to be effective, for the Married Women's Property Act became law in 1870, against all the odds.[31]

Yet despite his condescending boast of 'championing the sex – reasonably', along with his mention of women's 'little savings' and their property rights as a 'little item', it would be a mistake to overlook the value, in practical terms, of Dickens's support. His power to influence was noted as early as 1858 when Bagehot conceded that Dickens's 'sentimental radicalism', while artistically flawed in his opinion, was highly influential in effecting social change.[32] A year later David Masson in his book, *British Novelists and Their Styles*, also noted Dickens's powers as a reformer when he stated (in reference to *Little Dorrit*) that:

> The Administrative Reform Association might have worked for ten years without producing half of the effect which Mr Dickens has produced in the same direction, by flinging out the phrase, 'The Circumlocution Office'. He has thrown out a score of phrases, equally efficacious for social reform; and it matters little that some of them might turn out to be ludicrous exaggerations.[33]

Yet, as Nicola Bradbury has noted in relation to *Bleak House*, while Dickens could be 'indignant about the evils of England', he was often 'impatient with notions of reform'.[34] His approach to the woman question and feminists' demands for reform was rife with contradictions, for his concern to 'champion the sex' and 'to help the weak and injured party' appears to have been an intuitive impulse, rather than the result of any political or intellectual sympathy with feminists.[35] Dickens, as his

---

29   Griffin, p. 83.

30   [J.C. Parkinson,] 'Slaves of the Ring', *All The Year Round*, 4 July 1868: 85–6.

31   See Holcombe, pp. 166–83.

32   Cited in Collins, p. 398.

33   Quoted in Collins, p. 357.

34   Nicola Bradbury, Introduction, Charles Dickens, *Bleak House*, Nicola Bradbury (ed.) (London: Penguin, 2003), p. xxi.

35   See Chris R. Vanden Bossche, 'Class Discourse and Popular Agency in *Bleak House*', *Victorian Studies* 47:1 (Autumn 2004): 13, and John Bowen, *Other Dickens: From*

letter to Parkinson indicates, also wanted to be fair to men who were 'the weak and injured party' in marriage, a harking back to his depiction of Stephen Blackpool in *Hard Times* (1854), a working-class man bound to an alcoholic wife who appropriates his property and earnings. His letter and the resulting article 'Slaves of the Ring' thus seem more preoccupied with sentimental images of wronged spouses whose lives are ruined by the effects of alcohol, than feminist critiques of the outdated property laws.

Yet property and the laws relating to it are often the focus of Dickens's anger and he satirizes them in *Bleak House* by means of the Chancery theme. He draws attention to the cumbersome English legal system divided into the common law on the one hand and the law of equity on the other. As the novel suggests, this fragmented and often incoherent legal system was both inadequate and costly, entailing numerous bureaucratic processes and 'cartloads of papers' (BH 118). John Jarndyce states that the Jarndyce property is subject to 'an infernal country-dance of costs and fees' because 'Equity sends questions to Law, Law sends questions back to Equity; Law finds it can't do this, Equity finds it can't do that' (BH 118–19). This vacillation between the different channels of English law was, before 1870, at the root of the problem facing the majority of women on marriage, whose fortunes and earnings were subject to the common law of coverture because equity settlements entailed the expensive 'country-dance of costs and fees' of Chancery. *Bleak House* expresses the popular feeling of the 1850s against the costs (human and financial) of the inefficient legal system, for this was a decade which saw the establishment of the Law Amendment Society and the publication of a Society report which severely criticized the existence of 'two different sets of courts dispens[ing] diametrically opposite rules'.[36]

While Dickens was highly critical of the law and its ponderous mechanisms, his engagement with feminists and their calls for reform was, as I have suggested, riven with contradictions. Sharon Marcus has stated that by the 1860s 'unmarried women became visible as activists, philanthropists, and artists whose labor earned them a place in society made more porous by a general emphasis on reform'.[37] Dickens appears to have had a mixed response to the new generation of publicly active and 'visible' women of the mid-Victorian period. He considered most feminists to be 'masculine' destroyers of femininity, informing his acquaintance Whitwell Elwin in 1861 that a 'male female is repulsive'.[38] Although he ridicules and condemns what he considered to be 'unfeminine' activists in the forms of Mrs Jellyby, Mrs Pardiggle, Miss Wisk, and later in *A Tale of Two Cities* (1859) Madame Defarge and her fellow female revolutionaries, he does offer readers of *Bleak House* an alternative model of the female community. This group of women

---

Pickwick to Chuzzlewit (Oxford: Oxford University Press, 2000), p. 24 for discussions of what Bowen terms Dickens's 'contradictory, radical anger'.

[36]   Holcombe, p. 65.

[37]   Marcus, p. 208.

[38]   Quoted in Slater, p. 316.

consisting of Esther, Ada, Caddy, Charley and Miss Flite (with Lady Dedlock on the margins) is unique in Dickens's work. Pam Morris sees this 'supportive female community' as particularly modern in its characteristics:

> This is not a local, known community in the traditional sense; it is much more modern in the almost contingent coming together of different lives within the flux of urban space and social mobility. The community is formed and stays 'in touch' by shared understanding and sympathetic interest.[39]

R.J. Morris has discussed the importance of this form of network in nineteenth-century society, which offered an important supplement to the family. Unmarried members of a network found within it a sense of community, 'care and companionship', and in their wills they often left their fortunes to members of their network.[40] In *Bleak House* Dickens shows the benefits of the female network which functions by means of an 'exchange of resources and services' which, in Morris's words, 'countered economic or demographic disaster or ... the unevenness of experience'.[41] Networks in Dickens's novel, whether the feminist network consisting of Mrs Jellyby, Mrs Pardiggle, Miss Wisk and Mr Quale (all of whom are presented negatively), or the female network Esther belongs to, offer examples of collective action. The sharing of skills between members also emphasizes the notion of labour as an important form of portable property for women. Esther and Miss Flite, for example, help Caddy Jellyby to achieve her potential as an effective labourer in the skills of housewifery and household management in order for her to take her place as the manager of her husband's business and household. This skill is shown to be more important to her than the portable property which is 'packed on the hired coach and pair' when Caddy leaves her parents' home (BH 484). Yet *Bleak House* is unusual in its promotion of female labour and financial and social independence: indeed, in its representations of women's personal property and things in general it is, as we will see, more radical than many of Dickens's other novels, for here he critiques traditional notions of female dependency and the valorization of private property.

The Feminine Communal Properties of *Bleak House*

Bleak House is centred on a disputed will, Dickens being aware of the drama, pathos and comedy to be generated by an individual's last instructions to the world. In March 1841 Dickens's pet raven Grip died, attended in his last moments only by Topping the groom. Dickens wrote to his friend Daniel Maclise with an account of the bird's death:

---

[39] Pam Morris, *Imagining Inclusive Society in 19th-Century Novels: The Code of Sincerity in the Public Sphere* (Baltimore and London: The Johns Hopkins University Press, 2004), p. 133.

[40] R.J. Morris, p. 330.

[41] Ibid., p. 335.

> [Grip] was heard talking to himself about the horse and Topping's family, and to add some incoherent expressions which are supposed to have been either a foreboding of his approaching dissolution, or some wishes relative to the disposal of his little property – consisting chiefly of half-pence which he had buried in different parts of the garden. … I deeply regret that being in ignorance of his danger I did not attend to receive his last instructions.[42]

The deathbed scene in Victorian literature usually involves a redistribution of property and affords authors an opportunity to mingle representations of pathos with materialism. Grip takes his place within these conventions and is shown to play his part as a dying property owner with dignity. During Dickens's lifetime most married women could no more create a legally binding will than Grip, yet this did not prevent them following deathbed conventions by giving their final instructions about the disposal of what they considered to be their worldly goods. All of Dickens's novels involve the redistribution of property, and none more so than *Bleak House*, which is based on the disputed will in the Jarndyce vs Jarndyce case. In this novel Dickens demonstrates women's fitness to care for, and bequeath, property, while most of his male characters seem to renege on their responsibilities as property owners.

Many critics have drawn attention to the importance of property in *Bleak House*. Hilary M. Schor, for example, suggests that the novel's central question is 'What is property?' a view which is supported by Pettitt, who notes that '[t]he word "property" occurs no less than fifty times'.[43] Certainly the main plot, with its focus on the labyrinthine workings of the Jarndyce and Jarndyce case demonstrates the consequences of property being subject to the arcane and often irrational processes of the law. Pettitt also argues that property in *Bleak House* is 'oddly dependent on death'.[44] The transmission of property generally depends on the death of its owners; however, it is certainly the case that in this novel it can be fatal simply to be a suitor in a Chancery case. Many, such as Richard Carstone, Gridley and Tom Jarndyce (who blew out his brains), are killed by the suspense and frustrations of Chancery processes. Yet despite the deadly effects of the property dispute, Dickens frequently plays with the concept of property to comic effect, especially as he mocks men's preoccupation with ownership. Sir Leicester Dedlock's gout is presented as a property he has proudly inherited from his family (BH 255). Mr Turveydrop possesses property both in his deportment and endless supply of anecdotes about the Prince Regent and, in a strange reversal of the rules of coverture, he is bequeathed as a legacy to his son Prince by the dying Mrs Turveydrop (BH 228, 773). At the end of the novel Mr Turveydrop bequeaths to his grandson 'a favourite French clock in his dressing-room – which is not his property' (BH 987). Mr Guppy's two marriage proposals to Esther also

---

[42]   12 March 1841, *The Pilgrim Edition of the Letters of Charles Dickens*, vol. 2, p. 231.

[43]   Hilary M. Schor, *Dickens and the Daughter of the House* (Cambridge: Cambridge University Press, 1999), p. 101, and Pettitt, *Patent Inventions*, p. 182.

[44]   Pettitt, *Patent Inventions*, p. 183.

present him in the light of the blatant appropriator of another's property: 'I have no capital myself, but my mother has a little property which takes the form of a small annuity' (BH 150 and 968), he tells her. Mr Smallweed seems to voice the property obsessions of most of the male characters when, after being put through 'the usual restorative process of shaking and punching, he still repeats like an echo, "the – the property! The property! – property!"' (BH 530). Even Skimpole's biliousness is 'a sort of property' (BH 240) and, in his perennial childishness, he playfully refuses to respect the property rights of others.

Both Skimpole and the elder Turveydrop act as though they were Victorian model wives. Neither of them does any financially remunerative work, both expending energy on maintaining a pleasing appearance. Skimpole is accomplished, in an amateur way, in music and art, both traditional feminine accomplishments. Both men presume that others will support them. Skimpole, in particular, is a parody of wives' situation under coverture. He is a 'child' (BH 92), 'a bright little creature' with 'a delicate face and sweet voice' (BH 89). Unable to fulfil the duties of his profession (he trains as a doctor), he feels himself more suited to falling in love (BH 89–90). He is happy to possess property vicariously, leaving the duties and responsibilities of ownership to others (BH 91). Like the law's notion of a wife, he 'had no idea of money' and 'never could contract any business' (BH 90). While he admires the 'strong will and immense power of business-detail' of his acquaintance Mrs Jellyby, like the ideal Victorian lady, he has no wish to join her in the public sphere (BH 91). Seeing himself as 'gay and innocent', he exhorts his companions to 'play with me!' (BH 92). As Victorian wives before the passing of the Married Women's Property Acts were not held legally accountable for their debts, Skimpole also has a 'husband' in the form of John Jarndyce who quietly pays them off for him. Esther is also placed in the husband's role when she is asked to pay one of his debts.[45] Her prudence in saving for years out of her allowance in case 'some accident might happen which would throw [her], suddenly, without any relation or property, on the world' (BH 97) contrasts sharply with the novel's financially incompetent and improvident men. Similarly, in other reversals of Victorian gender ideals, Ada uses her fortune to pay off Richard's debt to Mr Vholes and Caddy expertly manages her husband's business. With these representations of female financial acumen and male financial irresponsibility, *Bleak House* offers support to the feminists' arguments for married women's rights to control their own property and earnings.

In *Bleak House* property and the law are aligned as secretive processes opposed to human needs. Women in the novel successfully defy the forces of possessive individualism for they work collectively and the property they possess is shared communally. Here, the female collective can, to a certain extent, protect itself from the law, in contrast to the isolated woman who is represented as vulnerable to its powers. The most isolated female character in the novel is

---

[45]   For a discussion of Victorian husbands' obligations to pay their wives' debts, see Finn, 'Women, Consumption and Coverture', pp. 709–13.

Lady Dedlock; her youthful transgression leads to Tulkinghorn exerting control over her, resulting in the loss of everything she owns, even her life. Miss Flite, another female Chancery suitor, suffers acute poverty because she vainly hopes to secure property by means of the law. Miss Flite's obsession with her caged birds, reminiscent of the lonely Esther's need in childhood for a bird companion, reflects her situation as a Victorian woman, similarly trapped and caged. Her birds are named in memory of aspects of her traumatic Chancery encounters, foreshadowing the memorials to personal traumatic experiences created by Mrs Clennam in *Little Dorrit* and Miss Havisham in *Great Expectations*, both of whom, as we will see in the next section, use their property primarily as a means to express anger at their situations. Apart from her caged birds, the only property Miss Flite actually possesses is literally 'rubbish', 'some small litter in a reticule which she calls her documents; principally consisting of paper matches and dry lavender' (BH 15–16). Her madness illustrates the dangers facing women who lack property and encounter the law: she is dismissed as absurd and insignificant by the lawyers who profit from her dilemma. Her adoption of legal discourse indicates her immersion in a system which does nothing for her interests and fails to reflect her actual experiences. When she (absurdly) makes the dying Richard the executor of her will, she explains to Esther that she has '[n]ominated, constituted, and appointed him. ... My executor, administrator, and assign. (Our Chancery phrases, my love.)' (BH 922). Miss Flite's tragedy centres on the fact that she respects the law and identifies herself with it ('Our Chancery'), yet as Leigh Smith's *Brief Summary in Plain Language of the Most Important Laws Concerning Women* demonstrated, it was naïve for women to believe that the legal system would look after their interests. Miss Flite's confused idea that the processes of the Court of Chancery will result in divine judgment – 'I expect a judgment on the day of Judgment. And shall then confer estates' (BH 233) – indicates the dangers of trusting in a legal system which the Law Amendment Society had described as 'discreditable'.[46]

Dickens also suggests that lawyers, like the law itself, are not to be trusted. Tulkinghorn represents the exploitative, predatory nature of the law and its hostility to women. He believes that '[t]here are women enough in the world ... too many; they are at the bottom of all that goes wrong in it, though, for the matter of that, they create business for lawyers' (BH 259–60). His dedication to patriarchy and its laws is symbolized by the objects on his desk which, unlike the playful miscellany furnishing Dickens's writing desk, represent the codification and silencing of women enshrined within a legal system devised and administered by ruling-class men to protect the interests of ruling-class men. As he sits at his desk conceiving his plot against Lady Dedlock, he continually fingers 'the round top of an inkstand and two bits of sealing-wax' (BH 159), as though writing and the sealing of writing (both in terms of making it secret and fixing its meaning) are weapons he wields. Yet despite the endless writing and sealing associated with the

---

[46] Cited in Holcombe, p. 65.

law, the Jarndyce and Jarndyce case actually demonstrates that lawyers are unable to fix or locate meaning adequately.

The destructive forces of the law, then, are levelled against both Miss Flite and Lady Dedlock. Schor argues that the latter has a 'desire to own property and to transmit it to her daughter', adding that she 'cannot leave her daughter any property' because of the laws of coverture: yet, there is no evidence to support this assertion as Lady Dedlock does not bring any property to the marriage, other than her useless stake in the Jarndyce and Jarndyce case.[47] Indeed, Lady Dedlock seems profoundly bored by the property dispute and also seems unaffected by the possessions given to her by Sir Leicester, for she leaves behind her 'all her jewels and her money' (BH 856), those 'rum articles' which (although he has no evidence for this) Inspector Bucket presumes must have been hard 'to cut away from' (BH 861). Yet, like Edith Dombey before her, Lady Dedlock appears to abandon the luxurious things she gains on her marriage without a qualm, items which their husbands were entitled to expropriate at any time.[48] The only example we have of her acquisitiveness is her desire for her daughter's handkerchief. Embroidered with Esther's name (and strangely, interestingly, we never discover who gave her the surname 'Summerson', a cheerful and liberatory name for a bastard to possess whose childhood was blighted by shame), the trajectory of this handkerchief through time and between 'owners' is, as I will discuss below, circuitous. However, instead of creating discord, this item of female property leads to a form of communal ownership which establishes bonds between disparate women from different class groups. *Bleak House* is, then, radical in its depiction of an effective female community, a feature of the novel which has been singled out for attention by numerous feminist critics.

Yet Dickens's radicalism has been diluted for many critics by his representation of Esther Summerson, the novel's main female protagonist and one of its narrators; she 'has not proved a popular character with readers', as Pam Morris has stated.[49] Laurie Langbauer, for example, has referred to her as 'insipid and unbelievable', created to 'console the male order', while Dianne Sadoff complains about 'her nasty habit of being overly coy: she is, in short, a goody-goody'.[50] Esther even seemed remarkably out-of-date to some Victorian critics. John William Kaye, writing anonymously in *Bentley's Miscellany* argued that Esther's passivity 'transcends the limits of our credulity'.[51] Kaye adds that when she is exchanged between men at the end of the novel:

---

[47]   Schor, pp. 104 and 115.

[48]   Although Dickens does not emphasize the point, neither Edith nor Lady Dedlock legally own the things given to them by their husbands, for husbands held the right to expropriate the gifts they had given to their wives.

[49]   P. Morris, p. 131.

[50]   Laurie Langbauer, *Women and Romance: The Consolations of Gender in the English Novel* (Ithaca and London: Cornell University Press, 1990), p.151, and Sadoff, p. 59.

[51]   Unsigned review, *Bentley's Miscellany*, vol. 34, October 1853, pp. 372–4. Reprinted in Collins, p. 289. I am grateful to Ashgate's anonymous reader for identifying the author of this review.

We do not know whether most to marvel at him who transfers, or her who is transferred from one to another like a bale of goods. Neither, if we could believe in such an incident, would our belief in any way enhance our admiration of the heroine. A little more strength of character would not be objectionable – even in a wife.[52]

The tone of disbelief that Esther could be part of a primitive exchange between men suggests that by 1853 some readers were ready to accept that 'even a wife' should have some degree of autonomy. Charlotte Brontë also complained that Esther's narrative was 'too often weak and twaddling'.[53] Such views undoubtedly misrepresent Esther, although they serve to indicate the changes of sentiment which took place at this period in relation to gender roles and suggest why there was increasing support for the feminist-initiated reforms of the 1850s, 1860s and 1870s.

Nevertheless, *Bleak House* is a feminist text despite feminists' responses to Esther and John Stuart Mill's complaints that Dickens had 'the vulgar impudence … to ridicule the rights of women' in his depictions of Mrs Jellyby and Mrs Pardiggle.[54] However, Ellen Moers has identified *Bleak House* as 'the single "woman question" novel in the Dickens canon', where the female characters 'look different, as a group, from the other women of Dickens: more forceful, more independent, more capable'.[55] Michael Slater has also noted *Bleak House*'s feminist tendencies, linking this to Dickens's representations of more female characters in his middle period novels, all of which explore the 'dangers, frustrations and humiliations experienced by women in the male-orientated world of Victorian England'.[56] If they are not overtly feminist in their message, Dickens's novels of the 1850s do tend to endorse femininity (if not matriarchy) as a preferable alternative to patriarchy. More recently Lynn Cain has discussed Dickens's 'narrative transvestism' in using a female first-person narrator in *Bleak House*, arguing that this allows him 'temporary access to a culturally defined female voice and sensibility through which he can interrogate the preoccupations of his era, especially those concerned with sex and gender'.[57] *Bleak House* is then a novel which represents 'forceful, more independent' women, a 'parade of powerful women' in the forms of the feminist activists and the female network. The latter compensate for the failed fathers and inadequate men which dominate so many of Dickens's novels.[58] *Bleak House* thus exposes the inadequacies of fathers and patriarchal institutions (symbolized here by the absurd Jarndyce and Jarndyce case,

---

[52] Reprinted in Collins, p. 289. For a critique of the notion of heterosexual exchange in the context of the Victorian novel, see Psomiades, pp. 93–118.

[53] Quoted in Collins, p. 273.

[54] Letter to Harriet Taylor, 20 March 1854; cited in Collins, p. 298.

[55] Ellen Moers, '*Bleak House*: The Agitating Women', *The Dickensian*, 69:1 (January 1973): p. 13.

[56] The novels Slater discusses here are: *Dombey and Son*, *David Copperfield*, *Bleak House*, *Hard Times* and *Little Dorrit*, p. 243.

[57] Cain, p. 128.

[58] Moers, p. 13, and Cain, p. 127.

based on a property dispute which is meant to be – but fails to be – solved by the law) by contrasting them with the efficacy of the female community (although *not* with the feminist community), where property is shared, rather than subject to dispute.

Esther learns about the concepts of possession and property by means of her relationships with a doll and a pet bird.[59] The first image we have of her is as a small child attempting to communicate with her doll and her mention of her caged bird 'companion' (BH 36). An understanding of property ownership usually originates in childhood with the possession of toys. Susan Stewart has stated that '[t]he toy world presents a projection of the world of everyday life', thus functioning as an important conduit towards adulthood and an understanding of the material world.[60] Additionally, toys and pets are 'reciprocal' property in that owners can establish a sense of communication which ranges beyond materiality.[61] Dolls in particular offer girls a first experience of possession, allowing them simultaneously to perform the actions of owner, while coming to awareness of the doll's symbolism as a miniature female. Esther's first recorded speech in the novel is her address to 'Dolly': 'Now, Dolly, I am not clever, you know very well, and you must be patient with me like a dear!' (BH 27). Having no mother or mother-figure during her childhood, Esther addresses her doll as though it is a mother, sister or friend, rather than a substitute baby. She has no female intimate from whom she can learn the tactics of femininity and sociability; instead she appears to learn (or at least, practice) these traits by means of communicating with her doll. In the loveless home of Miss Barbary, Esther states that her doll is 'the only friend with whom I felt at ease' (BH 28–9). As Carolyn Dever has argued, dolls function as 'the child's first "not-me" possession [and] they provide symbolic instruction in the construction and negotiation of self–other relationships'.[62] For Dever, Esther's doll represents both a substitute mother and herself which:

> compensates for the multiply overdetermined markers of absence in her world. As she talks with her doll, she talks with herself, and by talking with her doll she constitutes herself; by means of apostrophe, she creates an Other, she makes an absence (at least provisionally) a presence, and manufactures the conditions of discourse.[63]

As a substitute friend, the doll allows the child to create herself, perform her identity, in relation to others; as a symbol of herself, Esther can thus view her doll

---

[59] For an interesting discussion of the role of household pets in Dickens's work, see Ingham, p. 21.

[60] Stewart, p. 57.

[61] See Melanie Klein's discussion of the child's search for objects (both things and people) as a way of alleviating the problems of growing up. For a summary of her theory see R.D. Hinshelwood, *A Dictionary of Kleinian Thought* (London: Free Association Books, 1991), p. 393.

[62] Dever, p. 88.

[63] Ibid.

as an object, understanding how others may see her; she can also take part in a mother–child dyad, acting the role of the 'not clever' child with the 'patient' 'dear' mother. The doll's beauty, her 'beautiful complexion and rosy lips' (BH 27), not only presents Esther with an example of an ideal feminine appearance, but also affords an opportunity for aesthetic appreciation and imaginative engagement with femininity: as Marcus has demonstrated, dolls initiate sexual awareness, enabling girls to admire freely and desire erotically the female form.[64] Esther, crucially, can also treat her doll as her property. She exerts her sense of ownership in order to gauge her power over objects and assess the boundaries between human and object.

Esther's burial of her doll on the death of her aunt suggests not only the premature end of her childhood as she is sent out alone into the world, but also a burial of her 'mother', as well as a reconstruction of the burial of her aunt which has recently taken place. She states, 'I wrapped the dear old doll in her own shawl, and quietly laid her – I am half ashamed to tell it – in the garden–earth, under the tree that shaded my old window' (BH 36). Why does she feel an element of shame in performing this burial? Perhaps, if the doll is a substitute mother, this is an attempt to rid herself of the 'disgrace' associated with her mother and herself, for Miss Barbary has told her that her mother is her 'disgrace, and you were hers' (BH 30). Yet the burial is also an assertion of her rights as a property owner to destroy or 'kill' what she owns, and there may be a sense of shame in exercising this right. As a child she probably believed her doll to be alive and a subject (possessing her 'own' property in the form of a shawl). The burial immediately follows the unsettlement brought about by her aunt/godmother's death and the dispersal of the familiar objects she has known. Esther is particularly moved by the vision of 'an old hearth-rug with roses on it, which always seemed to me the first thing in the world I had ever seen, [and] was hanging outside in the frost and snow' (BH 36). As David Trotter has suggested, '[t]he deathbed apart, there are few scenes more profoundly disturbing in nineteenth-century fiction than household clearance, or the process of "selling up"'.[65] For Esther, this familiar household object in an unfamiliar place, exposed and vulnerable, even perhaps 'dead' (suggested by her use of the word 'hanging') indicates the way in which death or financial failure can shift personal property from its meanings in the realm of affect into an unwelcome publicity or oblivion. This shock offers another reason why Esther feels she must bury her doll: to avoid a similar exposure of her beloved object within the unfamiliar, non-domestic and public space of the school.

However, in *Bleak House* female companionship, even within the disciplinary context of the school, connotes succour and support and her school friends take the places of the buried doll and the caged bird (neither are mentioned again once Esther leaves her aunt's house). Belonging to a female network, Esther no longer

---

[64] See Marcus's chapter on dolls pp. 109–66 for a fascinating discussion of the role of dolls in furthering female fantasies and desires.

[65] David Trotter: 'Household Clearances in Victorian Fiction', *19: Interdisciplinary Studies in the Long Nineteenth Century*, 6 (2008) [www.19.bbk.ac.uk].

needs to own private property; other than references to her savings (which she readily gives away), her handkerchief (again, given away), and the flowers she receives from Allan Woodcourt (which are preserved as a keepsake but have no monetary value), Esther is presented as unburdened with possessions. In this respect she is like Harold Skimpole, able to appreciate aesthetically the pleasing things she encounters without needing to own them. Installed at Bleak House, she awakes to find 'pleasure in discovering the unknown objects that had been around me in my sleep. ... [T]he picture began to enlarge and fill up so fast, that, at every new peep, I could have found enough to look at for an hour' (BH 115). Dickens suggests that ideally women do not need to own property in the form of objects or money because their bonds with each other, their skills and abilities to appreciate aesthetically, are more valuable than tangible property. Although this suggests a traditional and conservative view of women, it is actually related to the novel's radical message: that collective property is a more positive form of ownership than the property of possessive individuals. Indeed, this runs as a utopian thread throughout his work. As John Bowen states in *Other Dickens*, 'The virtues that Dickens's novels most admire – benevolence, reciprocity, selflessness, compassion, trust – are essentially collective ones that depend upon the existence of a community of others'.[66]

By far the most significant example of collective property in the novel is a piece of fabric labelled 'Esther Summerson', which becomes an important form of wealth for a number of female characters in the novel, moving between a range of 'owners'. It is worth noting the significance of this handkerchief, for fabric has long functioned as a source of wealth and status for women. Dickens, like most other Victorian novelists, often mentions textiles in relation to his female characters: their handkerchiefs, pincushions, dresses and other items of costume, ornamentation (such as ribbons), and 'work' in the sense of sewing and embroidery. Weiner has demonstrated the importance of 'soft' wealth to women, associated as it is with female forms of production and ownership. 'Soft' possessions, such as cloth and textiles, as well as woven items such as baskets, have traditionally been denigrated in favour of 'hard' wealth, such as metals or building materials, usually associated with men.[67] Yet, as she convincingly argues, cloth is politically important in 'cultures ranging from chieftaincies to large-scale class societies, as such possessions provide repositories of wealth to be kept as well as to be given away'.[68] Cloth has also been associated with magic and the sacred (think of altar cloths, royal robes, wedding gowns and shrouds, for example). Women have often been involved in all stages of its production from the transformation of plant materials such as flax into spun thread which is in turn woven into cloth, dyed, cut, sewn, embroidered and put to use. The ownership of fine cloth was important as a signal of social status (as Magwitch realizes when he admires Pip's display of the clean

---

[66]   Bowen, p. 19.

[67]   Weiner, pp. 12–13.

[68]   Ibid., p. 12.

fine linen of a gentleman in *Great Expectations*). Before the twentieth century, the handkerchief in particular was a signal of respectability as well as a source of wealth and form of currency and, as Adela Pinch has demonstrated, during the 1840s there existed 'an entire branch of London commerce devoted to the sale of stolen silk handkerchiefs'.[69] (To offer another example from Dickens, Fagin's gang in *Oliver Twist* makes its living mostly from the theft of handkerchiefs.) The handkerchief is also a good example of a feminine possession which transcends mere use value to become an intimate biographical possession. Women personalized such property by embroidering their names, initials, personal motifs and designs into the fabric, transforming cloth into a form of aesthetic self-expression. It was also used as an aid to communication by means of gesture (there were distinct meanings attached to the carefully dropped handkerchief, the handkerchief held to a corner of the eye, the handkerchief covering the mouth during moments of mirth, the handkerchief concealing the face to signal sleep, and so on).[70]

In *Bleak House* the sharing of this handkerchief also offers one of the novel's most radical images of communal property. No one asserts a claim to ownership and each woman accepts another's need for it. Lady Dedlock's payment for the handkerchief she takes from Jenny's slum home is more to appease Jenny's husband rather than a transaction between women. (Lady Dedlock and Jenny also exchange clothes, another example of a transference of soft property between women.) Like the exchange of the handkerchief between the middle-class Rose Maylie and the prostitute Nancy in *Oliver Twist*, the handkerchief is affective portable property, no longer a mere commodity: it gains new meanings beyond the marketplace. As we will see in the next chapter, George Eliot was also aware of the role of 'named' fabrics in women's lives, for Mrs Tulliver in *The Mill on the Floss* believes that she is losing a part of her identity when the biographical objects she has woven and named are sold to pay her husband's creditors. However, in *Bleak House* identity is not diminished but reinforced when biographical property is transferred from woman to woman, for the female network is extended and strengthened by its means.

The handkerchief which originates with Esther is an object with a particularly complex biography. Embroidered with her name, it is a token of her identity and (probably) her labour. It is then gifted to the working-class Jenny as a decent covering for her dead baby (BH 136). Jenny keeps it as a memorial of her child (a point to emphasize, because she could have raised money on this item to assuage her dire poverty). Later, it is surreptitiously taken by Lady Dedlock (who leaves money in its place) to function (in Miss Flite's words) as 'a little keepsake'

---

[69] Adela Pinch, 'Stealing Happiness: Shoplifting in Early Nineteenth-Century England', in Patricia Spyer (ed.), *Border Fetishisms: Material Objects in Unstable Spaces* (New York and London: Routledge, 1998), p. 128.

[70] Edel describes James's experience at the theatre when he was a boy, seeing 'little girls in the Palais-Royal giving a curious aesthetic role to the handkerchief' during a performance of *La Dame aux Camélias*, *Life*, vol. 1, p.110.

(BH 564) of her 'lost' daughter. Signifying that Esther, the 'dead' child, has survived, it later acts as a clue to the history and whereabouts of the dying Lady Dedlock. As though aware of the importance of this object, Inspector Bucket addresses it as though it were a subject: 'Are you her Ladyship's property, or somebody else's?' (BH 861). The handkerchief, doubly a biographical object, actually leads to the exposure of Lady Dedlock's biography. In the end we are left uncertain as to who has the best claim to own this property, although it begins and ends in Esther's care. Indeed, Dickens suggests that such property is never 'claimed' but is used and exchanged within a circle of women who find it consoling. It thus sharply contrasts with the Jarndyce property dispute, functioning as a sign and token of female friendship and female bonding, rather than conflict and emnity. Another significant feature of Esther's handkerchief is that it is not transferred from the older generation to the younger. With Esther and her mother the patrilineal codes of property transmission are reversed, for it is the mother who 'inherits' her daughter's property.

The handkerchief is also eroticized when it is in Lady Dedlock's keeping. Hidden away like a token of forbidden love, and acting metonymically for Esther the love-child, it is secreted in the most private place in her boudoir, a 'dainty little chest in an inner drawer' (BH 861). Inspector Bucket's discovery of this white handkerchief exposes it as perhaps the most cherished item of property she possesses, an object which she has also placed in her 'unquiet bosom' (BH 136) as representative of her love for her daughter and her dead lover, Captain Hawdon, as well as a reminder of her 'sin'. Such an object functions as a fetish, compensating her for everything she lacks. As we saw in the previous chapter in relation to another 'fallen' woman, Madame Bovary, the overriding need for fetishes, symbolic coverings in the forms of screens, clothes and curtains, is symptomatic of women's lack of adequate social 'coverings' in the forms of rights and freedoms. Lady Dedlock's need for her daughter's handkerchief (which has already been given away as a covering for Jenny's dead baby) signals her vulnerable position as a 'fallen' woman and aligns her with the working woman who is also not married to her child's father. The startling image of a policeman's 'great hand' penetrating Lady Dedlock's drawer in her 'spicy boudoir', as Inspector Bucket 'turn[s] over some gloves which [he] can scarcely feel, they are so light and soft within it' (BH 861), indicates the precariousness of women's 'soft' property/properties to the harshness of patriarchy and its laws.

Although Dickens, like many Victorian novelists, represents women as disadvantaged in a world controlled by men, *Bleak House* also demonstrates that female property relationships can work very differently and more effectively than the property relations enshrined in law. Dickens gives serious attention to the issue of women's property, demonstrating its ability to circulate in unregulated and unconventional ways. This is a utopian vision, offering an idealized female communal alternative to patrilineal forms of property transmission and possessive individualism. His female characters often selflessly look out for each other's interests, as with Esther's attempt to protect Ada when she fears 'that my dear girl's little property would be absorbed by Mr Vholes' (BH 782), and Miss Flite's generous offer to share with Esther and Ada the estate she expects to receive when her Chancery case is finally resolved (BH 76). However, although he returns to an exploration of the private female community in his later novels, *Our Mutual Friend*, with the bonds established between Lizzie, Jenny Wren, Bella and Miss Abbey Potterson, and in his final novel *The Mystery of Edwin Drood*, with the schoolgirl community, female bonding, with its sharing of property, is largely missing from *Little Dorrit* and *Great Expectations*.

Pale Decayed Objects: The Female Still Life in *Little Dorrit* and *Great Expectations*

A few years after the publication of *Bleak House*, Dickens wrote *Little Dorrit*, a novel in which the notion of the female community is largely missing. Even the most passionate female–female bond in the novel, the attachment between Miss Wade and Tattycoram, is depicted as possessive and reifying. Women here collude with the reification imposed upon them: Miss Wade places her arm around her companion's waist 'as if she took possession of her evermore' (LD 379). In a different spirit, Mrs Merdle puts up her 'bosom' for sale and Mr Merdle 'buys' it: 'Mr Merdle wanted something to hang jewels upon, and he bought it for the purpose' (LD 293). Marriage can also bring property in circuitous ways: Miss Rugg successfully gains 'a little property' in the form of damages conferred upon her by a breach of promise suit (LD 344). The novel's main focus on women and property, however, takes the form of a comparison between the renunciating Amy Dorritt and the possessive Mrs Clennam. The latter is represented as an embodiment of perversity, whose relationship to the material world is complicated by the intensely private language emanating from the objects which surround her. The idea of female perversity is explored later by Dickens in *Great Expectations* in his depiction of Miss Havisham. Both Mrs Clennam and Miss Havisham are presented as creators of museal worlds, the apparent deadness of which is belied by the violent energy which is emitted from their carefully presented display of objects.

In *Little Dorrit* and *Great Expectations* the utopian vision of *Bleak House* has soured and the female property owner has deteriorated into a possessive individual. While female friendship had an ability to neutralize the effects of patriarchy in the earlier novel, the later novels tend to focus on ineffective female relationships. Just as Miss Wade and Tattycoram fail to find an alternative to patriarchal paradigms, so too do Miss Havisham and Estella in *Great Expectations* as they fail to keep at bay the forces of masculine power they seek to undermine. As Susan Walsh argues, Miss Havisham hopes to use Estella 'to render men incapable of acting collectively, or conspiratorially, yet ends up only reinforcing the male unity she wishes to disrupt'.[71] This is a reversal of *Bleak House*, where the women work

---

[71]   Susan Walsh, 'Bodies of Capital: *Great Expectations* and the Climacteric Economy', *Victorian Studies*, 37:1 (Autumn 1993): 90.

collectively and the men fail to unify. In the later novel even the bond between Miss Havisham and Estella eventually breaks down. Estella is incapable of joining a female community: she appears to make no friends at school and later when she lives with Mrs Brandley and her daughter at Richmond, Pip notes that, 'Little, if any, community of feeling subsisted between them and Estella', Mrs Brandley 'ha[ving] been a friend of Miss Havisham's before the time of her seclusion' (GE 300). Both Estella and her mother by adoption deliberately seclude themselves from female companionship. This brief and isolated reference to Miss Havisham before her disastrous meeting with Compeyson tellingly suggests that her downfall involved a rejection of female friendship in favour of an investment in male support. This also involved a misguided investment of her property, for she allowed her fiancé to control her finances, readily accepting the rules of coverture before they were legally imposed on her. *Great Expectations* thus represents the consequences of female disunity. In *Bleak House* the female collective was active, mobile and effective: in the later novel it does not exist at all, with disastrous results for the female characters whose isolation leads to stasis and imprisonment.

Both *Little Dorrit* and *Great Expectations* explore the concept of the power-hungry, angry woman who seeks to control her world by means of an ordering of property into a grotesque domestic still life. Mrs Clennam and Miss Havisham, owners of real estate, create museal displays as representations of their situations. As Barthes has argued in 'The World as Object', the still life pays homage to the human ability to control the material world. The space and objects depicted in seventeenth-century Dutch still-life paintings, for example, are presented in terms of 'man's space; in it he measures himself and determines his humanity, starting from the memory of his gestures .... [T]here is no other authority in his life but the one he imprints upon the inert by shaping and manipulating it'.[72] Mrs Clennam and Miss Havisham control inert matter by designing settings in which to stage their traumas, their domestic still lifes functioning as memorials to these. Miss Havisham has created a display of objects dedicated to the failure of her wedding day when she was jilted by Compeyson; for Mrs Clennam, her display is representative of the trauma which immobilizes her within her home, that is, her discovery that her husband had a mistress and illegitimate child. Their still lifes are performative uses of property, protests against the female condition, of being bought and sold as objects in the marriage market, of being seen as embodiments of property and conduits for exchange, allowing them the fantasy of control, of being able to fix movable possessions, to retain permanently the objects they own. To achieve this sense of fixity and control, however, they must become immobile themselves. The domestic stasis they achieve is a comment on the demands on women to be feminine, for they take the notion of confinement in the private sphere of the home to its logical conclusion, thus offering ferocious parodic performances of the feminine ideal. Their still lifes also function as *vanitas* scenes, reminders

---

[72]   Roland Barthes, 'World as Object' in *Calligram: Essays in the New Art History of France*, Norman Bryson (ed.) (Cambridge: Cambridge University Press, 1988), p. 107.

of death and the transience of all things, as both women remind visitors that they intend to die in their museums. Yet ironically they also suggest the quality of permanence in their persistent refusal to move beyond their traumas. Their use of personal property as theatrical 'properties' is highly significant; a creative *and* destructive way of expressing oneself by means of an arrangement of objects.

Like the painters of Dutch still lifes, the women fill their domestic spaces with 'details that surreptitiously explain' (as Van Hoogstraeten stated of still-life paintings in 1678), creating uncanny museums of memorials invested with meanings which are not readily apparent to an outside observer.[73] The *vanitas* still-life painting is designed to remind the viewer that death frames our possession of the object world; indeed, that our possessions are capable of outliving us, thus rendering the *ownership* of things illusory. Nevertheless, there are a number of ambiguities about the *vanitas* still life; as Peter Schwenger has suggested in *The Tears of Things: Melancholy and Physical Objects*, the *vanitas* can suggest that:

> one has become an object … a melancholy reminder of the futility of amassing material things, and of the Last Things that await everyone. But to become an object may also be a positive aspiration. Beyond ownership, there is the lure of a more complete and intimate possession of an object. This is possession in the same sense that an alien spirit enters a human being, only reversed: a human spirit entering an alien entity.[74]

The blurring of the human and object, allowing one's possessions to possess one in turn, seems to be a significant feature of both Mrs Clennam and Miss Havisham's worlds. However, they, too, penetrate objects with their 'spirit', imbuing ordinary things with their own strangeness and power. Their self-imposed immobility within the real estate they own (and there are few female owners of real property in Dickens's novels), and the collection of objects which surround them, suggest this blending of the human with the object. Schwenger suggests that the 'desire to *be* an object' is related to the desire 'to exist outside of the demands of being, to achieve the autonomy of Sartre's *en-soi*'.[75] Both Mrs Clennam and Miss Havisham, as a way of coping with pain, work to achieve a level of object-ness, attempting to become things centrally positioned within their displays of things.

Pip notices early on Miss Havisham's limited mobility and her obsessive relationship to the objects which surround her:

> I noticed that Miss Havisham put down the jewel exactly on the spot from which she had taken it up. As Estella dealt the cards, I glanced at the dressing-table again, and saw that the shoe upon it, once white, now yellow, had never been

---

[73] Quoted in E. de Jongh, *Questions of Meaning, Theme and Motif in Dutch Seventeenth-Century Painting* (Leiden: Primavera Pers, 2000), p. 130.

[74] Peter Schwenger, *The Tears of Things: Melancholy and Physical Objects* (Minneapolis and London: University of Minnesota Press, 2006), p. 76.

[75] Schwenger, p. 77.

worn. I glanced down at the foot from which the shoe was absent and saw that the silk stocking on it, once white, now yellow, had been trodden ragged. Without this arrest of everything, this standing still of all the pale decayed objects, not even the withered bridal dress on the collapsed form could have looked so like grave-clothes, or the long veil so like a shroud. (GE 60)

Here Dickens seems to suggest that the enforced stasis of her interior design, the refusal to circulate (either herself or her things), 'this standing still', creates the aura of death which Pip registers unconsciously, a knowledge which bursts forth upon him when he explores the grounds and experiences the hallucination, seeing a vision of Miss Havisham alive but hanging from a beam. The ghostly white (or off-white) world of the bridal things is a counterpart to the death-like qualities of Mrs Clennam's black 'quiet room', and it is interesting to compare Dickens's treatment of the still life created by the mistress of Satis House with the *vanitas* scene created by Mrs Clennam. The latter demands proximity to a number of key objects, including her books, handkerchief, steel spectacles and the gold watch with its silk watch-paper with the initials 'D.N.F.' worked upon it in beads:

The usual articles were on the little table; the usual deadened fire was in the grate; the bed had its usual pall on it; and the mistress of all sat on her black bier-like sofa, propped up by her black angular bolster that was like the headman's block.

Yet there was a nameless air of preparation in the room, as if it were strung up for an occasion. From what the room derived it – every one of its small variety of objects being in the fixed spot it had occupied for years – no one could have said without looking attentively at its mistress, and that, too, with a previous knowledge of her face. Although her unchanging black dress was in every plait precisely as of old, and her unchanging attitude was rigidly preserved, a very slight additional setting of her features and contraction of her gloomy forehead was so powerfully marked, that it marked everything about her.[76]

Mrs Clennam is as much an object as her 'deadened' things and the *vanitas* motifs are here underlined, from the 'deadened fire', the 'pall' on the bed, the 'black bier-like sofa' and the references to executions in 'the headman's block' and the 'strung up' room. Like Satis House, Mrs Clennam's interior space also appears fixed and dead, but actually emanates energy, a disturbing force, a 'nameless air', demonstrating their abilities to make objects appear animate. Each appears to embody the ambiguous qualities of the uncanny, recalling Freud's definition of the term as indicating a confusion between the animate and the inanimate, raising 'doubts whether an apparently animate being is really alive; or, conversely, whether a lifeless object might not be in fact animate'.[77]

---

[76]   Charles Dickens, *Little Dorrit*, John Holloway (ed.) (London: Penguin, 1987), p. 832. Subsequent page references will be cited in the text following the abbreviation 'LD'.

[77]   Sigmund Freud, 'The Uncanny' (1919), reprinted in Julie Rivkin and Michael Ryan (eds), *Literary Theory: An Anthology*, 2nd ed. (Oxford: Blackwell, 2004), p. 421.

In the still lifes created by Mrs Clennam and Miss Havisham clocks and watches (traditional *vanitas* motifs) are foregrounded. For Miss Havisham, the stopped timepiece gives her an illusory power as the controller of a moment in time. Mrs Clennam, on the other hand, sees the words 'Do Not Forget' in the fabric of the watch-paper before her as a reminder that she must not cease to remember her anger while time continues. The forms of temporal and spatial arrest both women try to maintain are also denials of the marketplace, with its need to keep things circulating. It is also a refusal to allow the market an entry into their intimate, private worlds, a dramatic protest *against* circulation. Similarly, neither woman uses things as they were designed to be used: for Mrs Clennam the watch she keeps in view before her is not used to tell the time, just as the words 'Do Not Forget' have a meaning for her which is denied to Arthur Clennam and the rest of the world; she states, 'I do NOT forget, though I do not read it as he [her husband] did' (LD 846). The commodity's meaning is linked only to its exchange value, its price tag; however, the meaning of things which have, in Marx's words, 'fallen out of circulation', such as those displayed by Mrs Clennam and Miss Havisham, are more difficult to read.[78]

Dickens's representations of objects thus reflect the unsettling qualities of the Dutch *vanitas* still life, offering a pronounced literary version of what the art historian Hal Foster has termed 'the strange energy that emanates from the objects of Dutch still life', particularly in *pronk* paintings (from *pronken*, to 'show off'), with their 'lavish displays of fine objects and extravagant food'.[79] Indeed, the dinner tables described in *Dombey and Son* and *Our Mutual Friend* offer good examples of *pronkstilleven* (still-life banquet scenes), particularly the Veneerings' table with its 'caravan of camels tak[ing] charge of the fruits and flowers and candles' (OMF 10). Dickens also captures many other features of the still life for, as Foster states:

> Often in Dutch still life the inert appears animate, the familiar becomes estranged, and the insignificant seems humanly, even preternaturally, significant, in a way that transvalues the ancient term for still life, *rhyparography*, the depiction of insignificant things. (Foster, 253–4)

The Victorian critic, E.B. Hamley, writing in *Blackwood's Magazine* in 1857, accused Dickens of rhyparography, stating that his novels resembled the work of a Dutch painter in his attention to 'insignificant things'. He suggested that Dickens depicts scenes and characters 'with a minuteness far surpassing that of the most laborious limner of the Dutch school, till still life has no atom left in natural indistinctness'.[80] In other words, an emphasis placed on *every* object militates against the conventions of realist representation, where some things need to be

---

[78]   Marx, *Capital*, p. 76.

[79]   Hal Foster, 'The Art of Fetishism: Notes on Dutch Still Life' in Emily Apter and William Pietz (eds), *Fetishism as Cultural Discourse* (Ithaca and London: Cornell University Press, 1993), p. 253.

[80]   Cited in Collins, p. 359.

in the background or not described at all. An attempt to depict everything results in the 'hilarious' lists Freedgood identified as characteristic of Dickens's work. Miss Havisham is also guilty of rhyparography in her arrangement of her portable property as she creates scenes reminiscent of the later phase of *pronk* still lifes which, according to Hal Foster, represent objects as 'at once phantasmagorical and palpable ... caught between worlds – not alive, not dead, not useful, not useless ... . And the pictorial effect is often one of deathly suspension or ... of eerie animation'.[81] Each object is presented as significant, yet remains inexplicable. No aspect of Miss Havisham's display is allowed to fade into 'natural indistinctness'.[82] When he first meets her, Pip states: 'I took note of the surrounding objects in detail' (GE 58), as though, like an artist, her arrangement of her things promotes an unusually heightened perception of them in observers.

In *Great Expectations* the objects associated with femininity are always imbued with uncanny qualities and this is most evident in Satis House where they are displayed, positioned or used inappropriately. This is the quality captured by the contemporary British artist Tracey Emin in her confessional autobiographical work, particularly her installation, 'My Bed' (1999–2000), which, like Miss Havisham's room, is an attempt to exhibit a private moment frozen in time and space, a biographical display of intimate objects. Sally Munt has argued that 'Emin is perhaps the contemporary Foucauldian artist *par excellence* experimenting with extreme forms of living, making her own life a work of art, rhetorically implicating the practice of self-making with the politics of representation'.[83] Like Pip, who wishes to 'tear down the cobwebs' in Satis House (GE 231), cleaners in various museums and art galleries have unsuccessfully attempted to clear up the clutter of the detritus of Emin's installation (which consists of an unmade bed, stained underclothes, used condoms, empty vodka bottles and other signs of intimacy, exhaustion and abjection). The uncanniness of Emin's display, like that of the Dutch still life, is centred on the depiction of a privacy which has been inexplicably rendered available to public viewing. Similarly, Miss Havisham's dishabille is presented as an art exhibit, constituting her representation, her interpretation of the female condition by means of memorabilia. Emin, too, depends upon souvenirs from her own past to construct her art. Munt's comments on Emin's artistic method can equally well be applied to that of Miss Havisham:

> The collection of these totemic items of memorabilia can be read as autistic, but it [sic] also a habitual symptom of a person who needs to externalise their history in order to remind themselves that they have "a self", i.e. whose self-existence has been previously threatened.[84]

---

[81]   Foster, p. 257.

[82]   For an interesting discussion of the female museum in relation to Gaskell's *Cranford*, see Dolin, p. 39.

[83]   Sally R. Munt, *Queer Attachments: The Cultural Politics of Shame* (Aldershot: Ashgate, 2007), p. 209.

[84]   Munt, p. 212.

Significantly, the assertion of a self appears to involve both Emin and Miss Havisham in acts of rebellion against the traditional feminine domestic practices centred on tidiness, cleanliness and order.

The elaborate stage-managing of Miss Havisham's trauma results in a disintegration of the conventional trappings of femininity and a blurring of the qualities of bride and corpse. Susan Walsh, noting Miss Havisham's dedication 'to angry spinsterhood', argues that she 'keeps the idea of a sexual self always before her, gleefully watching the gap widen between bridal promise and atrophied reality'.[85] The retention of her virginity is displaced on to the retention of her bridal possessions, including her wedding feast. She attempts, and to some extent succeeds, in achieving the impossible: the conversion of food into an inalienable possession. As Weiner states, 'Of all objects … food is the most ineffectual inalienable possession because its biological function is to release energy rather than to store it'.[86] Miss Havisham has attempted to redirect the energy of her wedding feast. When Pip first sees it he is unable to recognize it as food:

> [E]very discernible thing in [the room] was covered with dust and mould, and dropping to pieces. The most prominent object was a long table with a tablecloth spread on it, as if a feast had been in preparation when the house and the clocks all stopped together. An epergne or centre-piece of some kind was in the middle of this cloth; it was so heavily overhung with cobwebs that its form was quite indistinguishable; and, as I looked along the yellow expanse out of which I remember its seeming to grow, like a black fungus, I saw speckled-legged spiders with blotchy bodies running home to it, and running out from it … .
> (GE 84)

Miss Havisham, who proudly announces 'It's a great cake. A bride-cake' (GE 85), has achieved an edible memorial which is at the same time an inalienable possession, retaining its energy: it becomes a 'home' for spiders, a 'fungus', a formless centre-piece which, although portable property, offers the illusion of fixity as it rots in its place on the table. Yet while it never moves from here, its form and substance do change, evolving through various stages of decay and growth, its inhabitants – the mice and spiders – invoking its grotesque energy. This piece of property also serves to release its owner from the feminine rituals of hospitality, as once every year Miss Havisham's relatives visit her at the scene of her unappetizing *unstill* life, a powerful reminder of her rejection of domesticity and her prerogative as a property owner to do as she likes with her possessions. As Ingham has suggested, women in Dickens's novels tend to 'provide and/or dispense food' as 'a sign that the natural order of things is being maintained'.[87] Miss Havisham, like Mrs Clennam, is dedicated to overturning the 'natural order of things'. The former and Estella appear not to need food within Satis House. Only Pip is fed, like

---

[85]   Walsh, pp. 90–91.

[86]   Weiner, p. 38.

[87]   Ingham, p. 30.

'a dog in disgrace' (GE 62), in the yard when he visits as a boy. In this respect, Miss Havisham is a more extreme rebel against domestic virtues than Mrs Clennam, for the latter still maintains a link between domesticity and nourishment by regularly consuming dainty meals brought to her on a tray by her servants.

Miss Havisham's wedding feast, then, offers a grotesque version of the intimacy of the Dutch banquet still life, a genre which also points towards transient pleasures and the forces of time and decay upon the material world in its depiction of partially consumed food and used glasses and plates. She is able to maintain an intimacy between herself and Estella (and to a lesser extent Pip) as a ploy to exclude members of her own family from her world and her property. As many art historians have noted, the domestic scenes in close-up depicted in seventeenth-century Dutch still-life paintings, the half-eaten feasts or breakfasts, the jumble of things on a table, and personal property in the form of miniatures and bouquets, suggest a voyeuristic glance into a private life, invoking modern notions of privacy.[88] Intimacy, as Arendt has argued, is actually a 'modern discovery' which constitutes 'a flight from the whole outer world into the inner subjectivity of the individual'.[89] In *Great Expectations* Miss Havisham successfully thwarts her relatives who seek to gain her property after her death by her perverse withdrawal into the intimacy of her home. For her, no possession must leave the interior of Satis House to enter the marketplace.

The only exceptions she makes to this rule are Estella and the jewels. However, both are released into circulation for a purpose, as Miss Havisham's emissaries. Estella tells Pip that she must write regularly 'and report how I go on – I and the jewels – for they are nearly all mine now' (GE 270). Miss Havisham is unusual in that she does not wait until her death to bequeath her jewellery to Estella, for they are needed in the latter's armoury of weapons. Estella refers to these jewels as though they possess agency, they, like her, can 'go on' in the world. (We will see in the next chapter that George Eliot's novels display a similar tendency: in *Daniel Deronda* Grandcourt's diamonds also appear to possess agency, an agency which overshadows and overwhelms that of his wife Gwendolen and mistress Lydia Glasher.) Indeed, Marcus has noted that not only is Estella Miss Havisham's doll, she is also objectified in Pip's narrative as being '[l]ike jewelry ... hard, brilliant and coveted'.[90] Miss Havisham acts as though Estella is her property, quite literally portable, for she is sent out into the world to act on her 'owner's' behalf. According to Pip, Estella, like her foster mother/owner embodies the uncanny qualities of the automaton; she is neither fully human, nor fully an object, Pip presuming that Estella is Miss Havisham's property and that she will bequeath her to him as his bride.

---

[88]	See Hanneke Grootenboer, *Rhetoric of Perspective: Realism and Illusionism in Seventeenth-Century Dutch Still-Life Painting* (Chicago and London: University of Chicago Press, 2005), p. 16, Foster, p. 260 and Stewart, pp. 29–30.

[89]	Arendt, p. 69.

[90]	Marcus, p. 180.

Both Mrs Clennam and Miss Havisham are mistresses of reification. They ground things and people (including themselves) as components in museums dedicated to their traumas. They also disrupt the customary relationships humans have with the material world. In this way they intensify an awareness of objects, freeing things into new meanings and new uses, bestowing upon them a level of 'independence'. A shoe is not simply an item of footwear for Miss Havisham, for one shoe never meets her foot, but is carefully placed on the table before her. Both characters maximize the impact of the things they own by allowing their possessions to exist, simply to *be*, without being put to conventional use. They are embodiments of anti-fashion and upholders of the inappropriate. Bill Brown has noted the ways in which the misuse of objects increases awareness of those objects:

> 'Unnatural' use, uncustomary use, is what … discloses the composition of objects. Forced to use a knife as a screwdriver, you achieve a new recognition of its thinness, its hardness, the shape and size of the handle.[91]

By keeping their property still and refusing to use it according to custom, Mrs Clennam and Miss Havisham not only have opportunities to focus on what Brown terms the 'thing-ness' of their things, but also to invest them with private meanings.

In *Bleak House* property circulated freely and communally among women. However, for Dickens the female property owner who does not put her property into circulation is presented as a problem, largely because she refuses to support social relationships and, in Miss Havisham's case, acts as the enemy of the male economy. As Walsh has argued, Miss Havisham 'blocks her financial capital from circulating within the proper channels of investment and trade, thus rendering it economically barren'.[92] In this she does not resemble Magwitch, for he is sent to prison for putting stolen notes into circulation (GE 350), an illegal action which is nonetheless necessary as capitalism's 'shadow' economy. Crime may take from the legitimate economy, yet it feeds what it takes back again; as criminals satisfy their desires with their stolen wealth, they stimulate supply, thus perpetuating the capitalist cycle of supply and demand. Magwitch also differs from Miss Havisham in that he is unable to avoid objectification. While the wealthy owner of Satis House can put her property to private uses in order to emphasize her independence and autonomy, Magwitch's lack of property leads to him being 'locked up, as much as a silver tea-kettle' (GE 345). Both are imprisoned, although Miss Havisham voluntarily relinquishes her liberty as part of her project for revenge.

While Magwitch feels the restrictions of being treated like an object, Miss Havisham chooses to become an object within her domestic world; she holds a central place in her own interior design. In this way she acts as though she is her own property, putting into practice Locke's theory that '[e]very man has a

---

[91] Brown, *A Sense of Things*, p. 78.
[92] Walsh, p. 90.

property in his own person'.[93] The fact that she voluntarily abdicates her liberty of movement by fixing herself in Satis House indicates that she sees liberty as a property which she is free to alienate. However, conversely, Miss Havisham does not choose to alienate the objects which constitute her still-life scenes. The paradoxical nature of such freedom has been discussed by Radin in her serious pun on the two meanings of property: as an attribute and as an owned object. She exposes some of the problems of liberal property theory by addressing the question:

> Does this mean I abdicate personhood if my liberty is voluntarily relinquished? Apparently yes, if property means attribute-property. But if at the same time property also means object-property, then voluntarily relinquishing my liberty is also an instance of contract alienation, and in traditional liberal ideology this is an instance of self-expression and fulfilment of personhood rather than its negation. Abdication of liberty is both destructive of personhood and expressive of it. The pun is the surface manifestation of a deep fissure in liberal ideology.[94]

Miss Havisham (like her forerunner, Mrs Clennam) falls into this fissure. In order to express herself, she and her possessions must cease to circulate; in order to be free to express herself she must deny herself liberty. In some ways, however, this is the ultimate expression of freedom: the voluntary abdication of one's liberty indicates that one is free to alienate it. This perversity can be read as a tactic which exposes the paradoxical situation whereby patriarchy and capitalism are based on notions of liberty and property which work in opposition to women's needs by denying them liberty and property. In this respect, Miss Havisham's assertion of liberty (by alienating it) and property (by removing it from the processes of investment and imposing stasis on it) exposes the gender conflict at the heart of liberal ideology.

Great Expectations also represents another angry woman in the form of Pip's sister, Mrs Joe (actually Georgiana Gargery née Pirrip, although her own names are denied her throughout the novel). As a perverse arranger of her own still lifes to reflect her sense of frustration and anger, Mrs Joe is a working-class version of Miss Havisham. She creates a still life scene in 'the little state parlour ... which was never uncovered' (GE 22), in which are displayed 'four little white crockery poodles on the mantelshelf, each with black nose and a basket of flowers in his mouth, each the counterpart of the other' (GE 23). The four ceramic poodles were originally manufactured as commodities designed to be purchased as domestic fancy goods, expressions of lower-class feminine taste. Yet, like Miss Havisham's bridal property, Mrs Joe's ornaments are used for more sinister purposes, as parodies of feminine affect and hostile displays of uncomfortable domesticity. Like Esther's handkerchief and Miss Havisham's bridal things, Mrs Joe's property is white, signifying both purity and coldness, associated with innocence and death.

---

[93]   Locke, p. 274.

[94]   Radin, p. 194.

Mrs Joe owns 'hard' property: as well as the ceramic ornaments, she also owns two decanters which Pip 'knew very well as ornaments, but had never seen used in all my life' (GE 280). It is only at her funeral that Pip sees them in use (filled) for the first time. Just as Miss Havisham refuses to dispense food and drink, Mrs Joe's empty decanters signify her rebellion against her role as a dispenser of nourishment. They also reinforce her expressions of her sense of emptiness and discontent with her lot as a wife. She, like Miss Havisham, does not use her possessions conventionally; the stasis that Pip finds so deathly in the domestic scenes both 'mothers' create is actually an expression of their oppositional ways of 'using' objects to express anger. By denying the processes of circulation, exchange and use, Dickens's women can fix portable property within the home as a deeply ironic way of exerting their sense of control and communicating their rebellious impulses.

Yet Mrs Joe, unlike Miss Havisham, also has portable property which she takes out for public display. When she goes to visit Uncle Pumblechook she:

> lead[s] the way in a very large beaver bonnet, and carrying a basket like the Great Seal of England in plaited straw, a pair of patterns, a spare shawl and an umbrella, though it was a fine bright day. I am not quite clear whether these objects were carried penitentially or ostentatiously; but, I rather think they were displayed as articles of property – much as Cleopatra or any other sovereign lady on the Rampage might exhibit her wealth in a pageant or procession. (GE 99)

This display indicates her frustrated desire to exist as a public figure. Aware of the power of objects in creating a public image, Mrs Joe uses her things, all of them usually associated with conventional femininity, strategically. She converts 'feminine' things into 'masculine' expressions of power and aggression. Indeed, Pip learns the uses of such property from both his sister and Miss Havisham, both of whom intimidate and impress him with the power of their things and the ways in which they display them. As Marcus has argued, Pip, like a girl, learns femininity (which he confuses with gentility) through emulating the ways in which women use and display their possessions.[95] The careful interior design of his rooms in London and his many anxious purchases from his tailor and jeweller cause him to get into debt. Yet Pip lacks the creative energy of his sister and Miss Havisham for they, in their display of objects, are like artists creating autobiographical expressions of themselves, while he blindly follows fashions.

Wemmick does not personalize objects; he is a speculator and investor in things, rather than an arranger of the inert world of matter. Although he possesses a collection of mourning rings and cabinet of curiosities filled with the memorials of hanged men and women, objects which are intimately associated with the violent deaths of the donors, none of them actually function for him as *vanitas* objects. This is because Wemmick does not fetishize them; he views them always in terms of their exchange value. They are not reminders of death, they do not function as a source of affect or memory, but instead exist as property, exchangeable

---

[95]   Marcus, pp. 180–90.

commodities whose primary function is to physically sustain the living. In this respect, Wemmick who, as I mentioned earlier, is one of the most vocal fictional advocates of the advantages of portable property, has no sentimental interest in the objects themselves. They are 'curiosities', but nothing more than that. Wemmick thus represents the rational approach to the object world which underpins the marketplace. He is not even guilty of commodity fetishism, for he perpetually holds in mind the monetary value and origins (albeit with the condemned convict donors who have bought or stolen them, rather than the workers who have made them) of the things he amasses. Mrs Clennam, Mrs Joe and Miss Havisham, on the other hand, show that once they have 'fallen out of circulation', the objects they own can be stilled, arranged within a context of their own making and used as fetishes; their things vacillate in a complex process of avowal and disavowal. This level of control over objects suggests a desire to resist becoming an object or being treated as one. Although each of these female characters ultimately fails to achieve this desire, their protest is sustained over long periods of time, causing pain to those caught within the frames of their still lifes.

While Pip eventually leaves for Cairo to remake himself as a 'self-made' man, Estella becomes more enmeshed within Miss Havisham's elaborate memorial and complicated revenge plot. Yet she, too, eventually escapes although Dickens is highly ambivalent towards Estella as a free woman and property owner. She ends up (in the published version of the novel's ending) unmarried and the owner of real estate.[96] This level of freedom, as we will see in the next chapter, is reserved in George Eliot's work for her most ambivalent heroine, Gwendolen Grandcourt, another young widow who has 'behaved badly'. In *Great Expectations* we learn that Miss Havisham leaves everything to Estella in her will, except for a redeeming 'coddleshell' (as Joe terms her codicil) which suggests Miss Havisham's recapitulation to the demands of the patriarchal economy when she leaves £4,000 to her relative, Matthew Pocket. The Satis House collection is finally made public with an auction of its 'Household Furniture and Effects'. Indeed, Satis House itself is dismantled and converted into movable property: 'The House itself was to be sold as old building materials and pulled down' (GE 473). Miss Havisham's refusal to recycle her property during her lifetime is suitably punished in an action which suggests that even real estate can become portable. (This collapse of a woman's real estate had of course already happened in *Little Dorrit* when Mrs Clennam's house fell down at a suitably dramatic moment of crisis.) Yet Estella's dismantling of her property is actually a strong assertion of her possession: as an owner she can choose to destroy what she owns. She tells Pip that although her brutal husband, Bentley Drummle, had taken all of her personal property for himself, she made a 'determined resistance' to retain ownership of Satis House. Her statement: 'The ground belongs to me' (GE 482) is an unusual moment in Victorian fiction, a suggestion of the heroine's renunciation of renunciation by

---

[96]   In the original version of the ending, Dickens represented Estella as married to a Shropshire doctor (GE 508–9).

means of a projected future based on the ownership of real estate. As Lyn Pykett has stated, Satis House 'is awaiting redevelopment',[97] and Estella, as the owner of the ground, is free to redevelop as she chooses. Yet, as with Gwendolen Harleth, also free to redevelop herself and her property, critics have tended to focus on the more overt images of a 'broken' woman, beaten and bullied into submission. While Dickens and Eliot present their young widows with real estate as subdued by their experiences, they also present them as free to transcend women's usual lot. As Schor has stated, *Great Expectations* is 'Estella's novel'.[98] Her autonomy points towards a 'redevelopment' of the ground of the narrative away from Pip's version of events: while Pip presumes they will never part, Estella states to Pip that they will 'continue friends apart' (GE 484). In his later novels, *Our Mutual Friend* and *The Mystery of Edwin Drood*, Dickens presents a number of female characters trapped in an infantile relationship to property: Bella Wilfer's sophisticated knowledge of herself being 'willed away like a dozen of spoons' is eventually transformed (once she has been tricked and humiliated) into her acceptance of her place as a doll in a doll's house; Georgiana Podsnap must be saved from herself by Mr Boffin as she 'throws away' her property on her friend, Sophronia Lammle; Rosa, denied ownership and knowledge of her mother's ring, never grows out of her 'little' girlish things. Estella, then, is one of the few grown-up heroines Dickens offers to readers. The next chapter will demonstrate that George Eliot increasingly felt the need to move her young heroines away from the conventions of feminine renunciation and infantilism into the maturity of self-possession and property ownership.

---

[97] Lyn Pykett, *Charles Dickens* (Basingstoke: Palgrave, 2002), p. 166.

[98] Schor, p. 154.

Chapter 3
Makeshift Links:
Women and Material Politics
in George Eliot's Novels

The 1850s, as Nancy Paxton has argued, was a 'catastrophic decade' in terms of the anxiety generated by the heated debates on gender, sexuality and marriage in the run-up to the passing of the 1857 Matrimonial Causes Act.[1] During the early 1850s George Eliot (at this time calling herself Marian Evans) supported feminist campaigns for reform, and in 1856 she signed the petition drawn up by Barbara Leigh Smith which called for the rights of married women to control their own property and earnings.[2] As Jennifer Uglow has stated, this was the 'most "feminist" stage in her career'.[3] Yet Eliot's feminism, according to Paxton, was 'understandably complicated, not least because she was ostracized by women in polite society because Lewes could not marry her'.[4] Already married, but unable to divorce the wife who had left him for another, George Lewes was not in a position to offer his name, just as Eliot was not bound by the laws of coverture which conferred property rights and authority on men. Eliot's ambiguous position did not, however, prompt her to strengthen her political bonds with her feminist friends; on the contrary, she felt progressively more ambivalent towards the Woman Question. In a letter to Emily Davies in 1868 she expressed her fear that increasing women's legal rights would lead to their de-sexing, or what she termed the loss of 'that exquisite type of gentleness [and] … tenderness suffusing a woman's being with affectionateness'.[5] Such fears of gender confusion emerged in her novels, most notably in her representations of power-seeking women, such as Mrs Transome in *Felix Holt* (1866), Rosamond Vincy in *Middlemarch* (1872), and the Princess Halm-Eberstein in *Daniel Deronda* (1876). Yet she also emphasizes the vulnerability of wives, from Mrs Tulliver's loss of her 'household gods' in *The Mill on the Floss* to the humiliation experienced by Mrs Bulstrode on learning of her husband's disgrace in *Middlemarch*, a humiliation which she symbolically performs by ridding herself of her ornaments and fine clothes.

---

[1]   Nancy L. Paxton, *George Eliot and Herbert Spencer: Feminism, Evolutionism, and the Reconstruction of Gender* (Princeton: Princeton University Press, 1991), p. 15. See also Poovey, *Uneven Developments*.

[2]   Paxton, p. 34.

[3]   Jennifer Uglow, *George Eliot* (London: Virago, 1987), p. 115.

[4]   Paxton, p. 36.

[5]   *George Eliot Letters*, vol. 4, p. 468.

Because of her liminal situation as a *feme sole* masquerading as a *feme couvert*, Eliot's position towards ownership was unusually complex. Before she began to live with Lewes in 1854, Marian Evans was the possessor of £2,000 which she had inherited in 1849 from her father. This yielded a modest annual income of £90 a year.[6] Whether Robert Evans would have disinherited his daughter had he lived to witness her 'fall' from respectability, or whether he would have evinced any Dodson-like feeling of family bonds and sense of duty is a matter for speculation. Certainly her brother Isaac Evans disowned her once she became Lewes's common-law wife. On entering this relationship she chose to behave as though she were a married woman, voluntarily binding herself by the restrictions of coverture, calling herself 'Mrs Lewes' and relinquishing her earnings to her lover. She arranged for cheques to be paid into Lewes's account, and gave him control of her investments in canal, gas and railway companies. Her income from *Middlemarch*, for example, was invested by Lewes in American railway shares, and a proportion also went towards the support of Lewes's estranged wife, Agnes, and her four illegitimate children.[7] Eliot's generosity (after all, she had complete control over her property and earnings) indicates that the relinquishing of property was not just an ideal adopted by the saintly heroines in her fiction, but an ethical stance which she enacted in her own life.

Coverture, as Eliot's own desire for it indicates, always had the potential to be an ambiguous feature of marriage. As Finn has suggested, 'There is much to commend in the feminist emphasis on and critique of the legal status – or legal nonentity – of women under coverture, but there is also much that is excluded from its ambit'.[8] Coverture, as we have seen in previous chapters, while an evil for some married women, could actually suit the purposes of others. Pettitt has argued that the pseudonym 'George Eliot' acts in itself as 'a kind of *coverture*, which imprisons her while also protecting her'.[9] Marian Evans thus occupied an equivocal position: ambiguously placed as 'Mrs Lewes', a 'wife' holding conservative views on roles in marriage and welcoming coverture as a form of protection, and as 'George Eliot', an educated professional writer with radical views on female education who remained legally a spinster until late in life. While Victorian feminists sought to abolish the laws of coverture, Eliot's attitude towards women's property was not so straightforward. She admitted that because she felt 'too deeply the different complications' of the Woman Question she was unable to commit herself wholeheartedly to the feminist cause.[10] For Eliot, marriage remained the principal concern of her heroines, and indeed marriage is central to most of her plots. Yet she vacillates between condemning women's social exclusion (particularly from education) and lack of property rights in marriage and critiquing those women who are overly fond of property and power and use husbands as a conduit for this.

---

[6] Rosemary Ashton, *George Eliot: A Life* (London: Penguin, 1996), p. 68.

[7] Ashton, pp. 332–3.

[8] Finn, 'Women, Consumption and Coverture', p. 705.

[9] Pettitt, *Patent Inventions*, p. 243.

[10] To Mrs Nassau Senior, 4 October 1869, *George Eliot Letters*, vol. 5, p. 58.

George Eliot's attitude towards the legal ambiguity of Victorian women was, then, by no means clear cut. While she tends to satirize property-seeking women, she is nevertheless fascinated by women's fascination with the material world. In *Adam Bede* (1859) and *The Mill on the Floss* Eliot draws on popular eighteenth-century satires of women's desires for china and other household goods in her presentation of women such as Mrs Poyser, Hetty Sorrel, Mrs Tulliver and Mrs Pullet.[11] However, she can also be sensitive to the fact that this desire was often bound up with notions of identity and personhood. In her discussion of the consumption of luxury goods in the eighteenth century, Berg has shown that 'people not infrequently valued their possessions at rates even higher than their houses', and the tendency of the middle classes to privilege portable property continued well into the nineteenth century.[12] Eliot herself was anxious about the idea of buying a house, writing in a letter that she and Lewes were 'wondering what would be the right thing to do – hardly liking to lock up any money in land and bricks'.[13] As we have seen in previous chapters, portable objects, while theoretically capable of being more easily exchanged for money (unlike the 'locked up' assets in real estate), were frequently assessed by Victorians in more complex ways than any simple market valuation would suggest. For women whose legal hold on things was tenuous, their personal property could be both a source of pleasure and potential anxiety for, unlike the wealth in real property, wealth in objects was more liquid and thus more easily alienated.

Eliot's representation of women's emotional attachment to things changed throughout her career. From the satirizing of 'things women' in her early novels she moved towards an awareness of the complex relationships women had with the material world and the extent to which political forces could control these. All of her novels explore the tactics women employ to bypass the law and custom; however, it is only in the later novels that she presents these tactics positively. In later life, Eliot expressed her appreciation of women's relationships with little things to her friend, Mrs Elma Stuart, one of her 'spiritual daughters', who frequently sent her small homemade gifts, from wooden carved boxes to fabrics crafted into clothes or bookmarks. In a letter to Elma in 1874, Eliot wrote:

> You will not surprise me by any stories of energy on your part, for you struck me as an incarnation of fun, industry, and lovingness – three best forms of energy. And it is cheering to think that there are blue clocks as well as troubles in the world. There is another spiritual daughter of mine whom I should gladly see eager about some small delight – a china monster or a silver clasp – instead of telling me that nothing delights her. One can never see the condition of the world truly when one is dead to little joys.[14]

---

[11] See Berg, p. 245 for details of eighteenth-century satires on women and commodities.

[12] Berg, p. 226, and R.J. Morris, pp. 223–63.

[13] To Mrs Charles Bray, 1 June 1863, *George Eliot Letters*, vol. 4, p. 87.

[14] 8 March 1874, *George Eliot Letters*, vol. 6, p. 27.

The object-world is here presented as offering fun, consolation and delight. As she became increasingly aware of the pleasures of the material world (pleasures which she had tended to condemn in her early writing) her letters to her female friends refer to the 'little joys' to be found in the possession of objects. For example, one of her most exuberant letters concerns her invention of 'braces to hold up my flannel and calico drawers', and she playfully boasts to Mrs Stuart, 'I am wondering whether I have the start of you in invention so that I can actually give you a hint of ease in return for all the thoughts and stitches you have given me'.[15] These letters were written as Eliot began *Daniel Deronda*, a time when she was frustrated in her research into the laws affecting real estate. Unusually, this was a subject she found difficult to master, writing to a lawyer friend, 'I have been looking into Williams on Real Property, but cannot get clear as to the frequency and strict necessity of resettlements of estates in tail'.[16] The complexity of the laws concerning the entail of land down the male line seem almost as baffling to Eliot as they were to Mrs Bennet in *Pride and Prejudice*. However, the world she shared with her female friends based on the affective powers of 'china monsters and silver clasps', or the excitement of inventing braces to hold up one's drawers, seemed as intelligible as it was enjoyable. The letters written during 1875 reveal her awareness of the split between different types of property, as she conveys her sympathies for the ownership of 'blue clocks' and china ornaments at the same time she expresses her irritation with the irrational laws governing primogeniture and the inheritance of real property.

This chapter charts her developing response to women's need for things they could call their own, a response which was related to the attempts on the part of some of her feminist friends to bring about changes in the law affecting women's property. Her depictions of English provincial communities are characterized by an uneasy nostalgia, as social tensions both threaten tradition and engender improvements. In the provinces, she suggests, the clever and imaginative individuals fail while the stupid triumph. Trapped within such communities, intelligent women appear to find little comfort, many of them seeking deprivation and renunciation as perverse goals in a world where objects are often valorized and given priority over human beings.[17] Eliot's questioning of the 'natural' order, particularly in her representations of the inefficacy of patriarchy, is at work in three novels of English provincial life: *The Mill on the Floss*, *Middlemarch* and *Daniel Deronda*.[18] This chapter considers how Eliot raises the issue of material politics in terms of women's rights to, and control of, property in these novels, where depictions of female dispossession are matched with exposures of patriarchy's weak spots.

---

[15]   24 March 1875, *George Eliot Letters*, vol. 6, p. 133.

[16]   To Frederic Harrison, 7 January 1875, *George Eliot Letters*, vol. 6, p. 110.

[17]   See Sedgwick for a useful discussion of renunciation as a performative.

[18]   *Daniel Deronda*, of course, ranges beyond the provincial community in its depictions of Jewish heritage and continental life. See Plotz for a discussion of this novel as marking a break with Eliot's focus on 'midland scenery' (p. 77).

Female Economies and 'transcendent treasures' in *The Mill on the Floss*

Written in 1859, the 'anxious' year when 'George Eliot's' identity as an author was publicly exposed after Liggins's fraudulent claim to be the author of *Adam Bede*, *The Mill on the Floss* is a novel fractured by the heroine's anxiety about her duty towards others.[19] It also suggests, despite its nostalgic tone, the impossibility of the family (or at least a certain type of middling-class family) as a site of intellectual and spiritual growth. By the time she came to write the novel, Eliot had defied convention and the exigencies of patriarchy by eloping with Lewes, an action which forced her outside the boundaries of respectability. Yet Eliot's critique of provincialism appears to override the nostalgia; the narrator directly addresses the reader with the words: 'I share with you this sense of oppressive narrowness', presuming that readers will view negatively the claustrophobic domestic and provincial world she represents.[20]

For many critics, *The Mill on the Floss* represents the trauma of constriction and ostracism Eliot experienced as a woman of wide intellectual powers trapped in a narrow world of 'respectable' appearances. Sadoff links the novel's exploration of family tensions to Mary Ann Evans's troubled relationship with her 'authoritative and prohibitive father'.[21] Similarly, Pauline Nestor reads the relationship of Maggie and her brother Tom as a replication of Evans's 'own relationship with her brother Isaac'.[22] Neil Hertz sees the novel as focused on 'the powerful obligations that kinship or "blood" imposes on people like the Dodsons and the Tullivers'.[23] Certainly, Eliot looks back in this novel to the period of her own childhood in the 1820s, a time when family identities were being dramatically transformed by the changing national and global economies. The 1820s, as R.J. Morris has shown, produced 'a system of relationships and ambitions … responding to a richness of wealth and income flows that had never been available to such a sizeable proportion of the population'.[24] This new wealth was expressed in a burst of consumer activity. William Cobbett in his *Rural Rides* describes a family whose income had steadily increased for decades, but it was only in 1825 that they felt the need to display this increase with new possessions.[25] For Eliot, middle-class family life in the 1820s inevitably involves the investment of income and property

---

[19] See Pettitt, *Patent Inventions*, p. 237 for further details of Liggins's 'theft' of Eliot's authorial identity.

[20] George Eliot, *The Mill on the Floss*, ed. A.S. Byatt (Harmondsworth: Penguin, 1985), p. 363. Subsequent page references will be cited in the main body of the text following the abbreviation 'MF'.

[21] Sadoff, p. 79.

[22] Pauline Nestor, *George Eliot* (Basingstoke: Palgrave, 2002), p. 57.

[23] Neil Hertz, *George Eliot's Pulse* (Stanford: Stanford University Press, 2003), p. 73.

[24] R.J. Morris, p. 51.

[25] Cited in Colin Campbell, *The Romantic Ethic and the Spirit of Modern Consumerism* (Oxford: Blackwell, 1987), p. 18.

accumulation; however, ironically, the Tullivers' ambition to increase their wealth and social status ultimately destabilizes the very concept of the family.

With Eliot's novels, current events trigger a process of looking back in time. Radical activity in the 1850s prompted her to study the reform movement of the 1820s which had resulted in the passing of the first Reform Bill of 1832. The 1820s was a period of economic volatility, where the wealth of some individuals increased dramatically while a record number of bankruptcies in 1826 brought about a financial crisis. This combination of increased access to wealth, particularly credit, and increased uncertainty about retaining that wealth led to the reinforcement of a 'sense of extended family' among the middle classes, constituting a complex support network designed to offer some defence against financial failure.[26] This defensive attitude, as Eric Hobsbawm states, meant that the bourgeois family increasingly became a 'unit of property and business enterprise ... [b]uttressed by clothes, walls and objects', an inaccessible, self-enclosed, self-protective entity which became 'the most mysterious institution of the age'.[27] In *The Mill on the Floss* George Eliot demystifies the concept of the family by exposing its limitations to full view, highlighting the toll exacted by the extended family on individual autonomy and desire.

The family 'unit of property and business enterprise' has its foundation in the rights and duties of property ownership, a theme which is central to *The Mill on the Floss*. Tanner, like Hertz and Sadoff, considers the novel to be based on the 'tensions between the obligations of property and the importunities of passion'.[28] Property, then, far from being a route to individual freedom is represented by Eliot as a 'tie' bringing 'obligations' and curbing individual desire, a point also made by Eric Levy, who discusses the novel's representation of property ownership as an ethical system which 'informs and influences the [characters'] sense of identity', but which ultimately has negative consequences in encouraging a tendency to treat human beings as property.[29] Maggie, trapped within a community of obsessive property owners, becomes a victim to this morality for 'she construes her identity in terms of claims and indebtedness, almost as if she were the incarnation of property'.[30] Levy relates Maggie's tendency to see herself as others' property to the legal situation of Victorian married women generally, arguing that the novel 'develops a penetrating critique of "the pleasure of property". Yet it is a critique which, at bottom, concerns ... the distortion of human relations by an array of rights and claims analogous to those conferred by ownership'.[31] Thus Maggie

---

[26]   R.J. Morris, p. 125.

[27]   Eric Hobsbawm, *The Age of Capital, 1848–1875* (London: Abacus, 2004), pp. 227–8 and 278.

[28]   Tanner, p. 67.

[29]   Eric P. Levy, 'Property Morality in *The Mill on the Floss*', *Victorians Institute Journal*, 31 (2003): 174.

[30]   Ibid., p. 180.

[31]   Ibid., p. 181.

becomes the property of her family, who ignore her agency by treating her as an object. *The Mill on the Floss*, conceived during the late 1850s when feminist debates on women's relationships to property were widely disseminated, is thus a highly topical novel.

George Eliot was aware that the idea of woman-as-property was not applicable to all women in Victorian society. Maggie, for example, fails to see that it is possible to evade objectification in some contexts. She remains unaware that the enclosed, restrictive world inhabited by her aunts is also a protective space which operates more positively (if not perfectly) as a semi-public alternative to the marginal, private feminized spaces of the attic Maggie haunts with only her Fetish for company, or the hidden and enclosed space of the Red Deeps. The women of St Ogg's have, ironically, occupied the centre of the community and developed tactics which allow them to retain this space for themselves, a space which was never intended to belong to them. As Michel de Certeau states in his *The Practice of Everyday Life*: 'a tactic is an art of the weak. ... Power is bound by its very visibility. In contrast, trickery is possible for the weak'.[32] The St Ogg's women find what Certeau calls 'cracks' 'in the framework of a system', successfully fooling the male community into believing that they have the power of property owners.[33] Husbands in St Ogg's seem generally ignorant of their legal powers, their wives being fully aware that the marriage laws cannot be effectively policed. Armed with this knowledge they adopt a material politics which allows them to shape the material world to suit their needs. However, those who do not make use of feminine tactics, such as Mrs Tulliver and her daughter (both of whom make the fatal error of trusting in the dominant male order to look after their interests), become subsumed by the patriarchal system the other women have successfully evaded. The key to the St Ogg's women's successful tactics is that they both appropriate the object-world and treat it with respect.

At the beginning of the novel, Maggie is shown to fail miserably in both, for she treats her possessions badly, and even her love of reading does not prevent her carelessly dropping her books in the fender (MF 65). This lack of care for the object world is related to her lack of care for herself, illustrated by her treatment of her doll, an item of personal property which, as we have seen in relation to *Bleak House*, allows girls a conduit into the social. For Maggie, however, her doll becomes the abused Fetish which 'she punished for all her misfortunes' (MF 78). Hal Foster has stated that the 'term *fetish* was first used in relation to the amulets of witches, that is, to marginal others within the culture, persecuted peasant women'.[34] Instead of treating her property as an 'amulet' or aid to living as Esther Summerson does, Maggie treats her doll as the other, an object which she can 'punish'; however, it also works as a metaphor for her own position as the punished child. Like the perverse

---

[32]   Michel de Certeau, *The Practice of Everyday Life*, Steven Rendall (trans.) (Berkeley, Los Angeles and London: University of California Press, 1988), p. 37.

[33]   Certeau, p. 38.

[34]   Foster, p. 254.

Miss Havisham who, according to Marcus treats Estella as her doll, Maggie can only use objects in similarly self-destructive ways.[35]

As we have seen, the doll usually offers girls their first encounter with ownership, an opportunity to perform simultaneously the actions of owner and make use of the doll's symbolic function as a miniature female. Thus dolls allow girls to enjoy ownership, while symbolizing their role as owned objects. Marcus has shown that Victorian girls were encouraged in children's literature to view their dolls as fetishes. She states that 'fantasies of girls punishing dolls and being punished by them appeared regularly in fiction for young readers'.[36] Discussing the 1880 book by Clara Bradford, *Ethel's Adventures in the Doll Country*, Marcus notes how Ethel, the young heroine, 'delight[s] in meting out punishment to her doll' in a narrative which represents 'polarized states of abjection and idolization' resembling pornographic 'birching narratives'.[37] Although Marcus does not discuss Maggie's Fetish, she does note Maggie's failure to align herself with female friends; indeed her isolation from the community of women is a failure to align herself with 'proper femininity'.[38] Femininity is, then, both a source of oppression and a survival tactic. It was only later in life that Eliot adopted such tactics with the encouragement of female friends such as Elma. Not only was the great Sibyl helped towards finding an ingenious way of holding up her drawers, but she also developed greater insights into the female condition by understanding women's engagement with the material politics of the everyday. The proper care of the doll promotes a care of the object world, which in turn encourages a care of the self. The women of St Ogg's have learned this lesson well, for they care for the objects they fetishize as symbols of themselves, while Maggie's treatment of her Fetish, its trunk 'entirely defaced by a long career of vicarious suffering' (MF 79), points towards her own lack of self-respect.

Maggie's problem, then, is that she does not adopt female tactics for survival; neither does she develop a positive fetishism towards the material world. She thus fails to secure herself in the world of cherished personal property by developing her identity through ownership.[39] Instead, she focuses her attention on her sense of duty towards her incompetent father and tyrannical brother, seeing herself as the object they turn her into. She thus becomes a Fetish, an object to be punished and forced into deprivation. Sadoff has accurately stated that:

> Tom's role as lawgiver established him as the figurative father whom Maggie desires will punish rather than love her. The narrative in fact insists metaphorically and structurally on the brother as figurative father ... . Tom is educated to business because Mr Tulliver fears his son's desire to usurp the

---

[35]   See Marcus, p. 150.

[36]   Ibid.

[37]   Ibid.

[38]   Ibid., p. 80.

[39]   See Radin and Arendt for discussions of the role of property ownership in identity formation.

paternal property, and the narrative indeed proves this desire true. ... He fills a place the father vacated and fills it with more authority than did the father. *The Mill on the Floss* splits the father in two: one father desires the desiring daughter, the figurative other prohibits and punishes all her desire.[40]

Because Maggie so thoroughly identifies herself as part of the 'paternal property' she renders herself a victim of what Levy terms 'property morality'. Unable to forge a meaningful relationship with women and their objects, she is unable to share their ability to define themselves as subjects in a world determined to objectify them. Maggie's childhood and youth are depicted in terms of punishments inflicted and self-inflicted, and this cycle of deprivation is continued in the latter half of the novel with her lack of agency and determination to rid herself of all desire.

However, Eliot in the first part of the novel elaborates on the ways in which women can gain power through property ownership. As Sadoff has argued, the novel 'demonstrate[s] the cultural decline of paternity as a legal and lawful category. Paternal precedence in fact no longer determines and defines ownership, its rights and duties'.[41] *The Mill on the Floss*, more than most Victorian novels, illustrates the power of wives to bypass the law by means of the tactics Certeau identifies as the strength of the weak. They gain power covertly. Ambiguity may have been a consistent feature of the lives of many Victorian women, caught up as they were before 1882 in the absurdities of the legal system when their relationships with the material world could be highly confusing in terms of ownership rights. However, as Eliot indicates, the pleasure of 'small delights' in objects could offer consolations and, as we have seen in Chapter 1, there were numerous ways in which women could bypass the law.

Sophy Pullet and Jane Glegg offer the example of wives who behave as though they are beyond the reach of the laws of coverture. Their role model is embodied in the widow Mrs Sutton of the Twentylands, 'an old lady as had doubled her money over and over again, and kept it all in her own management to the last, and had her pocket with her keys in under her pillow constant' (MF 113). Mrs Sutton thus controls her fortune during her life and then leaves it 'in a lump to her husband's nevvy', an invalid (MF 114). Sophy and Jane promote male weakness, marrying men who are unable to control them, unlike Maggie who admires men she sees as strong and dominant (her father and brother, as well as the sexually forceful Stephen Guest). Her rejection of the feminized invalid Philip Wakem, who promotes her wellbeing and encourages her to recognize the validity of her desires, leaves her sunken in the abjection of the isolated, objectified woman. To be a female subject in St Ogg's it is necessary to employ the tactics of the 'Dodson sisters' and Mrs Sutton by accumulating personal property and using it tactically to forge a sense of identity.

---

[40]   Sadoff, p. 85.

[41]   Ibid., p. 81.

Sophy and Jane have husbands who cannot prevent them retaining their own property and keeping for themselves the money they make from their investments and labour, such as butter-making (MF 95). Mr Pullet shows little inclination for asserting his rights as a husband and displays all the hallmarks of infantilization that were supposed to characterize Victorian women, with his delight in toys, such as the musical snuff-box he exhibits which allows him to offer visitors 'a programme for all great social occasions, and in this way [he] fenced himself in from much painful confusion and perplexing freedom of will' (MF 154). The argument put forward by those in support of coverture for married women rested on the idea that wives welcomed the removal of a 'perplexing freedom of will' onto their husbands' shoulders, and Mr Pullet's discomfort with male freedoms marks him out as a failure in patriarchal terms. Both Mr Pullet and Mr Glegg are considerably 'nervous' about investing their money (MF 160), unlike the aggressive risk-taker, Mr Tulliver. Mr Glegg also allows his wife control of her paraphernalia and investments, describing her as: 'A woman with everything provided for her, and allowed to keep her own money *the same as if it was settled on her*, and with a gig new-stuffed and lined and no end of expense' (MF 192; emphasis added). Eliot indicates here that even if a woman was unable to have a marriage settlement in equity to ensure her control of her property, it was still possible for her to develop tactics which would enable her to get round the law. Indeed, Mrs Glegg has made a will, and her identity is largely based on the power she enjoys in disposing of her property after her death:

> No one must say of her when she was dead that she had not divided her money with perfect fairness among her own kin: in the matter of wills personal qualities were subordinate to the great fundamental fact of blood; and to be determined in the distribution of your property by caprice and not make your legacies bear a direct ratio to degrees of kinship, was a prospective disgrace that would have embittered her life. This had always been a principle in the Dodson family. (MF 97)

Jane's avoidance of 'caprice' in her production of a 'rational' will further suggests an inversion of gender, for married women's lack of legal rights was based upon women's supposed irrationality. George Eliot's own will, signed on her wedding day in 1880 (two years before the passing of the second Married Women's Property Act), resembled a man's, in that the bulk of her property went to a direct male heir, Lewes's son Charles. However, it also had features associated with women's wills, for hers made provision for nephews and nieces, as well as her female friends such as Cara Bray.[42]

For women, the making of a will was not only an assertion of the identity of the property owner, a public statement that one possessed things to bequeath, it was also a way of writing oneself into history even, as Martha Howell suggests, a

---

[42]   See John Rignall (ed.), *Oxford Reader's Companion to George Eliot* (Oxford: Oxford University Press, 2000), p. 464, for details of Eliot's will.

way for women to 'play God'.[43] Women's desire to publicize themselves and their possessions by means of the last will and testament has a long history. Howell's study of late-medieval women's wills indicates that women's 'personal effects measured more than economic value, they carried and marked social and cultural value … each resonated with cultural significance, each forged a link between giver and receiver, each told a life-story'.[44] Berg's discussion of women's wills in the eighteenth century suggests a continuity in the female practice of reinforcing family bonds, for women continued to name their possessions item by item, bequeathing 'spoons, cups, sugar tongs, casters, salvers, and ladles [which] were frequently apportioned among several children to nieces and nephews as a form of family keepsake'.[45] A similar situation existed in the early nineteenth century with women affirming their sense of identity in relation to their families and communities by means of their wills. As R.J. Morris states: 'The will was not simply a document giving information of such relationships [i.e. the links between property, family and the individual]. It was *a part of* those relationships'.[46] It also had the potential to extend the will-maker's actions beyond the grave: 'As a representation, the will had a powerful agency. It was a symbolic description of a world but, taking the model of the gift as being central, it was a symbolic account designed to describe, strengthen and reorder that world'.[47] As Deanna Kreisel has noted, *The Mill on the Floss* offers 'a veritable hermeneutic of wills'.[48] Characters like Jane Glegg view the will as a text through which the world can be reshaped and her interpretation imposed on it. While Maggie passively reads texts, her aunts actually write them. Death is the factor binding the world of family and kinship bonds; death is the moment when the redistribution of property takes effect and the St Ogg's women enjoy the 'considerable potential for making a will to be a quasi religious action'.[49] It was also a chance to stage a drama, with its 'plot and the full cast of characters'.[50] Above all, it facilitated female engagement in material politics.

The will-making activities of women during the 1820s which Eliot represents in *The Mill on the Floss* were actually supported by the law. The Wills Act of 1837, however, restricted women's ability to create a will independently of

---

[43]   Martha C. Howell, 'Fixing Movables: Gifts by Testament in Late Medieval Douai', *Past and Present*, 150 (February 1996): 38.

[44]   Ibid., p. 39.

[45]   Berg, p. 241.

[46]   R.J. Morris, p. 89; emphasis added.

[47]   Ibid., p. 100.

[48]   Deanna Kreisel, 'Superfluity and Suction: The Problem with Saving in *The Mill on the Floss*', *Novel*, 35:1 (Fall 2001): 96.

[49]   R.J. Morris, p. 90.

[50]   Howell, p. 25.

their husbands.[51] On the eve of the Victorian period women lost this right: 'a married woman had no legal personality at common law and was unable to make contracts, to buy or sell property or even make a will. The few residual rights which remained to a married woman could easily be overridden by her husband and his lawyers'.[52] In many Victorian novels, however, it is the law and husbands who are easily overridden. The St Ogg's women have the ability to expose the idiocy of the law, yet the processes of female material politics are not always straightforward (after all, neither Maggie nor Tom live to reap the benefit of their aunts' hoarding of property for their future use). To a certain extent Jane is aware of the difficulty of guaranteeing property transmission to one's chosen heirs because she realizes that husbands and wives may have different family identities. She tells her sister Bessy:

> '*I* can't leave your children enough out o' my savings, to keep 'em from ruin. And you mustn't look to having any of Mr Glegg's money for it's well if I don't go first – he comes of a long-lived family – and if he was to die and leave me well off for my life, he'd tie all the money up to go back to his kin'. (MF 111)

In other words, as a widow, she may only gain a life-interest in her husband's property, and would then have no power to control its destination.

Weiner has shown that property transmission between sisters has a long history and is common to many cultures. She has identified certain items of family property as 'transcendent treasures' which must be retained within the family in order to maintain its status and identity.[53] While many anthropologists have focused largely on the exchange of women between men and the sibling incest taboo as central to understanding how family identities and kinship groups operate, Weiner's anthropological study of Oceania societies emphasizes the role of sisters in strengthening these bonds. The transference of family property (what Weiner terms 'inalienable possessions') between sisters has, she argues, tended to be overlooked. She states that the transmission of family treasures:

> gives sisters an autonomous source of power that men cannot match or attain, making women feared and venerated … . More important, such power, linked as it is to a multiplicity of sexual, reproductive, and productive domains, accords to high-ranking women as sisters political authority in their own right.[54]

The Mill on the Floss suggests the complexity of family identifications which often override marriage bonds, making the transference of property between groups of

---

[51]   See Allan Hepburn, 'Introduction: Inheritance and Disinheritance in the Novel' in *Troubled Legacies: Narrative and Inheritance* (Toronto and London: University of Toronto Press, 2007), p. 11.

[52]   R.J. Morris, p. 103.

[53]   Weiner, p. 33.

[54]   Ibid., p. 68.

people by no means straightforward. The Dodson sisters' strength lies in their belief in their unity as Dodsons, this identification offering them a way to deny the forces which seek to disperse and alienate their family identity and property. Consequently, there is a split between the Dodsons and Tullivers, each pulling in different directions between the impulses of saving and spending. Yet some critics have failed to understand the distinction between the Dodsons and Tullivers and they are often lumped together as examples of one 'type' of nineteenth-century provincial philistinism. Kreisel, for example, has argued that we can 'use their names somewhat interchangeably' because 'their economic philosophies are the same'.[55] Yet Mr Tulliver's concerns, indeed, his sense of identity and social function, are centred on his ownership of real property, whereas the Dodson world is largely made up of savings and a 'museum' of artefacts accumulated and preserved in order to be passed on to the younger generation. Mr Tulliver wants to cut an impressive figure in this life, the Dodson sisters in the next.

However, many critics have not taken into account Eliot's representation of the gendered nature of property in this novel, for the Dodson name stands for the feminized culture of portable property, while the Tulliver name is associated with the traditional notion of property as the ownership of land and business, where its transmission moves directly from father to son through the generations. It is significant that the patriarch, Mr Tulliver, loses his land and his life in this novel, for Eliot, like Dickens, suggests the obsolescence of the traditional patriarch in an evolving, progressive society. Mr Tulliver's identification with the real property he owns is made particularly vivid in the scene where he is roused from his coma only on hearing the lid fall on the chest containing his property deeds (MF 303). The chest (which, as we shall see, functions in the same way as the chest Daniel Deronda inherits from his grandfather) is a repository for 'male' property, here the symbols of real estate and the family business. Mr Tulliver miraculously recovers to defend this symbol of propertied manhood; the chest 'had belonged to his father and his father's father, and it had always been a solemn business to visit it' (MF 304). In fact, as we saw in Chapter 1, the deeds of a house are actually *part* of the real estate, rather than a portable supplement. It is important to note here that the ownership of real property ultimately depends upon texts, upon the deeds that 'name' the owner. As we have seen, Eliot's anxieties about the ownership of her texts, her intellectual property, indicate how much the name 'George Eliot' and the texts she produced were intimately connected to her identity. In a letter to John Blackwood in 1858, Eliot likens the exposure of her identity following Liggins's imposture to an iron chest being pried open; she stated that she felt reluctant 'to open one's iron chest to a burglar'.[56]

The link between texts, names and property is a vitally important one, as we have seen in relation to the Dodson sisters' pleasure in writing their wills.

---

[55]   Kreisel, p. 84.

[56]   1 December 1858, *George Eliot Letters*, vol. 2, p. 505. Pettitt discusses this quotation in relation to the issue of intellectual property in *Patent Inventions*, p. 255.

Yet, Bessy Tulliver finds that the linkage between text, name and property ownership can be easily destroyed by marriage. While Jane and Sophy have been careful in their choice of ineffective but prosperous marriage partners, ensuring that they do not have to experience the quality of assertive masculinity in a husband, Bessy fails to follow her sisters' example. Marriage to the dominant Mr Tulliver leaves her vulnerable, for he takes advantage of the law of coverture to appropriate her paraphernalia and fortune to invest in his business. It is all subsequently lost when he is made bankrupt, his recklessness leading to the loss of her possessions. Distraught, she complains that she 'had to sit by while my own fortin's been spent, and what should ha' been my children's too' (MF 283). Plotz, in his discussion of Mrs Tulliver's loss sees her problem as based on her 'resolutely unmetaphorical relationship to her things'.[57] He argues that her 'primitive attachment to her property' leaves 'no space for sympathy, either from her sisters or from the reader'.[58] Yet this overlooks the fact that Mrs Tulliver has lost legal possession of the things she owned as a spinster. Bessy's helplessness is contrasted with her sisters' power, for Mr Tulliver is even forced to borrow £500 from Mrs Glegg in order to maintain the image of being 'a much more substantial man that he really was' (MF 134–5). The vulnerability of wives like Bessy Tulliver and, as we will see, Rosamond Vincy, both of whom feel the force of the law of coverture, is made evident when their precious personal property is forcibly removed by a husband's creditors.

For the 'Dodson sisters', the Dodson name is not lost on marriage and no explanation is offered for the sisters' persistent assertion of their maiden name. All four have ceased to be Dodsons in legal terms, yet Jane and Sophy's retention of an identification with their maiden name matches their refusal to recognise coverture. Indeed, Jane's identification is confirmed when she states that a husband's family is not worth bothering 'to pinch yourself for ... . But it's a poor tale when it [property] must go out o' your own family' (MF 114). Clearly for Jane it is her sisters, not her husband, who constitute her 'own family'. Although Mrs Tulliver displays all the signs of Dodson-identification, seeing herself as a Dodson long after her marriage and showing a preference for her son based on her belief that he resembles a Dodson rather than a Tulliver (although, as Sadoff states, 'Tom in fact resembles his father'), she is powerless against her husband's appropriation of her paraphernalia.[59] The fourth Dodson sister, Lucy's mother Mrs Deane, is a more shadowy figure existing in the background, and the first of the sisters to die. While the 'Dodson women' appear to be firmly bonded as a social and familial (if not necessarily an emotional) unit, the Tulliver family is fractured, with a rift between husband and wife.

Bessy, not really thinking of herself as a Tulliver, at the very beginning of the novel appears to relish the idea of her husband's death as she refers with pleasure

---

[57]   Plotz, p. 8. Plotz refers to the things as 'her property'; however, once she married, Mrs Tulliver lost all rights to own property.

[58]   Ibid., p. 9.

[59]   Sadoff, p. 85.

to the 'best Holland sheets' (MF 58) which she has preserved to use as his shroud. Her ownership of linen is one of the greatest pleasures of Bessy's life, for much of it she spun herself, 'and I marked 'em so as nobody ever saw such marking – they must cut the cloth to get it out, for it's a particular stitch' (MF 282).[60] As she watches the departure of her possessions she states, 'I shouldn't ha' minded so much if we could ha' kept the things wi' my name on 'em' (MF 284), her name being 'Elizabeth Dodson'.[61] As we have seen with the handkerchief named 'Esther Summerson' in *Bleak House*, the marking of linen and other goods with the owner's name was a traditional practice for women; as Howell has demonstrated in her discussion of medieval women's wills, wives recognized:

> The logic of preserving and perhaps even stretching traditions which made a woman's most personal property – her clothing and jewels – fully her own, and she would have every reason to try and mark other goods as her own as well, to label them so unambiguously as hers that, when the marriage ended, she or her heirs would have no trouble identifying and claiming what was hers.[62]

Yet, the tactic of marking goods as personal property fails in the case of Mrs Tulliver. Bessy cannot continue to own either the things she has made, or those she has bought with her own money before marriage, because the law refuses to recognize or support her as a property owner. Her mistaken belief in the security of her stitched name as a signal of her ownership is symptomatic of her inability to realize the law that frames women's relationships towards the material world and underpins the fragility of women's ownership. When Sophy Pullet states, 'to think o' the family initials going about everywhere' (MF 293–4), she suggests disgrace, for a tangible fragment of family identity in the form of marked initials on the 'family' property is wrested from the hearth into 'the hateful publicity of the Golden Lion' (MF 321), where the auction of Mr Tulliver's goods (which of course include the property his wife supposed was hers) takes place.[63] Women's traditional practice of inscribing their names on objects suggests a false confidence and naïve belief in their ability to control these possessions after marriage. However, as Eliot demonstrates in her representation of Jane and Sophy, some women successfully asserted property rights they did not possess.

The issue of naming is thus a crucial one and those objects which are inscribed with a person's name become, as we have seen in previous chapters, what Hoskins has termed 'biographical objects'. Bessy Tulliver's named objects have become

---

[60] See Berg, p. 242 for the importance of personally marked linen as 'signifiers of family and memory'. See also Weiner, pp. 36–40 for a discussion of cloth as an 'inalienable' possession.

[61] Plotz refers to Mrs Tulliver's 'unappealing, primitively selfish attachment to writing' (p. 188 note 34) in the form of her name, a view of her which I do not share.

[62] Howell, p. 35.

[63] As we have seen in Chapter 2, Esther Summerson's handkerchief does not actually enter the marketplace but is cherished and preserved by Lady Dedlock and Jenny.

a vital part of her personality, contributing to her biography and developing a biography of their own, which is why she breaks down on seeing her inscribed tablecloths being taken from her (MF 281). 'Elizabeth Dodson' represents an identity of herself as a property owner, reminding her of the period before marriage when she legally owned her things. As George Eliot herself stated in her journal, 'The mere fact of naming an object tends to give definiteness to our conception of it – we have then a sign which at once calls up in our minds the distinctive qualities which mark out for us that particular object from all others'.[64] When the object is marked with the name of its owner it is doubly named, doubly distinct, and the boundary between human and object becomes blurred. The loss of her property signifies the 'painful separation and harm to personality' which Radin claims arises when 'the free-market view of alienation that assumes all objects are fungible' is brought to bear upon the individual.[65] Yet here, in this novel written long before the passing of the 1882 Married Women's Property Act, the free market is not so much the guilty party as the law and its favoured subjects, that is husbands, with their rights of coverture, for Bessy (as a cautious Dodson) would probably never have risked the loss of these markers of her identity. Bessy Tulliver's loss exposes the impossibility of controlling 'inalienable' possessions in the context of capitalism: unless the law supports ownership through contract or settlement, individuals are powerless to retain the objects they have created and made their 'own'.[66]

The passing of the second Married Women's Property Act in 1882 allowed women like Bessy to retain these 'marks' of selfhood against a husband's appropriation. The protection of such property could mean a protection of identity, for Bessy's loss of her 'mark' leaves her adrift in the world:

> The objects among which her mind had moved complacently were all gone: all the little hopes, and schemes, and speculations, all the pleasant little cares about her treasures which had made her world quite comprehensible to her for a quarter of a century, since she had made her first purchase of the sugar-tongs, had been suddenly snatched away from her and she remained bewildered in this empty life. (MF 368)

However, Maggie fails to sympathize with her mother's experience of loss. Resenting her mother's 'implied reproaches against her father [she] … neutralised all her pity for griefs about table cloths and china', and exclaims, 'Mother, how can you talk so? As if you cared only for the things with *your* name on, and not for what has my father's name too. And to care about anything but dear father himself!' (MF 284). On one level, Maggie seems to be emphasizing the importance of the human over the object world; yet on another level she fails to understand that her

---

[64]   Quoted in Nestor, p. 65.

[65]   Radin, p. 196.

[66]   See Weiner, p. 37 for a discussion of the paradoxical nature of 'inalienable' property.

mother's humanity resides in the things she spun and washed, the things she made and used and personalized with her own name, the tools of housewifery, objects associated with her labour and her social role. Maggie fails to see that her father has robbed his wife in a fundamental way, and that his desire to be thought 'a much more substantial man than he really was' (MF 135) has taken precedence over his wife's and children's wellbeing. This gives some indication of Maggie's tendency to see herself as property owned by others, for she does not understand that her mother's sense of agency is centred on the personal property she thought that she owned. Tom, however, does realize his father's selfishness in legally 'robbing' his wife, and he understands the extent of her loss when he says, 'I'd do anything to save my mother from parting with her things' (MF 294). Maggie, in contrast, fails to register the way in which her father has impoverished her, for the loss of her books leads to her disastrous embrace of renunciation where, as Kreisel argues, Maggie's real danger lies.[67]

The Dodson sisters' attachment to things which form the basis of their family identity and sense of well-being is also shared by Bob Jakin who, as a member of the labouring class, shares their tenuous social and legal position. Bob's relationship with the knife that Tom gives him resembles the relationship Bessy and her sisters experience with their cherished domestic objects. When Bob, as a young boy, throws his knife away after an argument with Tom, there was a 'sense in Bob's mind that there was a terrible void in his lot, now that knife was gone'; however, when he retrieves it, '[h]is very fingers sent entreating thrills that he would go and clutch that familiar rough buck's-horn handle, which they had so often grasped for mere affection as it lay idle in his pocket' (MF 106). When Bob turns up years later to console Tom and Maggie in their misfortune, he takes out the same 'rough-handled pocket-knife', now become a biographical object, saying 'there isn't such a blade i' the country – it's got used to my hand, like' (MF 323). Here, the object is sentient, having developed agency, as well as possessing the ability to stimulate emotion.[68] Yet Tom, brought up to believe himself linked to real estate, rather than feminized personal property, is 'a little ashamed of that early intimacy symbolized by the pocket-knife' (MF 323).

Eliot indicates here that personal property, with its affective attributes, is associated with women, children and the working classes, while real property is the preserve of wealthy and powerful men. Yet ultimately *The Mill on the Floss* does not take the issue of women's personal property seriously, for the Dodson sisters are presented largely in terms of a comic chorus. Even Mrs Tulliver's devastating sense of loss is seen not so much as a trauma affecting her sense of identity but as symptomatic of her provincial narrowness, an example of the materialism Maggie so deplores. Eliot, however, was to revise her approach to women's tactics and her later novels offer more complicated representations of women and property relations.

---

[67]   See Kreisel, pp. 70–71.

[68]   See Hoskins, p. 75.

For example, a powerful critique of patriarchal law is central to *Romola*, published serially from 1862 to 1863. As Paxton has stated, in this novel Eliot 'expresses her continuing support for reforms in married women's property laws' and it is perhaps the most openly feminist of her novels.[69] Indeed, here she directly addresses the issue of married women's vulnerability in relation to property. Set in Renaissance Florence, Romola's situation as a wife, helpless to control the property she inherited from her father, resembles the situation of many married women in Britain before the passing of the Married Women's Property Acts. Tito uses his 'legal right' to appropriate and sell the library that Bardo has bequeathed to his daughter.[70] However, rather than being a beneficiary, Romola is simply a conduit for the property from her scholar father to the Florentine public. She does, however, possess some portable property of her own: when she disguises herself and escapes from her husband, she takes some of it with her:

> [S]he set about collecting and packing all the relics of her father and mother that were too large to be carried in her small travelling-wallet. They were all to be put in the chest along with her wedding-clothes, and her chest was to be committed to her godfather when she was safely gone. First she laid in the portraits; then one by one every little thing that had a sacred memory clinging to it was put into her wallet or into the chest. (R 319)

Unlike Mr Tulliver's chest, or the chest Daniel Deronda inherits from his grandfather, both of which contain the texts associated with the patriarchal transmission of property from father and son, Romola's chest is full of personal relics and memorials, portraits and clothes, biographical objects with intimate associations. Romola, then, like the Dodson sisters, feels the importance of familial bonds and the objects which represent these. In her final novels, *Middlemarch* and *Daniel Deronda*, Eliot elicits increasing sympathy for female ownership practices as she continues to analyze women's problematic sense of ownership and their convoluted relationships to objects.

'I hate my wealth': Problematic Property in *Middlemarch*

Written shortly after the passing of the Second Reform Bill in 1867 and during the passing of the first Married Women's Property Act of 1870, *Middlemarch* began serialization in 1871. Eliot, clearly responding to the calls for reform, focused her novel on the issues of voting and property rights where the emphasis, as in her earlier novel *Felix Holt* (1866), was on the notion that rights entailed duties. Unlike *The Mill on the Floss*, however, *Middlemarch* treats seriously the power of wives and widows, although it remains cautious in its endorsement of female

---

[69] Paxton, pp. 130–31.

[70] George Eliot, *Romola*, Dorothea Barrett (ed.) (London: Penguin, 1996), p. 275. Subsequent page references will be cited in the text following the abbreviation 'R'.

power. D.A. Miller has identified a 'doubleness' in *Middlemarch* which 'seems to be traditional and to be beyond its limit, to subvert and to reconfirm the value of its traditional status'.[71] This duality is particularly evident in the novel's treatment of the female property owner. As Victorian feminists were emphasizing women's legal disadvantages in relation to property, Dorothea Brooke, the novel's wealthy heroine, states, 'I don't mind about poverty – I hate my wealth'.[72] She tells her husband that he has 'been too liberal in arrangements for me – I mean, with regard to property; and that makes me unhappy' (M 351). However, the widowed Dorothea's eventual rejection of the Casaubon property means that she only appears to embrace 'poverty', for she remains throughout in possession of her 'own fortune – it is too much – seven hundred a-year' (M 762). Dorothea may 'want' little, but she does have agency, a point which is obscured by the often perverse comfort she takes in renunciation and self-denial. She only *appears* to be a dutiful wife to Mr Casaubon: 'The need of freedom assert[s] itself within her', prompting her to defy her husband's wishes by refusing to commit herself to 'sifting those mixed heaps of material', his notes for the *Key to All Mythologies* (M 449). She also defies her uncle and her brother-in-law by marrying Will Ladislaw. For a heroine who has disappointed feminist critics because of her reluctance to wrestle with the conditions of an 'imperfect social state' (M 784), Dorothea stands in decided opposition to male power and uses her wealth and influence to rescue men in distress, notably Lydgate, Farebrother and Ladislaw. Even renunciation appears to be a luxury she indulges in, a desire she embraces on religious grounds (M 7).

In fact, the main female characters in *Middlemarch* largely succeed in getting what they want, as far as property is concerned. Dorothea bestows her fortune on the man she loves, who happens to come from a lower class position than she. Mrs Bulstrode makes arrangements for the transmission of her husband's property *before* his death. The humbled and humiliated Bulstrode asks her: 'Tell me anything that you would like to have me do, Harriet ... I mean with regard to the arrangement of property ... . [T]he land is virtually yours' (M 773–4). Like many women with property to bestow, Harriet chooses to reinforce family bonds by offering her nephew Fred Vincy the tenancy of Stone Court. Celia is also able to establish herself as the mistress of Freshitt Hall (despite the fact that its owner hardly notices her at the beginning of the novel) and refuses to remain estranged from her beloved sister despite her husband's wish to sever all ties with Will and Dorothea. The novel thus quietly inverts the usual patriarchal dispensation of gender power. Eliot no longer feels obliged to punish female resistance vicariously on behalf of the provincial community as she does with Maggie Tulliver's drowning.

---

[71]   D.A. Miller, *Narrative and Its Discontents: Problems of Closure in the Traditional Novel* (Princeton: Princeton University Press, 1981), p. 107.

[72]   George Eliot, *Middlemarch*, David Carroll (ed.) (Oxford: Oxford University Press, 1998), p. 762. Subsequent page references will be cited in the text following the abbreviation 'M'.

Like *The Mill on the Floss*, *Middlemarch* is set in the 1820s and 30s, both texts focusing on the transitional moment of a culture based on declining upper-class landed privilege and the rising bourgeoisie. Eliot returns again in the later novel to the shifts in class identities and gender roles of this period, and how these were manifested in material and cultural forms.[73]

The development of industrialization and the growth of bourgeois power during the eighteenth century led to a culture of material display as a domestic ideal.[74] The repeal of the English sumptuary laws in the seventeenth century had already opened up the possibility of class confusion for tradespeople and manufacturers could now 'counterfaite and be lyke a gentilman', as one member of the landed gentry complained.[75] By the eighteenth century the majority of the population were free to express any wealth they possessed in their displays of clothes and other objects. In 1757, Josiah Tucker in his *Instructions for Travellers* commented on this freedom to display wealth: 'England being a free country, where Riches got by trade are no disgrace, and where property is also safe against the prerogatives of either princes or Nobles, and where every person may make what display he pleases of his wealth'.[76] As Berg has shown, the repeal of sumptuary regulations resulted in women feeling liberated to express their status and taste if their resources allowed, with 'rich dresses, comfortable houses, and precious jewels', as well as furnishings and domestic ornamentation.[77] If the middle classes were free to display their ownership of fine clothes and jewels, then the women of the aristocracy and gentry encountered difficulties in signalling their difference. As Andrew Miller states, during the nineteenth century the 'interpretation of dress was more energetically insecure'.[78] The legacy of this 'problem' can be seen in Eliot's presentation of Dorothea and Celia's need to assert their refinement; they possess the 'pride of being ladies' who 'naturally regarded frippery as the ambition of a huckster's daughter' (M 7). *Middlemarch* depicts the growing political and economic importance of merchants, traders and manufacturers. As the narrator ironically states, in the 1820s, the 'gorgeous plutocracy which has so nobly exalted the necessities of genteel life' (M 9) had not yet been established, but it was poised to enter the mainstream of British national life. The sisters' avoidance of display needs to be seen in the context of the rise of the commercial classes, associated as they were with the manufacture of commodities and their consumption. Because

---

[73]   See Davidoff and Hall, pp. 229–71.

[74]   See Berg for a detailed discussion of eighteenth-century material culture.

[75]   Cited in Grant McCracken, *Culture and Consumption: New Approaches to the Symbolic Character of Consumer Goods and Activities* (Bloomington and Indianapolis: Indiana University Press, 1988), p. 33. On sumptuary law, see M. Esquirou de Parieu, 'On Taxes Upon Enjoyments', *Journal of the Statistical Society of London*, 24:2 (June 1861): 167–97.

[76]   Cited in Berg, p. 195.

[77]   Ibid., p. 39. See also McCracken, pp. 3–30.

[78]   A.H. Miller, p. 194.

middle-class women were now free to display their family's status, the Brooke sisters face the challenge of finding ways to signal that their family's wealth was not gained by trade. However, 'birth' can only be conveyed through subtle signs and part of Dorothea's difficulty is that she is caught within a semiotic system based on a complex transmission and interpretation of the rapidly changing signs of status. Her dream of a time when 'everyday-things ... would mean the greatest things' (M 27) suggests a desire to transcend the economic basis of her world.

Middlemarch's opening chapter raises other issues relating to women and their property, such as the problem of transmitting property to chosen heirs and of accepting property one doesn't want. These were explored in *The Mill on the Floss* in a comic register. However, in the later novel the renunciation of property also conflicts with family duties, for Dorothea cannot happily accept valuable property, even from her own mother. At the opening of the novel, the dead Mrs Brooke's legacy of jewellery has been strangely forgotten both by her brother-in-law and her eldest daughter, while her youngest daughter seems to value the jewels largely because of the public display she hopes to make of them. Celia reminds her sister about their inheritance only after the jewels had spent six months locked out of sight in a cabinet, reproaching Dorothea with the words, 'you have never thought of them since' (M 11), just as Mr Brooke had also forgotten about them for months. Celia's reproachful comment seems just: 'I think, dear, we are wanting in respect to mamma's memory, to put them by and take no notice of them' (M 11). The half-forgotten gems (and by implication their half-forgotten owner Mrs Brooke) are dismissed by Dorothea as a collection of 'trinkets' (M 13). Despite being anxious about ownership of them, Dorothea is eventually 'enchanted' by the colour of the emeralds: 'They look like fragments of heaven' (M 13), and she decides to keep them in order to have 'them by her, to feed her eye at these little fountains of pure colour' (M 14), although she fails to blend her sense of aesthetic and spiritual delight with the memory of the mother who bequeathed them to her. Such blending would offer her a legitimate way of keeping the jewels as private memorials and assuage her anxieties about their ornamental properties. Yet Eliot fails to suggest this compromise.

Not noted for her love of sartorial display, Eliot had nevertheless a sentimental attachment to certain items of jewellery.[79] In 1880 she records a 'streak of anxiety' she experienced when she lost a brooch, 'the most valued brooch I ever possessed'.[80] It was 'valued' rather than 'valuable'. Eliot was also aware of the power of objects as memorials to the dead, recording in her journal a visit she made in 1865 to the newly widowed Robert Browning where he showed her 'the objects Mrs Browning used to have about her, her chair, tables, books etc. An epoch to be remembered'.[81] Yet Dorothea feels no sentimental attachment

---

[79]   See the letter to Mrs Richard Congreve, 28 November 1863, *George Eliot Letters*, vol. 4, p. 116, where Eliot describes herself as 'dowdy'.

[80]   12 May 1880, *George Eliot Letters*, vol. 7, p. 277.

[81]   George Eliot, *The Journals of George Eliot*, Margaret Harris and Judith Johnstone (eds) (Cambridge: Cambridge University Press, 1998), p. 126.

to her dead mother's property: the jewels are not mentioned again after the first chapters and neither is the sandalwood box she keeps as a memorial of her mother. Other objects, significantly the collection of miniatures and the tapestry in her boudoir at Lowick Manor, all associated with women she never met, her dead mother-in-law and Ladislaw's grandmother, do become biographical objects for Dorothea, integrated into her experiences as a wife. Although Mrs Brooke, known to the reader only through her bequeathed property, died when Dorothea was twelve years old (M 8), her collection does not function at all as a memorial for her daughters. Dorothea easily gives it away, telling her sister, 'There – take away your property' (M 12), while Celia, equally lacking in sentiment, is most concerned about which jewels 'would suit her own complexion' (M 13).

It is possible that Eliot is not raising doubts about Mrs Brooke's qualities as a mother and the 'problem' of her property is perhaps not a 'problem' centred on Mrs Brooke herself, but on the nature of women's property more generally. For Dorothea, the difficulty she experiences with this particular legacy is that it is a collection of jewellery, loaded with all of the usual associations with feminine adornment and social display, the 'trimmings' (M 7) and 'trinkets' (M 13) which are adopted by the daughters of the Middlemarch manufacturers. This type of gendered property is problematized by Eliot even more than the linen and china cherished by Dodson sisters, for Dorothea seems unsure about the grounds on which she should condemn her mother's jewellery. Her disapproval appears to be based on the idea of the 'miserable men [who] find such things, and work at them, and sell them!' (M 13), although it is uncertain whether she refers to the men's misery because she sees them as exploited labourers or as the exploiters of others' labour. It is also unclear why those employed in the jewellery trade are more miserable than those who provide Dorothea with her coal, cloth and china, or indeed the sandalwood box inherited from her mother. As Elaine Freedgood has shown in her discussion of *Jane Eyre*, the importation of wood in the eighteenth and nineteenth centuries was linked to deforestation with its attendant social and ecological consequences.[82] In contemplating her sandalwood box, Dorothea does not think of those involved in the felling of trees in Malabar or the South Sea Islands, with destructive consequences to the landscape or local economy. Her objections are specifically linked to things associated with gender performance and display. Yet despite her initial misgivings, Dorothea is ultimately able to ignore the jewels' association with Mrs Brooke, feminine frippery and miserable men in order to 'find visual satisfaction from them' (M 14), suggesting a Puritan girl's guilty need for aesthetic pleasure.[83] In Dorothea's confused and contradictory response Eliot indicates that the material world is not innocent of complex, sometimes repulsive, associations and symbolic meanings, and her inexperienced heroine is unable

---

[82]   Freedgood, pp. 33–5.

[83]   See Jean Arnold, 'Cameo Appearances': The Discourse of Jewelry in *Middlemarch*', *Victorian Literature and Culture*, 30:1 (2002): 265–88, for a discussion of Dorothea's aesthetic response to jewellery.

to position herself in relation to objects which carry so many unwanted social connotations.[84] The side-effect of this self-consciousness is Dorothea's slighting of her mother's possessions and her reluctance to accept her bequest.

Celia, having rather more in common with hucksters' daughters than her sister, is more attracted to the 'bright parterre' made by her mother's jewels on the table. The attractions of the 'bright parterre', or garden, suggests the pleasures of real estate and this is echoed later in her thoughts of Sir James and his property. On the sisters' pre-nuptial visit to Lowick Manor, Celia dislikes its 'air of autumnal decline' and is prompted to contrast it with Sir James's property:

> 'I am sure Freshitt Hall would have been pleasanter than this'. She thought of the white freestone, the pillared portico, and the terrace full of flowers, Sir James smiling above them like a prince issuing from his enchantment in a rose-bush, with a handkerchief swiftly metamorphosed from the most delicately odorous-petals – Sir James, who talked so agreeably, always about things which had common-sense in them … . (M 68)

The identification of real property with flowers avoids the notion of vulgar display associated with the property of 'hucksters' and others involved in trade. Celia's fantasy manages to eliminate trade and manufacturing altogether, for in her vision Sir James's handkerchief originates with a rose petal rather than the mundane materials manufactured in the nearby town of Middlemarch, while his person and the hard materials of his real property become softened and feminized by her focus on roses. It is significant that Sir James's handkerchief is referred to again towards the end of the novel when, on finding himself helpless to advise or influence his sister-in-law, he is forced to remain silent, the narrator stating that, 'Sir James took out his handkerchief and began to bite the corner' (M 767). This feminization of Sir James (silenced and infantilized here) suggests the inversion of men generally in *Middlemarch*, for as well as Ladislaw's more obvious feminine traits (M 73, 176, 761) Eliot depicts Lydgate, Fred Vincy, Mr Vincy, Farebrother, Mr Brooke, Bulstrode and Casaubon as at times helpless and unable control their worlds.

As members of the gentry class, Celia and Dorothea need to refigure property as something else; thus jewels become 'fragments of heaven' and Sir James's estate becomes a rose-filled dream. However, women from the manufacturing classes, such as Rosamond Vincy and her Aunt Bulstrode, do not pretend that the property they desire is really something else. They seem content to call a jewel 'a jewel'. However, Eliot shows that for women who wish to signal their transcendence of 'yard-measuring or parcel-tying forefathers' (M 7), property ownership is more problematic because it can actually detract from one's status, rather than enhance it. As Elizabeth Langland states, for nineteenth-century ladies, 'the emphasis rests on subtle understatement … . Excessive finery becomes a trap to betray the nouveaux

---

[84]　See Kate Flint, 'The Materiality of *Middlemarch*' in Karen Chase (ed.), *Middlemarch in the Twenty-First Century* (Oxford: Oxford University Press, 2006), p. 85.

riches'.[85] This is perhaps why Dorothea seems more comfortable at Lowick Manor, where nothing seems new and everything within is 'subdued by time' (M 68), 'faded', 'pale' (M 69) and 'pallid' (M 349). Here:

> The furniture was all of a faded blue, and there were miniatures of ladies and gentlemen with powdered hair hanging in a group. A piece of tapestry over a door also showed a blue-green world with a stag in it. … It was a room where one might fancy the ghost of a tight-laced lady revisiting the scene of her embroidery. (M 69)

The tapestry was probably produced by the embroidering 'tight-laced lady' herself, rather than bought in a shop, and is thus an object seemingly removed from the world of circulating commodities. Indeed, Dorothea's preference for the faded boudoir with its 'patina', the sheen associated with the cared-for goods from the past, is very much in line with her class position. As Grant McCracken has stated:

> Patina is a physical property of material culture. It consists in the small signs of age that accumulate on the surface of objects. … In Western societies, this physical property is treated as symbolic property. … Patina has a much more important symbolic burden, that of suggesting that existing status claims are legitimate. Its function is not to claim status but to authenticate it. Patina serves as a kind of visual proof of status.[86]

Berg has also associated the valuing of family heirlooms with an 'aesthetics of "patina"' which exists in opposition to an industrialized culture based on 'fashion system and novelty'.[87] Dorothea, by cherishing the faded objects in her boudoir, objects which she has unofficially inherited from the former female inhabitant, is thus able to signal her rejection of fashion and novelty. Edward Casaubon's home offers Dorothea an illusion of escape from a modernity focused on manufacturing and trade; the property she unofficially inherits with the boudoir (which once belonged to her mother-in-law) is clearly easier to manage without guilt or anxiety than the 'bright parterre' of jewels bequeathed by her own mother, or the £700 a-year left to her by her parents, money which she states, 'buys me nothing but an uneasy conscience' (M 350).

This 'bare room' with nothing 'outwardly altered', has 'gathered within it those memories of an inward life', making Dorothea believe that the miniature portraits on the wall form 'an audience as of beings no longer disturbed by their own earthly lot' (M 349). The room not only represents that transcendence of property ownership, commodity circulation and consumerism that Dorothea so desperately seeks, but also provides an 'audience' for her thoughts, a way of communicating

---

[85]   Elizabeth Langland, *Nobody's Angels: Middle-Class Women and Domestic Ideology in Victorian Culture* (Ithaca and London: Cornell University Press, 1995), p. 35.

[86]   McCracken, p.32.

[87]   Berg, p. 42. See also Weiner, p. 38.

with the dead women whose 'hidden lives' (M 785) have been recorded only in the room's faded objects.[88] Although Dorothea seems not to cherish her mother's legacy, she does forge a reciprocal relationship with her husband's dead mother and aunt's possessions. This is an example of female property transmission which works tangentially, beyond law and custom, suggesting a ghostly power of affect which, as we have seen, Eliot noted on seeing the objects once used by the dead Elizabeth Barrett Browning.

Yet critics have viewed Eliot's representation of the object world in largely negative terms. *Middlemarch*, for Freedgood, is a 'novel of consumer development', whereby Dorothea Brooke moves from naivety, 'variously oblivious or indifferent to, or overwhelmed by things', to developing consumer awareness about 'how much everything costs'.[89] Andrew Miller sees Eliot as 'clearly devaluing feminine material culture' in the novel.[90] Similarly Ellen Bayuk Rosenman argues that Eliot's contempt for 'women's culture' is evident in her dismissal of 'clothing, jewelry, and furniture as so much detritus'.[91] However, the relationship Dorothea forges with her inherited collection of miniatures and the tapestry in her boudoir suggests Eliot's sympathies with an emotional need for material culture which transcends consumerism and fuels imagination. She also understands the 'aesthetics of patina' which motivates her heroine to prefer the faded to the bright. Eliot's representation of Rosamond Vincy, the ambitious daughter of a Middlemarch manufacturer, may have given rise to the view that she condemns 'feminine material culture'. However, Rosamond's approach to marriage as a route to status and her 'huckster's daughter' love of display is presented more negatively than the 'ardent' Dorothea. Eliot demonstrates through her the vulnerability of wives in relation to the material world. The objects Rosamond believes she possesses, such as the bridal presents from her husband consisting of 'some purple amethysts costing thirty pounds' (M 554) and the 'tiny ornamental basket' which contains Lydgate's gifts, are clearly not her own property (although Rosamond, unlike Mrs Tulliver, brought no property to the marriage) (M 560). Lydgate is legally within his rights in expropriating the jewellery he has given as gifts, just as Mr Tulliver legally owns his wife's possessions.

Women of Dorothea's class, likely to have a marriage settlement, are in a stronger position than the daughters of failing manufacturers, such as Rosamond. She is also in a position to bequeath property and gifts. From an early age Dorothea had been aware of her relationship to property, preoccupied with '[t]he historical, political reasons why eldest sons had superior rights, and why land should be entailed: those reasons impressing her with a certain awe, might be weightier than

---

[88]   See Arnold, p. 281 for the significance of the miniature in *Middlemarch*.

[89]   Freedgood, pp. 128, 118 and 119.

[90]   A.H. Miller, p. 192.

[91]   Ellen Bayuk Rosenman, 'More Stories About Clothing and Furniture: Realism and Bad Commodities', in Christine L. Krueger (ed.), *Functions of Victorian Culture at the Present Time* (Athens: Ohio State University Press, 2002), p. 59.

she knew' (M 349). She is baffled by the law (as Eliot was annoyed by the legal labyrinths associated with male primogeniture when she researched the novel) and defies it. Failing to understand the reasons for her husband's anger about her challenge to his right to control the Lowick property, Dorothea won't rest until the injustice done to her husband's Aunt Julia, has been put right:

> Here was a daughter whose child – even according to the ordinary aping of aristocratic institutions by people who are no more aristocratic than retired grocers, and who have no more land to 'keep together' than a lawn and a paddock – would have a prior claim. Was inheritance a question of liking or responsibility? All the energy of Dorothea's nature went on the side of responsibility – the fulfilment of claims founded on our own deed, such as marriage and parentage. (M 349)

This passage reads not simply as a moral message from the author; it also sends out another message to readers of the 1870s in the form of a reassurance that the reform of the marriage laws would not result in widespread chaos. With Dorothea's numerous contemplations of the rights and wrongs of property inheritance, Eliot suggests that wives were capable of rational thought and moral responsibility. The passage also indicates that lower middle-class people, such as grocers, could leave their property more responsibly than the gentry, a reminder that despite their comic treatment, the Dodson ethos of fair play in relation to family bonds constituted a valid social practice.

Dorothea's measurement of claims and duties results in the belief that her marriage settlement has conferred upon her 'an unfair concentration of the property' (M 350) and, unable to redistribute this wealth 'responsibly', she rejects it, bestowing her own fortune (and herself) upon the man who was disinherited. When the newly widowed Dorothea offers Will the miniature portrait of his mother 'as a family memorial' (M 512), it is because she cannot at that point offer him the fortune she feels has been 'stolen' from him; the miniature, as well as functioning reciprocally as a companion to Dorothea when she is alone in her boudoir, also works metonymically for the property Will has been denied. Again, Eliot represents a reversal of gender roles, as Dorothea has appropriated a man's (her future husband's) property at a time when the law entitled men to appropriate their wives' property. The reader is never informed about the inheritor of Lowick Manor once Dorothea leaves it, and we don't know if she left behind 'her' portable property, the miniatures and tapestry with which she consoled herself during her brief period as Mrs Casaubon. The legal system, privileging the ownership of real estate, imposed the qualities of transience and vulnerability on movable property and Eliot, as we have seen in *The Mill on the Floss*, was aware that women's use of things could be fleeting. In *Daniel Deronda*, published in 1876, she again critiques the 'imperfect social conditions' women faced in the nineteenth century, this time setting her novel in the 1860s.

'A doing-without more or less patiently': Makeshifts in *Daniel Deronda*

The writing and publication of *Daniel Deronda* took place between the passing of the first Married Women's Property Act of 1870 and the second Act in 1882. The initial germ for the novel came in September 1872 when Eliot witnessed a young woman gambling in a German casino. She recorded her disgust in a letter:

> I am not fond of denouncing my fellow-sinners, but gambling being a vice I have no mind to, it stirs my disgust even more than my pity. The sight of the dull faces bending round the gaming tables, the raking-up of the money, and the flinging of the coins towards the winners by the hard-faced croupiers, the hateful, hideous women staring at the board like stupid monomaniacs – all this seems to me the most abject presentation of mortals grasping after something called a good that can be seen on the face of this little earth. Burglary is heroic compared with it. I get some satisfaction in looking on from the sense that the thing is going to be put down. Hell is the only right name for such places.[92]

For Eliot this 'abject' acquisitive impulse to win money is infinitely worse than a desire for a collection of china or textiles, for the casino exposes a naked desire for property (albeit the most liquid form of property, money) which is furthest removed from domestic life. She returned to the subject a few days later: 'The saddest thing to be witnessed is the play of Miss Leigh, Byron's grand-niece, who is only 26 years old, and is completely in the grasp of this mean, money-raking demon. It made me cry to see her young fresh face among the hags and brutally stupid men around her'.[93] The opening of *Daniel Deronda*, with its reworking of the image of Miss Leigh at the gaming table, takes Eliot's exploration of women and materiality beyond the privacy of the domestic sphere and the limits of provincial life into public and cosmopolitan contexts. However, her representations of shops and shopping are unusual because they involve the recycling of goods rather than the consumption of newly manufactured commodities. Gwendolen inverts the consumer experience when she sells her necklace, while Deronda chooses a second-hand gift for Lady Mallinger in a bric-a-brac shop in London. Such scenes of commodity exchange highlight what Andrew Miller calls Eliot's concern with the self-division women face as 'consumers and things consumed'.[94] In what looks like a scene of commodity display and consumption, Deronda, window-shopping, sees:

> some fine old clasps in chased silver displayed in the window at his right hand. His first thought was that Lady Mallinger, who had a strictly Protestant taste for such Catholic spoils, might like to have these missal-clasps turned into a bracelet; then his eyes travelled over the other contents of the window, and he

[92] To Mrs William Cross, 25 September 1872, *George Eliot Letters*, vol. 5, p. 312.

[93] To John Blackwood, 4 October 1872, *George Eliot Letters*, vol. 5, p. 314.

[94] A.H. Miller, p. 195.

saw that the shop was that kind of pawnbroker's where the lead is given to jewellery, lace, and all equivocal objects introduced as *bric-a-brac*.[95]

He immediately associates this display of 'feminine' bric-a-brac with Lady Mallinger and her 'taste' for 'equivocal objects'. The idea of a miscellany, a jumble of recycled goods, is marked here as specifically feminine. This pause in the narrative to focus on Lady Mallinger's desire for bric-a-brac is not just typical of what Emily Apter terms the 'display-case narrative device' used by nineteenth-century novelists to convey the 'reality' of the material world, but also to suggest the emotional bonds and complexity of gift-giving which operate via objects.[96] For example, Deronda's gift of the missal clasps to Lady Mallinger would mean that she could legally own them as her personal property; however, if her husband gave her a similar gift, he would retain the rights of ownership. If, on the other hand, Lady Mallinger chose to steal her husband's gift back from him, she could do so with impunity because she lacks an independent legal identity.[97] Eliot's incursion into the imaginative possibilities of urban consumer culture in her last novel involves the blurring of consumer and product, seller and customer.

Like the 'equivocal objects' to which she is attracted, Lady Mallinger is also in a sense an 'equivocal object', for, like most of Eliot's female characters, she lacks agency, holding an ambiguous social position. As a married woman, she is not an autonomous property owner, seeing herself as a conduit facilitating the transmission of property between men. The mother of 'makeshift feminine offspring' (DD 611), she believes herself to be a 'failure' (DD 236) because she 'produced nothing but daughters in a case where sons were required' (DD 192). Attracted to 'equivocal objects', Lady Mallinger is also positioned as one herself. Lydia Glasher, a mistress rather than a wife, also holds an 'equivocal position' (DD 288). Lady Mallinger's 'makeshift daughters' are echoed in the situation of Deronda's mother, the Princess Halm-Eberstein, who complains of her role as a 'makeshift link' in the transference of property between men (DD 541). The heiress Catherine Arrowpoint resents the fact that her primary function is to 'carry the property gained in trade into the hands of a certain class' (DD 211) through marriage, indicating that she too is intended to be a 'makeshift link' between male owners. Whether legitimate upper-class wives or common-law wives, heiresses or female artists, penniless outsiders or genteel ladies fallen on hard times, Eliot draws attention to women's 'equivocal positions' as 'makeshift' social beings in a system that privileges men. Eliot repeatedly uses these terms in her final novel in relation to the female characters. In 1870, she complained of 'the perpetual makeshifts

---

[95]   George Eliot, *Daniel Deronda*, Graham Handley (ed.) (Oxford: Oxford University Press, 1988), p. 323. Subsequent page references will be cited in the text following the abbreviation 'DD'.

[96]   Apter, p. x.

[97]   See Holcombe, p. 29. Victorian feminists pointed out the absurdity of the law which meant that wives could retain ownership of gifts if they were not given by their husbands.

of a migratory life', expressing a longing 'for the order and habitual objects of home'; she went on to state that 'there are many in the world whose existence is a makeshift, and perhaps the formula which would fit the largest numbers of lives is, "a doing-without more or less patiently."'[98] Clearly, according to Eliot's definition, to live a 'makeshift life' is to be without a home, and this is reflected in her representations of women's exclusion from real property. Both heroines in *Daniel Deronda*, the English Gwendolen and the Jewish Mirah, are without a settled home, and even apparently established women, such as Lady Mallinger, have no control of real property, but depend upon husbands to provide this.

Daniel Deronda foregrounds women's inability to inherit, and their servitude in their function to transfer property between men. Leonora Charisi (later the Princess Halm-Eberstein) is, in her father's view, merely a conduit transferring the Jewish heritage between men (DD 541). Similarly, the Mallinger sisters are 'makeshift feminine offspring' (DD 611) because they are incapable of retaining their father's property and title. Gwendolen fails to understand her role as wife, expecting to 'manage' Grandcourt after she marries him (DD 115), despite witnessing her mother's own experience of a second marriage to the sinister Captain Davilow, the stepfather who (like Mr Tulliver and Lydgate) 'carried off his wife's jewellery and disposed of it' (DD 233). Gwendolen naively expects marriage to Grandcourt to confer upon her the power of ownership.[99] Indeed, when Eliot uses the word 'own' in relation to her heroines' pretensions to citizenship and status, it is usually ironic. In Chapter 31 for example, when the newly married Gwendolen travels by train to Ryelands, she looks forward to the 'incredible fulfilment about to be given to her girlish dreams of being "somebody" – walking through her own furlong of corridors and under her own ceilings of an out-of-sight loftiness' (DD 301). The link Gwendolen makes between being 'somebody' and property ownership reflects the social view of property as the guarantor of a valued social identity. Yet Gwendolen overlooks the fact that she will never actually 'own' the furlong of corridors or ceilings of Ryelands. Her husband owns all and, after his death, his son will assume ownership, whether a legitimate son borne by Gwendolen or the illegitimate son borne by Lydia (in the end Henleigh Glasher does inherit the estate). It is at this point, when she is most excited by the idea of ownership that Gwendolen is given the packet containing the box containing the jewel-case containing the diamonds and Lydia's letter (DD 302). Sarah Gates describes this letter as Lydia's 'last will and testament',[100] and as we have seen, the production of a will is an act of self-assertion, a woman's attempt to write herself into history and establish or confirm relationships with her heirs. Lydia's 'will', however, is a perverse bequeathing: 'These diamonds, which were once given with

---

[98]   To Barbara Bodichon, 23 June 1870, *George Eliot Letters*, vol. 5, p. 104.

[99]   For a discussion of fathers in the novel see Judith Wilt, '"He Would Come Back": The Fathers of Daughters in *Daniel Deronda*', *Nineteenth-Century Literature*, 42:3 (1987): pp. 313–18.

[100]   Sarah Gates, '"A Difference of Native Language": Gender, Genre and Realism in *Daniel Deronda*', *ELH*, 68 (2001): 720.

ardent love to Lydia Glasher, she passes on to you. You have broken your word to her, that you might possess what was hers' (DD 303).

Lydia's use of the third person indicates not only the alienation of the diamonds but also her own alienated state: at this juncture she has lost her chance of gaining the settlement and social identity conferred by marriage. Eve Kosofsky Sedgwick notes the considerable number of 'explicit performative speech acts' in this passage: 'a promise, a curse, a warning, a marriage vow, a commitment to the grave, a deed of gift', none of which conform to the definition of a speech act as a statement made in the first-person singular form.[101] Sedgwick calls this a 'periperformative', an indirection which 'foreground[s] the material and legal problematics of how a woman may be said either to own or transmit property'.[102] However, Lydia was already dangerously objectified by Grandcourt, who thinks: 'Her person suited diamonds and made them look as if they were worth some of the money given for them' (DD 289), a sentence indicating that he considers her to be the object in relation to the diamonds as subject. A similar objectification occurs later when Grandcourt, forcing his wife to sail with him to Italy, looks at her 'as if she were part of the complete yacht' (DD 575). Lydia insists on excluding Grandcourt from the transaction with 'his mother's diamonds' (although one wonders how far *she* actually 'owned' them and whether she, too, was a 'makeshift link' in the transference of an heirloom between father and son), and like Gwendolen she exposes her illusions of ownership in her letter by using the terms 'given' and 'possess'. Lydia fails to see that although Grandcourt describes the jewels as his 'mother's diamonds' (DD 289), he is the absolute owner and will remain so. As we have seen, Trollope's *The Eustace Diamonds* also demonstrates that women were never meant to 'own' heirlooms such as diamonds, but to receive and wear them as symbols of their links to men, primarily using their bodies as display-cases for exhibiting the family property.

Lydia may not literally or legally bequeath the diamonds to Gwendolen. However, she bequeaths her curse, and Eliot draws on melodrama to establish the relationship between the two women: 'Truly here were poisoned gems, and the poison had entered into this poor young creature. ... In some form or other the Furies had crossed [Grandcourt's] threshold' (DD 303). This situation is figured in equally gothic terms in references to Grandcourt's 'withered heart', 'dead' love, and the image Lydia uses of herself as 'the grave in which your chance of happiness is buried' (DD 303). Eliot had foreshadowed this moment in the epigraph to Chapter 14 where Gwendolen receives the first of Lydia's letters:

> I will not clothe myself in wreck – wear gems
> Saved from cramped finger-bones of women drowned;
> Feel chilly vaporous hands of ireful ghosts
> Clutching my necklace; trick my maiden breast
> With orphans' heritage. Let your dead love
> Marry its dead. (DD, 122)

[101] Sedgwick, p. 76.

[102] Ibid., p. 77.

Again, the images of death and jewellery are used to indicate the rivalry between women for the property they can possess only tenuously. The notion of gems taken from the fingers of drowned women is echoed later when Gwendolen, most abject in her bondage as a prisoner on Grandcourt's yacht, is described as having 'heavily-jewelled hands' (DD 580). The 'property' she wears symbolizes her manacled condition, although Grandcourt's drowning (with all the ambiguity surrounding it) offers her a fortuitous escape from her bondage. Indeed before her widowhood, Gwendolen links the word 'property' with Grandcourt's power, having 'certain associations … first with her mother, then with Mrs Glasher and her children' (DD 510). Gwendolen's misery comes about when she realizes that as a wife she is denied the power of the property owner, that her London home is a 'painted gilded prison' (DD 504) rather than the gratification of her desires she once believed it would be.

Both Lydia and Gwendolen are among Eliot's more troubled female characters, noted for their social and psychological ambiguities and desires for self-gratification, in contrast to the exemplary heroines, Dorothea Brooke, Dinah Morris and Romola. Yet *Daniel Deronda*'s desiring heroines are not straightforwardly condemned; their stories expose patriarchy's injustices, deflecting attention from their 'misdemeanours' (of bearing children out of wedlock, marrying to rescue the family fortune, or abandoning a child in order to pursue a career). The diamonds act for Gwendolen as a memorial of Lydia, as well as reminding her that she is legally her husband's possession. The terms 'self-possession' and 'self-control' are used ironically in relation to Gwendolen once she is married, as though Eliot wants to emphasize the opposite: that legally a husband 'owned' his wife (DD 304, 373, 475). As Barbara Leigh Smith stated in 1854, legally 'a married woman's body belongs to her husband; she is in his custody, and he can enforce his right by a writ of habeas corpus'.[103] Eliot dramatizes this legal bondage to Grandcourt in repeated 'flashbacks' to the image of Gwendolen's face as she loses at roulette, and her hopeless, but outwardly convincing, attempts to appear 'self-possessed'.

Jewellery functions in Eliot's work as a type of property that women find difficult to accept or bequeath. However, in *Daniel Deronda* the diamonds belong to men; there is no straight line of inheritance from Grandcourt's mother to his wife, for it is Grandcourt who controls the property. Lydia's temporary and illusory possession of the diamonds 'poison' them for Gwendolen, not because Lydia as her husband's mistress has contaminated them, but because Gwendolen feels the guilty usurper when she becomes the legitimate wife. The 'poisoned gems' are put to work repeatedly to illustrate the outcome of Gwendolen's speculation upon the marriage market, and Eliot again draws upon melodrama to emphasize her psychic pain; for example, she deliberately 'hurt[s] herself with the jewels that glittered on her tightly-clasped finger pressed against her heart' (DD 521). The association between pain and jewellery is later repeated when Gwendolen considers murdering her husband with the jewelled pin in her cabinet: as she tells Deronda,

---

[103] Cited in Nunokawa, p. 83.

'There it was – something my fingers longed for among the beautiful toys in the cabinet in my boudoir – small and sharp, like a long willow leaf in a silver sheath. I locked it in the drawer of my dressing-case. I was continually haunted with it, and how I should use it. I fancied myself putting it under my pillow. But I never did' (DD 592–3). Gwendolen's escape from her condition as a man's property is signalled by another jewellery image, for when Deronda sees her for the last time, we are informed that her hands are now 'unladen of all rings except her wedding-ring' (DD 656), the latter no longer a symbol of her marriage but of her widowhood, an image which echoes the earlier one of Dorothea Casaubon with her hands 'free' of all jewellery except her wedding ring.[104]

If the Grandcourt diamonds act as a 'poison' on Gwendolen, the 'shabby' (DD 377) turquoise necklace she pawns at Leubronn acts as the antidote. In a process of association, Gwendolen reads her own redemption in the redemption of the necklace by the priestly Deronda.[105] At the New Year's Eve ball 'she longed, in remembrance of Leubronn, to put on the old turquoise necklace for her sole ornament. … Determined to wear the memorial necklace somehow, she wound it thrice round her wrist and made a bracelet of it …'. (DD 377). The complex history of this particular object offers some indication of how meanings develop in relation to inanimate things. When she sells the necklace at Leubronn, the narrator explains that the stones 'had belonged to a chain once her father's', and that these 'three central turquoises' were of 'superior size and quality'. At this point, however, Gwendolen believes it to be 'the ornament she could most conveniently part with' (DD 13), and clearly it does not function as a 'memorial' to the father who died when she was three years old. However, once it is returned to her (with the addition of a cambric handkerchief), the necklace takes on new meanings: it is converted into a makeshift bracelet ('in its triple winding [it] adapted itself clumsily to her wrist' DD 380), a biographical object representing Gwendolen's career as a gambler, eventually becoming a fetish of Deronda himself, a symbol of his faith in Gwendolen's moral redemption.[106] Although it appears as Gwendolen's most precious possession, for her husband it is a 'hideous thing' (DD 380). So what started out as a man's chain, with the addition of some 'superior' stones, becomes Gwendolen's expendable necklace, a property she sells; it then becomes a source of irritation as a symbol of her losing gamble, and finally becomes a symbol of hope, associated with the man who redeemed it from the pawnbroker's and with her own redemption. As with Lady Mallinger's makeshift bracelet made from missal-clasps, Eliot is interested in the way objects can be adaptable and transformable, both in terms of their physical make up and their possible meanings. She reinforces the

---

[104] See Arnold, pp. 212–22 for a discussion of the role of jewellery in Eliot's novels.

[105] Susan Ostrov Weisser sees Deronda not so much as a priest but 'like some irritating modern psychoanalyst' in 'Gwendolen's Hidden Wound: Sexual Possibilities and Impossibilities in *Daniel Deronda*', *Modern Language Studies*, 20:3 (Summer 1990): 7.

[106] Plotz notes the number of 'sentimental fetishes' in *Daniel Deronda* (p. 84).

point she has emphasized throughout her work: that women, with their equivocal rights of ownership, have tangential relationships with the material world.

Earlier male characters, such as Silas in *Silas Marner* (1861), and Rufus Lyon in *Felix Holt*, act as protectors of women's property and Deronda also sympathizes with women's attachment to particular objects. He not only redeems and returns Gwendolen's necklace, but is sensitive to Lady Mallinger's taste in, and need for, ornaments. Similarly, he carries his inherited diamond ring from England to his mother in Italy, while Jacob's mother and grandmother are delighted with the 'portable presents' (DD 441) he gives to the children. Such sympathy, Eliot suggests, is more likely to exist in men who are disadvantaged by their own equivocal social positions, for Rufus is a dissenter, Silas a social outcast and Daniel fears he is illegitimate, and thus excluded from the property rights enjoyed by most men of his own class. Eliot emphasizes the dangers of primogeniture in the figures of Gwendolen and Deronda, the latter suffering some of the impediments usually experienced by women. Like women, he also feels that he has been excluded from a legitimate occupation: 'He found some of the fault in his birth and the way he had been brought up, which had laid no special demands on him' (DD 308). However, the female complaint of 'nothing to do' is more easily remedied for Deronda, able to travel and communicate freely and read what he likes.[107] Yet Deronda is only shown to be a victim of primogeniture for part of the novel. When he discovers his origins as a Jew he takes a privileged place in an alternative, more ancient, patriarchal tradition.

Deronda's 'place' is embodied in the 'precious chest' (DD 638) he inherits from his grandfather, containing 'preserved manuscripts, family records stretching far back' (DD 640). It becomes Deronda's most valued possession (DD 618), the 'precious' contents contained within a highly decorative chest 'made heavy by ornamental bracers and handles of gilt iron. The wood was beautifully incised with Arabic lettering' (DD 618). The writing here is far removed from Mrs Tulliver's named goods, for the chest represents national and racial identity, rather than a store of individual and family memory. The bond between Deronda and Mordecai is strengthened by the 'blent transmission' (DD 643) of this patriarchal inheritance, yet Leonora Charisi sees it as a symbol of her oppression. Her desire to destroy it is a desire to disrupt the transmission of patriarchal culture from man to man. She tells her son:

> Once, after my husband died, I was going to burn the chest. But it was difficult to burn; and burning a chest and papers looks like a shameful act. I have committed no shameful act – except what Jews would call shameful. I had kept the chest, and I gave it to Joseph Kalonymous. He went away mournful, and said, 'If you marry again, and if another grandson is born to him who is departed, I will deliver up the chest to him'. I bowed in silence. (DD 546)

---

[107] For a discussion of the Victorian woman's plight of 'nothing to do', see Florence Nightingale, *Cassandra*, reprinted in M.H. Abrams (ed.), *The Norton Anthology of English Literature*, vol. 2 (New York and London: Norton, 2006), p. 1600.

However, despite her strength and her talent, she is unable to avoid her role as the 'makeshift link' between men. Interestingly, Eliot represents Jewish culture as a precious inalienable possession, yet she uses the language of material property and finance to describe it; Mordecai views the doing of good works as 'a property bearing interest' (DD 491), while in relation to the Jewish spirit he states: 'let us make it a lasting habitation – lasting because movable – so that it may be carried from generation to generation, and our sons unborn may be rich in the things that have been, and possess a hope built on an unchangeable foundation' (DD 453).

For Plotz, Eliot emphasizes the ways in which culture can be made portable by being incorporated into people's minds.[108] Nevertheless as Kate Meyrick states, 'girls' doings are always priced low' (DD 418), and their role as transmitters of cultural property has tended to be devalued. The Meyrick household, dominated by women, suggests a miniature (in all senses of the word) alternative to patriarchy. Yet for Eliot, the Meyrick women (and Mirah, who joins their household) have an ideal relationship with the object world. Mrs Meyrick's house is one of 'the homes of a culture the more spotlessly free from vulgarity, because poverty has rendered everything like display an impersonal question, and all the grand shows of the world simply a spectacle which arouses no petty rivalry or vain effort after possession' (DD 166). Personal property, Eliot suggests, should reflect a 'nicely-select life, open to the highest things in music, painting, and poetry' (DD 167), rather than display the owner's status and wealth. However, as we have seen from her letters, she also values the less elevated charms of 'the china monster or silver clasp' which do not enrich in terms of cultural or cash value, existing only as sources of affect and pleasure.

While the Meyrick women embody an ideal, as Dorothea did in Eliot's previous novel, it is the less-than-ideal Gwendolen who dominates *Daniel Deronda*. Although most critics have read Gwendolen's suffering as a rite-of-passage towards the ranks of property-rejecting female characters such as Mirah and the Meyrick women, the ending of *Daniel Deronda* is highly ambivalent, where the moral and economic plots become blurred. Attention is divided between the story of Deronda's mission to the East and Gwendolen's future as a widow. Many critics read the resolution of Gwendolen's story in terms of her failure. Nestor sees her as a 'sad and diminished figure', while Gates considers her as having 'no script but that of the tragic scapegoat, since the domestic closure of wifehood given in the other Eliot novels to the romance heroines, has here been figuratively handed to the hero'.[109] She adds that Gwendolen, 'Not married, not dead, not exiled, and quite sane, … will live out a plausible tragedy, figured as a role-less and repetitive living and an end-less bettering'.[110] Sarah Willburn argues a similar point, noting that 'Grandcourt's possessions do not pass to Gwendolen through their marriage. Because Gwendolen is not allowed to be an independent

---

[108] Plotz, p. 79.

[109] Nestor, p. 154, and Gates, p. 720.

[110] Gates, p. 721.

proprietor, she is not allowed property, empire, or influence. Her father's company and Grandcourt have both failed her'.[111] Patricia Menon sees Gwendolen destroyed by the 'sadistic abandonment' of both Eliot and Deronda.[112] Although Alexander Welsh sees Gwendolen's future as 'unclear' he reads her statement 'I mean to live' as '[h]ysterical words …, promises not to kill herself', and he adds that she 'will not be much rewarded or consoled in the end'.[113] What is extraordinary about these interpretations is the presumption that Gwendolen is 'not allowed property', and critics seem to concur with Hans Meyrick, who thinks the only fitting outcome for Gwendolen's story should be her remarrying. Deronda, however, asks, 'Is it absolutely necessary that Mrs Grandcourt should marry again?' (DD 685), and Eliot, in a rare move, leaves her young heroine single and in possession of a comfortable inheritance of £2,000 a year for life, a substantial sum for a 'penniless' woman, despite Sir Hugo's exaggerated statement that she is 'no better off than a doctor's wife' (DD 648). To put her income into context, we are informed that Deronda receives an income of £700 a year (the same amount that Dorothea Brooke possessed in the late 1820s), Mrs Davilow is given a 'generous' allowance of £800 a year by Grandcourt, while Eliot, as I mentioned earlier, received only £90 per year when she first met Lewes in 1854. Clearly, Gwendolen's £2,000 a year is a great deal more than she had ever received before her marriage; it is certainly not the poverty to which critics refer. Added to this money is her ownership of Gadsmere, not her chosen home, but we are informed it could be leased 'on capital terms' (DD 651). After the passing of the 1870 Married Women's Property Act, Eliot now confers real estate on one of her heroines without it appearing to be a burden or a problem. Deronda's comment that Gwendolen need not marry again, and that her inheritance is one she 'will be quite contented with' (DD 614), turns us away from the traditional marriage plot of the Victorian novel to face a lack of closure quite untypical of Eliot's work, or for that matter, of the Victorian classic realist text. Gwendolen's repeated assertion that she 'shall live' (DD 691–2) is also part of the novel's irresolution. In one of the few positive readings of Gwendolen's fate, Gillian Beer notes her 'fierce will to survive' and that she 'escapes the marriage market'.[114] That so many modern readers see marriage as the only 'happy' ending for Gwendolen, whose sexless regard for the 'feminine' Deronda as a mentor-figure is the only positive relationship she has with a man, indicates that Eliot's reinstatement of her as a *feme sole*, this time with property to control and enjoy, has not been sufficiently registered and appreciated.

---

[111] Sarah A Willburn, *Possessed Victorians: Extra Spheres in Nineteenth-Century Mystical Writings* (Aldershot: Ashgate, 2006), p. 17.

[112] Patricia Menon, *Austen, Eliot, Charlotte Brontë and the Mentor-Lover* (Basingstoke: Palgrave, 2003), p. 178.

[113] Alexander Welsh, 'The Later Novels' in George Levine (ed.), *The Cambridge Companion to George Eliot* (Cambridge: Cambridge University Press, 2001), p. 70.

[114] Gillian Beer, *George Eliot* (Brighton: Harvester, 1986), pp. 226 and 227.

George Eliot, according to Andrew Miller, kept a 'wary distance from material culture', largely because she 'understood art as ideally existing apart from trade'.[115] Yet Eliot's growing attachment to personal property, the 'china monsters and silver clasps' which provided valid emotional channels for women, complicates the view of her as an anti-materialist. This chapter has charted her progress from her ridicule of the Aunts Pullet and Glegg to her sympathetic portrayal of Dorothea's attachment to dead women's possessions and Gwendolen's fetish necklace, with its connotations of hope and redemption. Henry James, as we will see in the next chapter, also explored the affective qualities of material culture, emphasizing the ways in which people and the things they possess fuse together. His female characters rarely use personal property as a route towards sociability or as symbols of moral education; instead things function for them experientially, offering aesthetically satisfying sensations and enrichments of subjectivity, as well as offering provocations to violence.

---

[115] A.H. Miller, pp. 216–17.

Chapter 4
Property With Violence: Female Possession in the Work of Henry James

In previous chapters we have seen that Dickens and Eliot's property plots, despite their ambiguity, usually lead to the eventual 'settlement' of the heroines. For example, Esther is safely established at the new 'Bleak House', while Estella inherits the 'ground' of Satis House; Mary Garth is made mistress of Stone Court, while Gwendolen inherits Gadsmere. Such denouements largely elide the troubled issues of gender and property which formed the basis of the novels, thus reiterating the traditional link between land and stability. Henry James, on the other hand, saw no future for the narrative leading to female settlement. His heroines are vulnerable to instability; the apparent solidity of real estate which materializes so 'unexpectedly' at the close of most Victorian novels, fragments in his work into women's tenuous possession of bric-a-brac, what-nots and collectables. Largely concerned with people on the move or trapped, rather than settled, his novels depict female strategists who plot to achieve a stability that seems impossible at the *fin de siècle*. For many of his heroines, attempts to gain a sense of settlement fail; instead they are left cherishing their portable property as salvage, *disjecta membra*, usually melancholy memorials to an idea of settlement they will never attain. Increasingly, his heroines embrace the provisionality of their fates. As Donatella Izzo argues, in James's later work the female characters reject 'all remaining subjection to sanctioned nineteenth-century roles, seem[ing] to experiment with them in a self-aware performative fashion'.[1] This is where James differs from his predecessors, for unlike them he is in a position to consider the issue of female property ownership in the aftermath of the passing of the Married Women's Property Acts in Britain and America.[2]

James was writing in the final decades of the nineteenth century, a period when traditional roles were being assaulted on a number of fronts by intellectuals, artists and political activists such as the 'New Woman'. Indeed, Carroll Smith-Rosenberg has claimed that James was responsible for the term 'New Woman

---

[1] Donatella Izzo, 'Nothing Personal: Women Characters, Gender Ideology, and Literary Representation', in Greg W. Zacharias (ed.), *A Companion to Henry James* (Oxford: Blackwell, 2008), p. 356.

[2] See Dianne Sachko Macleod, *Enchanted Lives, Enchanted Objects: American Women Collectors and the Making of Culture, 1800–1940* (Berkeley, Los Angeles: University of California Press, 2008), pp. 46 and 80 for changes to the marriage laws in America.

[which] originated as a literary phrase popularized' by him.[3] Elaine Showalter has demonstrated that the New Woman targeted all aspects of the establishment, with its 'system of inheritance and primogeniture, its compulsory heterosexuality and marriage'.[4] The New Woman, above all, challenged the Victorian ideals of womanhood which Dickens and Eliot had promoted. As Sally Ledger has argued, contemporary commentators on the New Woman frequently registered their sense of social panic, raising the spectre of a reversal in gender relations and an overturning of what had once seemed to be stable sexual identities.[5] For example, *The Westminster Review* carried an article in 1889 arguing that the New Woman would bring about a social crisis because her demand for rights was 'causing incalculable upheaval and destruction'.[6] James found these developments highly interesting: in a notebook entry of 1895 he recorded a French social critic's observation on 'the masculinization of the women' in modern Britain, adding that this would offer a 'fertile ... subject, for the novel, for the picture of contemporary manners'.[7] James depicts women who desire property as having 'masculine' traits; indeed, for him to be a woman of property involves an element of gender inversion. It also involves violence and eroticism, for in his work women with property are ready to fight for their things and defend them as well as bonding strongly with them, experiencing an intense tactile pleasure.[8] This chapter explores the ways in which James draws upon anxieties about the social impact of assertive New Women, anxieties which were fuelled by hostile media coverage of their demands for property rights, education, employment opportunities and the suffrage.

James's major novels were written at a time when the changes in legislation appeared to be moving in women's favour, and he makes an important distinction between the New Woman who confidently takes possession of her new rights and more vulnerable women who are trapped within the cage of Victorian femininity. Legal reforms, he suggests, do not by themselves have the power to

---

[3]   Carroll Smith-Rosenberg, *Disorderly Conduct: Visions of Gender in Victorian America* (New York: Alfred A. Knopf, 1985), p. 176. However, this assertion is not supported by evidence.

[4]   Elaine Showalter, *Sexual Anarchy: Gender and Culture at the Fin de Siècle* (London: Bloomsbury, 1991), p. 11.

[5]   Sally Ledger, *The New Woman: Fiction and feminism at the fin de siècle* (Manchester: Manchester University Press, 1997), p. 128.

[6]   Quoted in Linda Dowling, 'The Decadent and the New Woman', *Nineteenth-Century Fiction*, 33:4 (1979): 439. See also 'Character Note: The New Woman' (1894) in *The Fin de Siècle: A Reader in Cultural History*, Sally Ledger and Roger Luckhurst (eds) (Oxford: Oxford University Press, 2000), pp. 80–83.

[7]   Henry James, *The Notebooks of Henry James*, F.O. Mattiessen and Kenneth B. Murdock (eds) (Chicago and London: University of Chicago Press, 1981), pp. 191–2.

[8]   See Thomas J. Otten, '*The Spoils of Poynton* and the Properties of Touch', *American Literature*, 71:2 (June 1999), for a perceptive discussion of James's representations of female pleasure in the tactile. Macleod also discusses women collectors' satisfaction from touching objects, p. 14.

change entrenched mental states or deep-rooted traditions. As Izzo states: 'few male writers have devoted to women the sustained and coherent attention that Henry James displayed throughout his career', noting the 'complex and pervasive presence of the "woman question"' throughout his work.[9] Indeed, as we will see in the following section, his engagement with the Woman Question began long before he had published his first novel.

'Modern Women' and the Long Revolution

In a book review written for *The Nation* in 1868, James made a number of telling comments about what he perceived to be the contrast between American and British society, differences which to him centred on the customs of property transmission and their effects upon gender relations. The book in question was *Modern Women and What is Said of Them*, reprinting a series of articles which had originally appeared in the conservative periodical, *The Saturday Review*. Among the essays was Eliza Lynn Linton's controversial 'The Girl of the Period', which condemned the modern young woman as exhibitionistic, both in dress and manners.[10] James, writing anonymously and addressing an American readership, stated:

> The American reader will be struck by the remoteness and strangeness of the writer's tone and allusions. He will see that the society which makes these papers even hypothetically – hyperbolically – possible is quite another society from that of New York and Boston. American life, whatever may be said, is still a far simpler process than the domestic system of England. We never read a good English novel (and much more a bad one), we never read either Mr Trollope or Mr Trollope's inferiors, without drawing a long breath of relief at the thought of all that we are spared, and without thanking fortune that we are not part and parcel of that dark, dense British social fabric. An American is born into a so much simpler world; he inherits so many less obligations, conventions, and responsibilities. And so with the American girl. You have only to reflect how her existence, in comparison with that of her British sister, is simplified at a stroke by the suppression in this country of that distinguished being the 'eldest son', of that romantic class the 'younger sons'.[11]

Here he identifies the convention of primogeniture as the basis of the 'remoteness and strangeness' of British life. The English novel, preoccupied as it is with the themes of property and inheritance, is for Americans an important source of information about the 'dark, dense' Old World society which contrasts so sharply with their 'simpler world'. Indeed, European society, particularly the American

---

[9]   Izzo, pp. 343 and 355.

[10]   See Lyn Pykett, *The Improper Feminine: The Woman's Sensation Novel and the New Woman Writing* (London: Routledge, 1992), pp. 69–70 for a discussion of the impact of Linton's article.

[11]   [Henry James,] 'Modern Women', *The Nation* (October 22 1868): 333.

encounter with Europe, and later the 'darkness' of Europeanized Americans themselves, was to afford James the material for most of his major fiction.[12]

James had long been alert to the situation of 'modern women'. While the essays in *Modern Women and What is Said of Them* condemn women's deployment of the 'tricks of the marriage market', James argues that an unmarried woman is actually left little time 'for study, for reflection, or sentiment' because her social business is 'the care of her person', the cultivation of a fashionable appearance.[13] He goes on to elaborate:

> It is impossible to discuss and condemn the follies of 'modern women' apart from those of modern man. They are all part and parcel of modern civilization, which is working itself out through innumerable blunders. It seems to us supremely absurd to stand up in the high places and endeavour, with a long lash and a good deal of bad language, to drive women back into the ancient fold. Their extravagance is a part of their increased freedom, and their increased freedom a part of the growth of society. The lamentable results – the extremely uncomfortable 'wreck' society would be sure to incur from an attempt to fasten again upon womankind the tether which was sufficient unto the aspirations of Miss Hannah More and Miss Edgeworth, the authors of these papers would be the first to denounce. We are all of us extravagant, superficial, and luxurious together. It is a 'sign of the times'. Women share in the fault not as women, but as simple human beings. As women, they strike us as still remarkably patient, submissive, sympathetic – remarkably well-disposed to model themselves on the judgment and wishes of men. They reflect with great clearness the state of the heart and imagination of men.[14]

What this early review also indicates is that in the years before he made his permanent home in Europe his knowledge of European society, its mores and conventions, was gleaned largely through the medium of the novel. Later, of course, he was to make an intensive personal study of Europe and more sophisticated readings of its representations of itself. Even so, his review of *Modern Women* demonstrates that he had already given considerable thought to the Woman Question and was astute enough to realize that social 'wreckage' would ensue from any attempt to turn back the course of history.

Thirty-two years later James again addressed this issue in an essay called 'The Future of the Novel' which first appeared in the *New York Times* in August 1900. However, while the 1868 review imagined women as the victims of patriarchal violence, being subjected to 'a long lash' and driven 'back into the ancient fold', the later essay represented women as prone to inflicting violence and liable to self-assertion. He wrote:

---

[12]   On American women's relationships with Europe, see Macleod, p. 177.

[13]   [James,] 'Modern Women', pp. 333–4.

[14]   Ibid., p. 334.

[N]othing is more salient in English life today, to fresh eyes, than the revolution taking place in the position and outlook of women – and taking place much more deeply in the quiet than even the noise on the surface demonstrates – so we may very well yet see the female elbow itself, kept in increasing activity by the play of the pen, smash with final resonance the window all the time most superstitiously closed. … It is the opinion of some observers that when women do obtain a free hand, they will not repay their long debt to the precautionary attitude of men by unlimited consideration for the natural delicacy of the latter.[15]

In a discussion replete with references to gender inversion (albeit ironic references to the 'native delicacy' of men), he mentions the pent up violence of women writers who desire to 'smash' their way out of their social confinement. The feminist revolution which James had identified in his review of *Modern Women* turned out to be a long revolution, but never without the potential for violence, as indicated by the later suffragette protests. In his representations of women and property James, as we will see in subsequent sections, focuses on the New Woman's capacity for violence and self-assertion.

The subject of women has preoccupied most accounts of James's work; indeed, many critics have argued that he psychologically identified with them. John Carlos Rowe, for example, has suggested that 'James's uncanny ability to represent the complex psychologies of women … is in part attributable to his identification with their marginal and powerless situations'.[16] This view is shared by Elaine Pigeon, who has argued that James's 'sympathetic treatment of women', despite his avowed lack of sympathy with the feminist movement, was the result of 'his marginal position as a writer during the second half of the nineteenth century [which] facilitated identification with his female protagonists, for James produced his writings from behind the scenes, within the privacy of the domestic, feminine sphere'.[17] Tessa Hadley also relates his interest in 'the particular history of women' to his 'own ambiguously gendered position'.[18] Alfred Habeggar even suggests that James's 'strong point of view on the women's rights movement' needs to be seen in relation to the fact that 'his own masculinity was problematic in the extreme', a view which fails to take into account (and indeed falls victim to) the very problems

---

[15]   Henry James, 'The Future of the Novel: An Analysis and Forecast by Henry James', *New York Times*, 11 August 1900, reprinted at: http://query.nytimes.com/men/archive (accessed 08/02/2009).

[16]   John Carlos Rowe, *The Theoretical Dimensions of Henry James* (London: Methuen, 1984), p. 9.

[17]   Elaine Pigeon, *Queer Impressions: Henry James and The Art of Fiction* (London and New York: Routledge, 2005), p. 1. It is not, however, clear in what sense James was 'marginal'.

[18]   Tessa Hadley, *Henry James and the Imagination of Pleasure* (Cambridge: Cambridge University Press, 2002), p. 13.

of gender categorization which James himself addressed in his fiction.[19] As this brief survey indicates, critics have presumed that in representing women, James was actually representing himself. This is an extraordinary presumption to make in relation to a writer who so self-consciously crafted his material, and it does not in the end take us very far towards an understanding of James's undoubted attraction to the subject of women, their social positions and sexual relationships.

As well as attempting to measure the extent of James's masculinity and/or femininity, numerous critics have also sought to give an accurate measurement of his feminism. Habeggar, who adopts the most extreme position, offers what can only be called a diatribe against James, seeing him as a confirmed anti-feminist.[20] There is, of course, some evidence to support the 'anti-feminist' argument, particularly in *The Bostonians* and *The Princess Casamassima*, both published in 1886; however, it would be rash to oversimplify James's complex engagement with the Woman Question. In April 1883, when he planned to write *The Bostonians*, he stated his wish to explore 'the most salient and peculiar point in our social life ... the situation of women, the decline of the sentiment of sex, the agitation on their behalf'.[21] Victoria Coulson strikes, I think, exactly the right note in her combination of literary analysis and biographical enquiry when she states 'that James can best be understood as both subject to, and the compelling artist of, a potent ambivalence about the social authority of conservative gender patterns', adding that what is needed is 'a sufficiently nuanced perspective on James from which to apprehend the psychological and aesthetic complexity of his work'.[22] She notes that James's major work is coincident with one of the most dramatic periods in the history of feminism, a time when women gained a public voice and achieved new legal rights.[23] While James's depictions of women and property draw on the renunciating heroines of Victorian fiction, they also explore other styles of femininity in representations of women who assert their ownership of things.[24] This chapter considers one of the central tropes James employs, that of the penetrating woman; penetrating in her understanding of situations and people,

---

[19]   Alfred Habeggar, *Henry James and the Woman Business* (Cambridge: Cambridge University Press, 1989), p. 6. For more nuanced discussions of James and sexuality see Denis Flannery, *Henry James: A Certain Illusion* (Aldershot: Ashgate, 2000) and Eric Haralson, *Henry James and Queer Modernity* (Cambridge: Cambridge University Press, 2003). See also Hugh Stevens, *Henry James and Sexuality* (Cambridge: Cambridge University Press, 1998), pp. 27–8 for an interesting discussion of James's representation of the New Woman in relation to *The Wings of the Dove*.

[20]   Habeggar, p. 5.

[21]   Quoted in Edel, *Life*, vol. 1, p. 738.

[22]   Victoria Coulson, *Henry James, Women and Realism* (Cambridge: Cambridge University Press, 2007), pp. 22 and 8.

[23]   Ibid., pp. 1–4.

[24]   See Hadley, who argues that James works within a 'moral framework inherited from his great Victorian predecessors' (p. 2). She also sees him having 'roots' in the work of George Eliot (p. 12).

but also capable of physical penetration – with her elbows, her feet, her eyes and with her keys. Indeed, in his essay on Sainte-Beuve, James listed 'penetration' as a specifically 'feminine' quality.[25] As we will see, James categorizes his female characters in terms of those who 'penetrate' and those who do not.

The safe settlement or resting place found by the heroines of Victorian novels by means of marriage or inheritance is, then, almost impossible for James's female characters. However, some do not want to be settled at all, such as Mrs Touchett in *The Portrait of a Lady* (1881), one of many of James's American characters who moves easily between countries and continents, carrying their property with them, sometimes investing it if the opportunity arises. When her husband dies, Mrs Touchett makes a final visit to his London home and, '[a]fter selecting from among its furniture the objects she wished to transport to her other abode [in Florence], she left the rest of its contents to be disposed of by the auctioneer'.[26] When we are given an example of a woman who is fixed in one place, such as Juliana Bordereau in *The Aspern Papers* (1888), isolated in her deteriorating rented Venetian palace too large for comfort, her settlement seems to be a matter of inertia and entrapment rather than choice. Adela Gereth, the dispossessed widow in *The Spoils of Poynton*, is determined to stay at home only to find that the law supports her eviction from Poynton and the forcible repossession of her cherished collection of *objets d'art*. Writing after the passing of the Married Women's Property Acts, James's fiction of the 1880s and 1890s represents the tensions between women's sentimental ownership of things traditionally associated with femininity, and the more 'masculine' acquisitiveness of the New Woman, demonstrating that in spite of the reforms of the property and marriage laws, there was little sense of resolution. Some women continued to be viewed as property or as sources of property, and his contemptuous reference in *The Spoils of Poynton* to the 'cruel English custom' of primogeniture suggests a sympathy with women who could find consolation and a sense of identity in the material world through those items of personal property they believed they owned.[27]

Yet James, like Dickens and Eliot before him, complicates the human–object boundary by exploring the possibility of reciprocity between person and thing. As Brown has stated, James was intrigued by the 'ontological democratization of person and thing', as well as the unstable boundary between the animate and the inanimate.[28] In *The Portrait of a Lady* Madame Merle (famously) finds both

---

[25] See Kelly Cannon, *Henry James and Masculinity: The Man at the Margins* (New York: St Martin's Press, 1994), p. 5 for a discussion of James's essay on Sainte-Beuve.

[26] Henry James, *The Portrait of a Lady*, Nicola Bradbury (ed.) (Oxford: Oxford University Press, 1998), p. 231. Subsequent references will be cited in the text following the abbreviation 'PL'.

[27] Henry James, *The Spoils of Poynton*, Bernard Richards (ed.) (Oxford: Oxford University Press, 1982), p. 9. Subsequent references will be cited in the text following the abbreviation 'SP'.

[28] Brown, *A Sense of Things*, pp. 137–8.

consolation and a sense of identity in the objects she owns, indicating the reciprocal relationship she has with them:

> What shall we call our 'self'? Where does it begin? Where does it end? It overflows into everything that belongs to us – and then it flows back again. I know that a large part of myself is in the clothes I choose to wear. I've a great respect for *things*! One's self – for other people – is one's expression of one's self; one's house, one's furniture, one's garments, the books one reads, the company one keeps – these things are all expressive. (PL 222–3)

Merle, despite her tendency to see herself (and other people) as an object, shows an unusual level of awareness of what society expects from women, how the object world can aid the expression of a social identity, and what strategies and consolations women can take. Indeed her views closely match those definitions of natural law made by Locke in his assertion that 'making a thing one's own means making it part of oneself'.[29] Serena Merle's eloquent speech outlining her view of her identity as overflowing into, and out of, her belongings suggests that for her this reciprocity is important to her, perhaps even exceeding, her relationships with people. The excess implied by the word 'overflow' also appears to eroticize her relationship with her things. Similarly, Mrs Gereth's identification with her collection of *objets d'art* is so complete that when she is forced to relinquish her things she feels castrated, as though an 'amputation – as she called it, had been performed. Her leg had come off – she had now begun to stump along with the lovely wooden substitute; she would stump for life' (SP 46). This chapter will consider the ways in which James's would-be female property owners destabilize traditional gender roles. It also asks whether his female fetishists are alienated subjects, according to Marxist notions of the reifying effects of capitalism, or if James is suggesting, as later feminist critics do, that fetishism offers women an important defence mechanism in a hostile world?[30]

Before I go on to discuss female characters and their personal property in three key texts, *The Portrait of a Lady*, *The Aspern Papers* and *The Spoils of Poynton*, it is worth pausing to consider a little-discussed short story 'Paste', originally published in James's collection, *The Soft Side* (1900). This tale not only shows the deeply emotional, even erotic, relationships that women have with objects, but also the difficulties they face in maintaining these relationships. It highlights the problems of bequeathing and inheriting possessions which have intimate and compromising connotations. This story, dismissed by James as insignificant, is actually one of his most significant representations of human–object relations, not only in an ontological sense, but also as a sociological and anthropological exploration of women and the things they value.

---

[29] See Olivecrona, p. 225.

[30] See Mulvey and Apter.

'They're things of passion': Women's Secret Possessions in 'Paste'

'Paste' opens with a search through a dead woman's possessions and the discovery that among her mediocre effects is a pearl necklace of great price. This scene echoes James's earlier unsettling experience of handling a dead woman's effects when in 1894 his friend, the novelist Constance Fenimore Woolson, committed suicide in Venice. James's subsequent search through her things was fraught with anxiety, for he suspected that Woolson had wished to be intimate with him and may have left a record of her feelings. The fear of being compromised underpins the image with which Lyndall Gordon opens her biography of James, an image of him unsuccessfully 'drowning' her legacy of dresses in the Venetian lagoon.[31] Edel also describes his painstaking search through Woolson's possessions:

> He was all too aware how many trunks Fenimore possessed; he had seen her constitutional difficulty in extricating herself from the clutter of her days. He could imagine – he who was intensely private and secretive – what piles of paper, notebooks, possibly even diaries, there might be lying at this moment in the rooms of the temporarily sealed apartment in the Casa Semitecolo. Fenimore had spoken of a will, shortly before her death; none was found. She had even – he learned later – told Francis Boott that her last testament would contain a 'surprise'. When Boott told James this, he replied it was 'just one of those numerous strangenesses that illustrate (as one looks back) her latent insanity'. In the absence of a will, Clara Woolson Benedict in New York, Fenimore's sister, fell heir to all her possessions.[32]

Like many nineteenth-century women, Woolson was aware of the dramatic potential of a will; yet she also created a drama by not making one. James arranged to escort her heir, her sister Clara Benedict, to Venice to arrange for the removal of Constance's effects, an action which, in Edel's words, also involved him being 'at hand to cope with whatever privacies might require safeguarding among the dead woman's papers. His task was the opposite of that of his narrator in *The Aspern Papers*'.[33] In other words, he hoped to destroy anything which may have been compromising or revealing. James found this time-consuming and exhausting, writing to his siblings William and Alice about the delay caused by 'the winding-up of Miss W's so complicated affairs… [A] most devouring, an almost fatal job'.[34] Clara wrote to a friend that 'Henry James met us at Genoa, and never never left us until all her precious things were packed and boxed and sent to America',[35]

---

[31] Lyndall Gordon, *A Private Life of Henry James: Two Women and his Art* (London: Chatto and Windus, 1998), p. 1.

[32] Edel, *Life*, vol. 2, p. 82. For a different view of the James–Woolson relationship, see Coulson.

[33] Ibid.

[34] Letter to William and Alice James, 25 May 1894, reprinted in *Henry James: A Life in Letters*, Philip Horne (ed.) (London: Allen Lane, 1999), p. 269.

[35] Quoted in Edel, *Life*, vol. 2, p. 84.

the repetition of 'never' offering here a hint that James was determined not to leave his friend's sister alone with her newly acquired possessions for a moment, until he had examined each document carefully.

While Edel traces the links between the death of Woolson and *The Aspern Papers*, seeing James's role as an inversion of that of the acquisitive narrator of the novella, the nervous search through a dead woman's possessions with its attendant sense of fear about the secrets which may be uncovered was translated into the story 'Paste', ostensibly a reworking of Guy de Maupassant's 'The Necklace' (1884), but really an exploration of the dramatic impact of a woman's secrets being uncovered by death.[36] In 'Paste' the secret is embodied in an object which continues the narrative of its owner's life after death. James thought this one of 'the least valuable' of his short stories, instructing his French translator not to 'waste your time at it, it isn't worth it'.[37] Interestingly, the narrator of 'Paste', a vicar's son whose stepmother had been an actress before she married his father, dismisses her pearl necklace as 'waste', mere paste, for to admit that the pearls were genuine would expose his dead stepmother's history as less than respectable, for he implicitly believes that an impoverished actress could only come by a beautiful set of pearls if she had been involved in a sexual liaison. Indeed, James often represented actresses as transgressing boundaries, as disadvantageously placed in relation to 'domestic' women.[38]

The story opens with the anxious and socially correct bourgeois Arthur Prime being assisted in the search through his dead stepmother's effects by his cousin, Charlotte Prime, a governess who was fond of her aunt. As she searches for a suitable 'relic' to remember her by, she finds on an inaccessible shelf in an unused cupboard a tin box full of 'things of the theatre', jewellery made of 'tinsel and glass'.[39] Despite their 'vulgarity', Charlotte finds something in these long-treasured 'gewgaws that spoke to her', 'melancholy' evidence that Mrs Prime had kept memorials of her undistinguished career on the stage (P 311). Arthur, embarrassed by this evidence of his stepmother's past, asks Charlotte to take the box of 'shameless pinchbeck', insisting that Mrs Prime would have thrown them away if she had not forgotten them. Yet Charlotte senses that the box was carefully hidden, rather than forgotten, imagining Mrs Prime to have 'a mind divided and a vision vaguely troubled' by her possession of these memorials (P 312). Later she discovers among the fakes a genuine pearl necklace, the value of which is revealed by her friend Mrs Guy, a forceful woman staying as a guest of Charlotte's employers. Mrs Guy brings the neglected pearls back to life, she 'handled them, understood them, admired them

[36]   Letter to Auguste Monod, 17 December 1905, reprinted in Horne, p. 431.

[37]   Ibid., p. 431.

[38]   See in particular his novel of 1890, *The Tragic Muse*, which offers his fullest treatment of the actress' situation. See also Coulson, p. 80.

[39]   Henry James, 'Paste', *Fourteen Stories by Henry James*, David Garnett (ed.) (London: Rupert Hart-Davies, 1946), p. 310. Further references will appear in the text following the abbreviation 'P'.

and … wakes them up', telling Charlotte, 'They're alive, don't you see?' (P 318). Indeed, the pearls function as reciprocal property: Mrs Guy hears the story they speak and deduces the hidden history of the dead Mrs Prime: during her time as an actress, she had once been 'kind' to an admirer (P 320).

Charlotte, now the owner of the pearls, faces the same dilemma as her aunt: she wants them and values them but cannot wear them publicly. Mrs Guy, wealthy and physically powerful, with 'white shoulders' on display and 'very red lips' (P 322) borrows the 'darlings' to wear at the dinner party Charlotte (as governess) cannot attend (P 323). Charlotte, now aware of the full significance of her memorial to her aunt, senses that the pearls have become 'more and more alive', her imagination is fired by Mrs Guy's comment that 'they're things of love!' (P 323), 'things of passion!' (P 324). Charlotte finds it 'touching' that Mrs Prime (in a reworking of Poe's 'The Purloined Letter') needed to hide her pearls, 'mixed … in her reliquary, with false things, in order to put curiosity and detection off the scent' (P 324). In an action that echoes Mrs Prime's 'illegitimate' possession, Charlotte wears the necklace 'in secret sessions; she wore it sometimes under her dress; she came to feel, verily, a haunting passion for it' (P 324). Yet, despite these passionate 'sessions' with the pearls, Charlotte is also aware that, 'in her penniless state', she would probably sell them if she actually owned them. Although she feels that she must inform Arthur of their true value and return them to him, she procrastinates for several months in order to continue her 'secret sessions', fantasizing that Arthur will allow her to keep them in 'a grand magnanimous moment' (P 324). Eventually, Charlotte (not satiated, but feeling too guilty) returns the pearls to Arthur, he angrily insisting they are 'rotten paste' (P 325). Yet despite his assertion of their worthlessness, he refuses to allow Charlotte to keep them, later informing her that he has destroyed them. Charlotte shortly afterwards sees them worn by Mrs Guy and feels a 'really morbid' (P 325) suspicion of betrayal that a bargain had been struck between Arthur and her friend.

'Paste' is a story of forbidden love, forbidden possessions, sensuous involvement with objects as a conduit to the past, a means of identification and communication with a dead woman, a depiction of things acting as narrators of hidden stories, of women as victims of deceit and betrayal, the uncanniness of the continuation of material things after the owner's death, and the problems entailed by 'inappropriate' objects for those who survive. Charlotte and Mrs Prime are owners who feel that they cannot own, while the worldly and sexually aware Mrs Guy (whose name signals both her relationship to the 'masculine' qualities of the New Woman and the name of de Maupassant, whose story provided the basis of James's tale) has no difficulties in possessing and wearing the pearls. She has no need of 'secret sessions' with them because her wealth and flamboyant sexuality (wearing them she makes advances to 'a very beautiful young man' (P 326)) allow her to display and make use of them. Yet Mrs Guy as their eventual owner ensures that the pearls lose their 'aura', their meanings as 'things of love', biographical objects, hidden memorials. They had the potential to be inalienable property, a status which would have remained intact if Charlotte had continued the practice of secret possession instigated by her aunt. However, Arthur alienates them, releasing them into other, more banal meanings and, significantly, impoverishing his cousin Charlotte in a double sense for she must continue her life as a governess, as well as being denied the sensuous pleasure she gains from them. Yet Charlotte, of course, could not have kept the pearls as well as selling them, and although she does not have to face this particular dilemma, she does have to cope with the fact of their loss. As we will see, this dual approach to possession – the tenuous, emotionally charged connection with things and the determinedly grasping intention to own – characterized many of James's earlier representations of women and property. The following sections explore, through a series of close readings of *The Portrait of a Lady*, *The Aspern Papers* and *The Spoils of Poynton*, James's fascination with women's 'secret sessions' with their things in the aftermath of the Married Women's Property Acts.

'Property erects a kind of barrier': *The Portrait of a Lady*

As 'Paste' suggests, women value property most when they can establish reciprocal relationships with it, either secretly as Charlotte and Mrs Prime do, or as Mrs Guy does in her flamboyant public display. However, reciprocal property, as we have seen, can also have a didactic function. Esther Summerson, for example, in *Bleak House* uses reciprocal property in the forms of her doll and pet bird as a route into the social, offering knowledge of the boundaries between the self and others. Numerous female characters in nineteenth-century fiction forge such pupil–teacher, mother–daughter, or sister–sister relationships with their portable property in childhood. The young Isabel Archer in *The Portrait of a Lady* (like Jane Austen's Fanny Price, isolated in the East Room of Mansfield Park and surrounded by her 'nest of comforts')[40] is educated into sociability through her relationship with things. However, significantly, while Fanny Price, settled within the Mansfield Park estate even after her marriage, may continue to access her 'nest of comforts', Isabel's travels from America to Britain to Italy mean the loss of all connection with the things from her childhood, the discarded relics of her grandmother's house stored in:

> [a] chamber of disgrace for old pieces of furniture whose infirmities were not always apparent … and with which, in the manner of children, she had established relations almost human, certainly dramatic. There was an old haircloth sofa in especial, to which she had confided a hundred childish sorrows. (PL 40)[41]

---

[40]   Jane Austen, *Mansfield Park*, James Kinsley (ed.) (Oxford: Oxford University Press, 2003), p. 120.

[41]   See Macleod, p. 177 for a discussion of the ways in which American women forged relationships with objects in Europe. She also briefly discusses James in this context.

Communion with the things in her grandmother's house doesn't prepare her for the complexity of the social functions of objects in the wider world, however. As Merle later states, Isabel appears only 'to have the vaguest ideas about [her] earthly possessions' (PL 224). She admits to her aunt that she is 'not stupid; but I don't know anything about money' (PL 43), resembling the economically vulnerable heroines she reads about. Although her reading of Browning and George Eliot (PL 51) allows her access to the knowledge that 'the unpleasant' is 'a source of interest and even of instruction' (PL 49), she fails to learn sufficiently from Eliot's novels that the 'unpleasant' in fiction often emanates from women's negative experiences of property ownership and marriage. Similarly, Browning's 'My Last Duchess' offers a prescient view of the male collector's desire to objectify his bride as a trophy for his collection, as well as the inherent violence and eroticism of the Duke's objectification of women. Indeed, once she is married to Osmond, Isabel comes to see herself as 'some curious piece in an antiquary's collection' (PL 353). In her youth, however, sheltered from the transactions of the marketplace, Isabel fatally misunderstands the role of objects and possessions in forging a social identity and, more significantly, the fact that women themselves can be viewed as property. Despite her early attachment to the things in her grandmother's lumber room, Isabel later comes to undervalue the material world, presuming that it is unimportant. She resists Madame Merle's proclamation that she has 'a great respect for *things*!' by stating, 'Nothing that belongs to me is any measure of me; everything's on the contrary a limit, a barrier and a perfectly arbitrary one' (PL 223). Isabel's error makes her vulnerable to Serena Merle's more sophisticated knowledge of the social role of things.

Serena Merle, one of the most articulate and complex of James's 'things' women, suggests that the boundaries are virtually nonexistent between people and the objects they own (PL 222–3). Agnew suggests that she is a character who 'is perhaps one of the most celebrated instances of an achieved marketplace identity'.[42] While marketplace values do not apply to her possession of things, for like most of the 'fallen' women of Victorian fiction she works hard to keep her things *out* of circulation, she does embody a 'marketplace identity' as far as her relationship to her self is concerned. Her portable property consists of a few precious bibelots which are not for sale, and her own labour, which is:

> When Madame Merle was neither writing, nor painting, nor touching the piano, she was usually employed upon wonderful tasks of rich embroidery, cushions, curtains, decorations for the chimney-piece; an art in which her bold, free invention was as noted as the agility of her needle. She was never idle ... She laid down her pastimes as easily as she took them up; she worked and talked at the same time, and appeared to impute scant worth to anything she did. She gave away her sketches and tapestries; she rose from the piano or remained

---

[42]   Jean-Christophe Agnew, 'The Consuming Vision of Henry James' in *The Culture of Consumption: Critical Essays in American History, 1880–1980*, Richard Wightman Fox and T. Jackson Lears (eds) (New York: Pantheon, 1983), p. 85.

there, according to the convenience of her auditors, which she always unerringly divined. She was in short the most comfortable, *profitable*, amenable person to live with. (PL 213; emphasis added)

James suggests that her productivity resembles the ceaseless activity of industrial production as she churns out the products of the traditional labour of the Victorian lady. The widow of a Swiss businessman, she has adopted the career of the lady of leisure, which is ironic in that she labours so tirelessly. However, while others find her 'profitable' she, like the exploited industrial worker, makes little profit in herself, although she does manage to live off others by functioning, Skimpole-like, as a regular guest in her wealthy friends' homes. The 'precious' portable property she has acquired over the years has come to her by some mysterious process; as Osmond's sister states, 'No one knows, no one has ever known, what she lives on, or how she has got all those beautiful things' (PL 580). Yet Merle's identification with her things – 'valuable curtains of time-softened damask' (PL 554) and 'delicate specimens of rare porcelain' (PL 558) – means that she must remove them from circulation as a form of self-protection which leaves her financially vulnerable, for she refuses to invest them or sell them. Yet her 'precious' things are also vulnerable to decay and deterioration, evident when Osmond mentions the existence of 'a wee bit of a tiny crack' in a precious cup (PL 558). The flaw nicely suggests Serena's subjection to reification and her economic vulnerability, a point that is reinforced when Isabel admires her possession of many skills, and she answers, 'What have my talents brought me? Nothing but the need of using them still' (PL 221). Her choice of a career as a 'lady' is, James suggests, an unproductive and exhausting one, a dead-end that firmly positions her on the margins of the world to which she aspires to belong. However, her attachment to her collection of things is also a source of consolation (as it is for Mr Rosier however, who sells his bibelots in an attempt to 'buy' Pansy, an action which proves fruitless).

Serena's possession of property being tenuous, she is envious of Isabel's good fortune. When she hears of Mr Touchett's will:

> The idea of a distribution of property – she would almost have said of spoils –
> just now pressed upon her senses and irritated her with a sense of exclusion.
> I am far from wishing to picture her as one of the hungry mouths or envious
> hearts of the general herd, but we have already learned of her having desires that
> had never been satisfied. (PL 229)

Madame Merle's 'sense of exclusion' aligns her with (although the narrator is also careful to try and distance her from) the hunger and envy of the labouring classes, whose work goes largely unrewarded. She schemes to bring about a redistribution of property when she engineers a marriage between Isabel and Osmond, her former lover and the father of her child. It is unclear whether she hopes to gain personally from this, or whether, having 'renounced all visible property in the child' (PL 579), she hopes that her daughter Pansy's future will be secured by Isabel's riches. Serena's view of Mr Touchett's property as the spoils of war (an image

James uses repeatedly, especially in *The Spoils of Poynton*) indicates that one aspect of her labour, albeit a covert one, is her need to fight for what she gets. Having adopted her chosen career of 'lady', she must hide the fact that she is 'perversely yearning' for the things she cannot have, being 'careful not to betray herself' (PL 229). Her response to the news of Isabel's fortune of £70,000 is to exclaim, 'Ah, the clever creature' (PL 230), indicating her belief that Isabel had to work in the same covert way that she herself works for gain. Madame Merle's description of Osmond, 'No career, no name, no position, no fortune, no past, no future, no anything' (PL 214), is equally true of herself, for she has also accepted a genteel stagnation rather than reject the values of the class she aspires to.

Henrietta Stackpole, on the other hand, like Isabel, has no 'sympathy with inanimate objects' (PL 161), preferring instead an ideal based on human community and the relations between people. Henrietta treasures her talents for, like Serena, her labour is her property. She comes from a poverty-stricken background and has seized the opportunities offered to the New Woman to enter the public world of the workplace. Isabel esteems her 'courage, energy and good humour', for Henrietta is 'without parents and without property' (PL 70), yet manages to earn enough not only to support herself, but also the children of her widowed sister. When Henrietta first hears of Isabel's inheritance she sees it as a problem because, as she accurately predicts, it will isolate her within those European social conventions she despises: 'Your newly acquired thousands will shut you up more and more to the society of a few selfish and heartless people' (PL 238). Mrs Touchett also sees wealth as marking social boundaries, creating distinctions; however, she approves of the fact that 'property erects a kind of barrier. You can do a great many things if you're rich which would be severely criticised if you were poor'. (PL 242). Although Henrietta also inherits a fortune from Ralph she, unlike Isabel, invests it in herself. Ralph's bequest of his extensive library of 'many rare and valuable books' is portable property she puts to use: as Mrs Touchett explains, 'as she can't carry it about the world in her trunk he recommends her to sell it at auction' (PL 618). (As we have seen, Mrs Touchett is well-practiced in raising money on dead men's property.) Henrietta invests this inheritance in establishing her own newspaper and, despite her plans to marry Mr Bantling, she has the New Woman's belief in herself and her rights to employment.

In what appears to be a reversal of the advances of feminism, Isabel values the fortune left to her by her uncle only to the extent that she can give it away. Yet she is as prone to the attractions of gender reversal as James's more overtly feminist characters. When she marries she experiences 'the happiness of a woman who felt that she was a contributor, that she came with charged hands … . At bottom her money had been a burden, had been on her mind, which was filled with the desire to transfer the weight of it to some more prepared receptacle' (PL 458). This renunciation, however, far from being an act of feminine submission, appears to be the price that Isabel is prepared to pay to effect a gender reversal: she *provides* while Osmond becomes a *receptacle*. Isabel is, of course, deceived into thinking that Osmond lacks masculine assertion when he states, in the manner of the feminine woman, that he wants 'to be as quiet as possible ... not to strive or struggle. To resign myself. To be content with little' (PL 288–9). Fooled into viewing him as feminized, Isabel revels in the idea of owning him as her property: 'the subtlest-manly organism she had ever known had become her own' (PL 459). Yet, it later becomes evident that Merle has once 'owned' Osmond and now 'bequeaths' him to Isabel. The latter also desires to reverse gender roles and play the part of a man by acquiring an objectified husband through the power of her money. As Denis Flannery has argued, Isabel, Serena and Osmond 'have their gendering open to question. For James's novel, the making of gender is a very open and reversible process'.[43] Isabel's failure to interpret Osmond correctly, to see that his adoption of a passivity associated with femininity actually hides a patriarchal tendency to reify women, leads to her profound unease about human–object relationships generally. From her early dismissal of things as unimportant, she moves into a Dickensian nightmare where objects 'show for conscious things, watching her trouble with grotesque grimaces' (PL 604).

Isabel has an early intimation of the danger of confiding in her new friend Serena, feeling 'as if she had given to a comparative stranger the key to her cabinet of jewels. These spiritual gems were the only ones of any magnitude that Isabel possessed, but there was all the greater reason for their being carefully guarded' (PL 208). Serena Merle is a penetrating woman in all senses of the word. Indeed, Flannery has noted that the word 'merle' appears in Oscar Wilde's *Teleny* as an Italian slang word for 'penis'.[44] In another example of James's tendency to play with gender categorizations, the phallic connotations of the key are ironized when Ralph Touchett also believes 'he had keys in his pocket' to access Isabel, although 'he had a conviction that none of them would fit' (PL 81). However, Serena Merle's key not only 'fits' Isabel but is one of a bunch of many, for Isabel also believes that her new friend has 'somewhere in the capacious pocket of her genial memory ... the key to Henrietta's value' (PL 211). The key and the pocket, suggesting both phallus and vagina, indicate the ambiguity of Merle's gender identity, a topic which has been perceptively discussed by Flannery. Yet Isabel, who misreads Osmond, also fails to read these early signs of Serena's capacity to control locks and keys and she becomes caught in what the Countess Gemini calls the 'steel trap' of her marriage (PL 384), while Ralph views her as being 'put in a cage' (PL 368).

Adrian Poole has referred to James's 'recurrent focus in the material structures to which his writing gives such close attention', namely his 'images of houses, rooms, doors, windows and balconies'; he goes on to add that this is part of James's interest in boundaries.[45] The caging of Isabel is a direct result of her ownership of property (Osmond would not be interested in her if she had no money) and her own inability to cross the boundary line of Victorian femininity. Poole refers to

---

[43]   Flannery, p. 32.

[44]   Ibid., p. 28. James may, of course, have been aware of this usage.

[45]   Adrian Poole, *Henry James* (Hemel Hempsted and London: Harvester Wheatsheaf, 1991), p. 28.

the ways in which boundary lines are fetishized in *The Portrait of a Lady* where 'intense anxieties and desires affix themselves to bolts, keys, locks and knockers'.[46] These anxieties and desires encourage a reading of the novel which relates Isabel to the physically imprisoned heroines of traditional gothic fiction. The issues of imprisonment and freedom for women, along with the examination of women with property and women as property, themes which surface in the gothic eroticism of *The Portrait of a Lady*, are also developed in James's novella *The Aspern Papers*, a gothic tale of violence and grotesquerie which explores both the vulnerability and the strength of women who possess desirable personal property. It also focuses on the sexual aspects of such property, in this instance a woman's love letters. While Isabel remains trapped in the cage of feminine propriety, Juliana and Tina Bordereau, the female protagonists of *The Aspern Papers*, unexpectedly find the door of their cage open.

Wild Dreams of Possession: *The Aspern Papers*

In 1865, six years before the publication of his first novel, James possessed himself of a locket belonging to the seventeen-year-old Lilla Cabot. She recorded the story of the 'theft', a story which is worth quoting in full:

> I was staying with Aunt Anna Lowell and was going to Harvard Square to post some letters after supper in late May. I heard steps running after me and H.J. asked if he might go with me. After posting the letters I said goodnight as I had to go to my cousin's for a locket I had left there the night before. He proposed that I sh'ld. [sic] let him go with me and go for a walk afterwards. I got my locket and dropped it when he picked it up and gave it to me. I was a shy girl and feeling embarrassed by his man of the world manner and by knowing he was 'an author' I accidentally dropped it again and this time he picked it up and put it in his pocket and said it was the will of Providence he sh'ld always keep it. I had the dignity of shy youth and said nothing meaning to ask for it again when he took me home from our walk but we went to the top of a hill to see a view he knew of and he talked so interestingly that we did not get home till 10.30 and I hurried into the house and forgot the locket till the next morning when I wrote him a stiff little note asking him to give my locket to the bearer and finding it very stiff and prudish I added a P.S. 'Did you see Miss Poke's poem in the Cambridge Chronicle this morning called the "Rape of the Locket"'. This is his reply and I kept it because I knew he was *an Author*! My brother who was my messenger … said 'Well Lilla I never knew a man take so long to write a short note'.[47]

James's carefully thought-out reply to Lilla's 'stiff' note was:

> I had of course wildly dreamed of keeping, wearing and cherishing your locket – but I must part from it just as I'm getting used to it – In sterner truth I had quite

---

46   Ibid., p. 29.
47   Quoted in Horne, pp. 6–7.

forgotten having taken it – it was sojourning sweetly in my waistcoat pocket, just over my heart, when your note was handed to me.[48]

The flirtatious tone, along with the hint of transvestism suggested by his 'wild dream' of wearing Lilla's locket (suggesting Charlotte's surreptitious wearing of 'inappropriate' jewellery in 'Paste'), emphasizes the playful contradictions he presents in this carefully phrased letter, whereby he implies that desire motivated both the theft of the locket and his 'wild dream' of keeping it, at the same time that he had forgotten it.[49] The loss of her locket renders Lilla both anxious and sarcastic (there was, of course, no poem by Miss Poke in the *Cambridge Chronicle*). James's teasing tone, his condescension and the trickery suggested by his sleight of hand and slippery language are the sorts of behaviour traditionally suffered by teenage girls from men five years their senior. However, the juxtaposition of desire and deceit in relation to a woman's portable property is here a playful version of the desire and deceit which so often emerges in relation to women's possessions in his fiction. The narrator of *The Aspern Papers* adopts a similar linguistic slipperiness in his 'wild dream' of appropriating an elderly woman's intimate property: her letters from her dead lover, the poet Aspern. Adopting a '*nom de guerre*' for his attack,[50] the narrator justifies his obsessive quest for the papers by arguing that Aspern is the 'property' of the human race (AP 87), although actually his main motive for appropriating the letters is an emotional one based on his own romanticized image of the dead poet, his wish to have the Aspern relics 'sojourning sweetly' in his possession.

The Aspern Papers echoes *Great Expectations* in its depiction of the woman of property, for James focuses on a disabled elderly woman, Juliana Bordereau, who undergoes a self-imposed imprisonment in a deteriorating house with a younger female companion, her niece, Tina. The folk tale qualities of *Great Expectations* are also evident, for as Millicent Bell has indicated of James's novella, 'the questing hero strives to penetrate a stronghold, a moated castle, in order to seize a treasure. The guardian of the castle is ancient and formidable, possessed of dark powers'.[51] Unlike Pip, however, who hopes that the young Estella is destined to become his bride, the unnamed first-person narrator of *The Aspern Papers* is actually horrified to find that Juliana offers Tina to him in exchange for the letters. In both stories, the property-owning older woman is presented by the male narrator as a grotesque figure trapped in an equivocal social position: Miss Havisham is a bride who will never marry, while Juliana was a mistress who never married. Juliana's position, however, is extremely ambiguous for she is a spinster placed in the position of

---

[48]   Reprinted in Horne, p. 7.

[49]   Constance Woolson noted that James wore 'six rings on one hand', a sign of his interest in the display of personal property. See Edel, *Life*, vol. 1, p. 704.

[50]   Henry James, *The Turn of the Screw and The Aspern Papers*, Anthony Curtis (ed.) (London: Penguin, 1986), p. 52. Further references will be cited in the text following the abbreviation 'AP'.

[51]   Millicent Bell, *Meaning in Henry James* (Cambridge: Harvard University Press, 1991), p. 203.

Aspern's widow; ostensibly Tina's aunt, there is a strong implication that she may actually be her mother (Aspern being Tina's father); she lives in penury in a big Venetian palace, practicing 'self-effacement' in a 'city of exhibition' (AP 48); she possesses valuable relics, *disjecti membra poetae*, and is herself a 'relic' (AP 60); and, like Osmond and Merle, she was born an American, but her long sojourn in Europe has meant she has lost 'all national quality' (AP 45). As the narrator awakens her awareness of the marketability of her spare rooms, garden and (importantly) her relics, Juliana moves from being a faded relic from the past towards a self-assertion associated with the New Woman when she discovers her skills as a financial negotiator. Katherine Snyder argues that both Juliana and Tina become New Women and that Tina's 'choice of non-marriage marks her as belonging to a later generation of New Woman than Juliana'.[52] This point is also made by Joseph Church, who sees Tina at the end of the narrative as 'in possession of the man's wealth ... [she] has begun to be mobile, to circulate', in other words to attain some status and freedom.[53] Here, James depicts the female possessor of property as enabled to do things usually associated with men.

The Aspern Papers and *The Spoils of Poynton*, both depicting women's personal property under threat from men, originated in accounts James heard of actual women. While the reporting of a Scottish widow's dispossession formed the basis of the later novel, the idea for *The Aspern Papers* (first recorded in James's notebook in 1887) came from an account of an American 'Shelley-worshipper', Captain Silsbee, who tried to appropriate the papers of the aged Claire Clairmont, Byron's former mistress.[54] An old woman dying in isolation in Florence with her middle-aged niece acting as her housekeeper, Claire Clairmont's power to retain possession of her letters from Byron and Shelley seemed to be negligible. Yet on her death the papers were transferred to her niece, Pauline Clairmont, who made it clear to Silsbee that only by marrying her could he gain possession of them. The 'price' of the papers seemed too high and he swiftly withdrew from the field. The 'picture of two faded, queer, poor and discredited old English women – living into a strange generation, in their musty corner of a foreign town – with these illustrious letters their most precious possession' was particularly significant for James, for here was an example of a woman proposing marriage to a man, a reversal of traditional gender roles brought about by her belief in the power of her possessions.[55]

Claire Clairmont was reputed to have had an affair with Shelley in 1814 when she was sixteen years old and she became Byron's mistress two years later, giving birth to his daughter Allegra in January 1817. Allegra was placed in a convent by her father where she died in April 1822. These years of wild adolescent

[52]   Katherine V. Snyder, *Bachelors, Manhood and the Novel, 1850–1925* (Cambridge: Cambridge University Press, 1999), p. 132.

[53]   Joseph Church, 'Writing and the Dispossession of the Woman in *The Aspern Papers*', *American Imago*, 47:1 (Spring 1990): 30.

[54]   James, *Notebooks*, p. 71.

[55]   Ibid., p. 72.

freedom were followed by Clairmont's lifetime of respectable employment in Europe as that archetypal Jamesian figure, a 'faded, queer, poor' governess and paid companion.[56] Clearly, economic vulnerability was her lot in life. Her most 'precious possession', in James's view, originated from her sexual liaisons with Byron and Shelley, as though she were a prostitute 'paid' with 'papers' in the form of letters; not the usual paper currency, but unique texts.[57] However, the publication of the letters would remind the world of her discreditable youth; so, in gaining credit financially she would lose the credit of respectability slowly gained over the years. James represents the paradoxical nature of Claire Clairmont's credit in Juliana Bordereau's similar inability to profit from her lover's texts. As her niece states, 'she lived on them!' (AP 135) as emotive relics from her youth; yet ironically she was unable to 'live on them' in financial terms because once in the public realm as commodities the letters would expose her. Mrs Prest tells the narrator that the Misses Bordereau 'live on nothing, for they've nothing to live on' (AP 50), their only property cannot be used. As J. Hillis Miller has shown, the narrator is also trapped within the same paradox, for if he was

> [m]arried to Tina, the narrator would have had a husband's obligation to keep his wife's family secrets. He cannot have the papers if he remains an outsider, so cannot publish them. He can have them if he becomes an insider, but then he cannot publish them. He will have incurred a family duty that will far outweigh his responsibility as a literary historian. Either way he will be baulked.[58]

Juliana's property is related to her sexuality, linked to her 'illicit' relationship with Aspern and, as so often in James's work, sexualized property is associated with violence. The narrator's desire for the letters is imaged in terms of his preparedness to commit violation and theft: he appears to feel himself justified when he plans to 'pounce on her possessions and ransack her drawers' (AP 60). (In the nineteenth century one of the meanings of 'ransack' was to violate a woman.)[59] He imagines her bedroom with 'some battered box that was shoved under the bed' (AP 112) and attempts to penetrate visually Juliana's most private spaces:

> None the less I turned an eye on every article of furniture, on every conceivable cover for a hoard, and noticed that there were half a dozen things with drawers, and in particular a tall old secretary with brass ornaments of the style of the Empire – a receptacle somewhat infirm but still capable of keeping rare secrets. (AP 112)

---

[56]   Jeremy Tambling, *Henry James* (Basingstoke: Macmillan, 2000), p. 78.

[57]   James, *Notebooks*, p. 72.

[58]   J. Hillis Miller, *Literature as Conduct: Speech Acts in Henry James* (New York: Fordham University Press, 2005), p. 25.

[59]   Church, p. 33.

His penetration, although visual, is nevertheless disturbing, even to himself, for his desire is to get close to Jeffrey Aspern. Penetrating a woman's 'secret' spaces is out of character, for he cannot imagine himself 'in any such box' as a heterosexual relationship (AP 48). Indeed, as we have seen, penetration is not for James an activity associated with men, and it is significant that the narrator ultimately fails to penetrate Juliana's secret. When he later 'turn[s]' his eyes 'once more all over the room, rummaging with them the closets, the chests of drawers, the tables', looking for which 'receptacle to try first', he realizes that his behaviour is 'well-nigh indecent'(AP 116). As Juliana lies dying, the narrator does enter her room and considers breaking into the secretary desk; he justifies his crime by believing that Juliana's room 'looked like the dressing-room of an old actress' (AP 116), as though women who exist beyond the pale of respectability cannot expect the consideration and legal protection accorded to legitimate wives. As with Mrs Prime, the former actress in 'Paste', the social situation, as well as the possessions, of a woman 'with a past' was precarious.

Juliana seems to the narrator to possess only the Aspern relics, the letters and the portrait of the poet painted by her father, for when he first enters her home he is surprised that:

> Miss Bordereau appeared not to have picked up or have inherited many objects of importance. There was no enviable *bric-à-brac*, with its provoking legend of cheapness, in the room in which I had seen her. Such a fact as that suggested bareness … . (AP 77)

He thinks that Juliana and her niece 'are worse off than Carmelite nuns in their cells' (AP 80–81); yet this male evaluation of what is valuable may be very far removed from what the two women prize. Juliana's furniture, such as her 'queer superannuated coffer, of painted wood, with elaborate handles … [which] would have made a strange figure arriving at a modern hotel' (AP 116) and her 'infirm' Empire-style 'old secretary' (AP 112), could be as important to her as her Aspern relics. James illustrates the fluid boundaries between valuable property and rubbish; what in one context can be 'tattered papers' (AP 138) can in another be 'treasure' (AP 140). When he came to revise *The Aspern Papers* for the 1908 New York edition he emphasized 'the papers [as] … palpable or visible objects ("material", "documents", "literary remains", "relics and tokens", "tangible objects", "mementoes", "spoils" etc.)', as though to give weight to the texts, to emphasize their solidity.[60] The papers are key examples of personal property; as texts written as a form of communication between two people they did not originate as commodities, yet by preserving them over the years, Juliana has transformed them in the narrator's view into commodities to be bartered for.

The Aspern Papers, then, offers an exploration of the differences between male and female forms of possession. Juliana's possession of the Aspern relics is intensely private, so much so that all of the assumptions made by the narrator

---

[60]   Bell, p. 194.

and Tina that she cherishes her love for Aspern are pure speculation, for there is no evidence to suggest that she still feels anything towards her dead lover; only that she values his texts, which is, of course, a very different matter. Tambling has argued a similar point, suggesting that Juliana 'is not wholly in thrall to [her] past ... there is a concealed aggression towards it, and its patriarchal implications'.[61] The narrator, on the other hand, makes his desire for the relics, his obsession with the past, and his love for Aspern very public. Not only does he communicate his desires to his accomplices, Mrs Prest and John Cumnor, but *The Aspern Papers* itself offers a public declaration, even confession, of the ways in which his desire prompts him to deceive. The narrator views property in a traditional, patriarchal way, as something which is transferred from man to man, bypassing women altogether. Although he has never even seen the letters, he asks himself, 'Was I still in time to save *my* goods?' (AP 140), as though he considers the women to have no right of possession. The narrator presumed that the Aspern relics will make his 'life continuous, in a fashion, with the illustrious life they had touched at the other end' (AP 73). This need to make a straightforward connection between the Aspern-worshipper and the dead Aspern himself is disrupted by two women, another signal in James fiction of the New Woman's ability to disrupt patriarchal traditions.

Juliana and Tina outmanoeuvre the narrator, their tactics resembling those of Victorian women who subverted the laws of coverture meant to contain them.[62] Coverture, meant to deprive married women of legal autonomy, is ironically invoked by Tina when she proposes marriage to the narrator, presenting Juliana's argument that the papers he so desires will legally become his own property once he marries. She states: 'Anything that's mine would be yours, and you could do what you like. I shouldn't be able to prevent you – and you'd have no responsibility' (AP 135). Yet because he initially rejects her offer, Tina then exercises the ultimate right of the property owner: to destroy her own property. James demonstrates that the women, far from being vulnerable, actually develop financial acumen, acquiring from the narrator the most liquid forms of portable property, money and gold, without giving anything in exchange. Tina takes the 'bag of chamois leather' from him 'with extreme solemnity ... weighing the money in her two palms' (AP 71), fully appreciating the tangibility of the property she receives. This mercenary quality is noted by the narrator, who repeatedly states his sense of unease that the women should 'so constantly bring the pecuniary question back' (AP 67).

Dennis Foster has seen Juliana as 'the old con' who recognizes in the narrator 'a perversity he would not acknowledge, and took him for most of what he was worth'.[63] This view is supported by the way Juliana teases the narrator with Aspern's portrait; she 'sport[s] with' him (AP 109) as she draws 'out of her pocket with an embarrassed hand a small object wrapped in crumpled white paper' (AP 108),

---

[61]   Tambling, p. 91.

[62]   Neither Tina nor Juliana is bound by the rules of coverture, however.

[63]   Dennis Foster, *Sublime Enjoyment: On the Perverse Motive in American Literature* (Cambridge: Cambridge University Press, 1997), p. 80.

to 'dangle it before [his] eyes and put a prohibitive price on it' (AP 109). Is her hand 'embarrassed'? Or is this the perverse interpretation imposed by a narrator prone to an excess of fetishism in relation to 'Aspern' objects? Indeed, the 'flushed' narrator exposes his own excitement when he states: 'I possessed myself of it with fingers of which I could only hope that they didn't betray the intensity of their clutch' (AP 108). As Rowe has stated, '*The Aspern Papers* involves a critique of the ways that *literature* may be said to serve the phallocentrism of patriarchal culture'.[64] The portrait stands for male literary culture and its traditions, and Juliana's teasing use of this object emphasizes James's interest in women's ability to disrupt patriarchy. The narrator wants to wrest Aspern and male literary culture from the possession of women, and Juliana's disruption resonates with the revolutionary effects of the 'female elbow' James would refer to later in his essay 'The Future of the Novel'.

Like Dickens and Eliot, James is also fascinated by women's illegitimate transmission of property. The Aspern relics become Tina's property, although Juliana made no will. Tina acts as the owner of this property for she gives the narrator the portrait of Aspern (AP 133) and burns the papers. Both of these actions, giving and destroying, signify her ownership and indicate a system of property transmission between women that frustrates the narrator's sense of what is 'proper'. Indeed, he later sends Tina 'the price of the portrait of Jeffrey Aspern, a larger sum of money than I had hoped to be able to gather for her, writing to her that I had sold the picture, she kept it with thanks' (AP 142). This is not just an act to assuage his guilt at having taken the portrait when she believed that this was the first instalment of his 'payment' for marrying her, but is also a way of excluding women from the bond he believes he has forged between himself and Aspern: by paying Tina off, thus clearing his 'debt', he rids himself of this unwelcome third party. However, in financial terms, Juliana and Tina have been able to make strategic investments in the narrator by means of the property he desires but never sees. Indeed, their tactics are even more astute (the narrator is 'awestricken by the astuteness' [AP 136] of Tina as she makes her proposal) if, as some critics believe, the papers never existed in the first place. It is, of course, equally feasible that the papers may have continued to exist and that Tina only told the narrator she had burned them as a way of getting rid of him. Like the fate of the priceless *objets d'art* in *The Spoils of Poynton*, the letters are never made explicit to the reader and there remains a question mark over whether they are actually destroyed.

Neither the female system of property transmission (illegitimate, but nonetheless effective) developed in *The Aspern Papers* nor the bequest based on the ability to appreciate aesthetically made later in *The Spoils of Poynton*, is represented by James as a utopian alternative to patriarchy, for he appears unable to represent women's possession as uninterrupted. Indeed, the relationships between the older and younger women in each story are not idealized. Tina says of Juliana, 'I've no control of her .... It's she who controls me' (AP 100), even to the extent of having no control over her own income (AP 102). *The Spoils of Poynton*, as we

---

64   Rowe, p. 114; emphasis in the original.

will see, further complicates the notion of female property transmission, focusing on a battle between two women for 'spoils' (that is, beautiful antiques) juxtaposed with a communion between two women based on an appreciation of the 'spoils'. The male owner of the property is marginalized. This novel, as we will see in the following section, affords James an opportunity to continue his exploration of the links between property, violence and eroticism; however, he also makes a more direct engagement with the figure of the New Woman.

Cruel English Customs: *The Spoils of Poynton*

The Spoils of Poynton depicts two New Women, the militant Adela Gereth, who was young in the 1850s, when the feminist campaign for the reform of the married women's property laws began in earnest, and Mona Brigstock, whose name echoes that of the feminist novelist, Mona Caird, the author of 'Marriage', a controversial article linking post-Reformation marriage with the bourgeois marketplace.[65] James's exploration of the issue of women's social and financial independence in his 1897 novel was, then, particularly topical, for here he focuses on militant New Women prepared to fight for property. Although Poole has argued that the novel exposes the fact 'that all property is itself a fiction', this view would not have consoled those women for whom property ownership was quite literally a fiction or fantasy under English law, and James emphasizes this point in his representation of a widow who, because of 'the cruel English custom' of primogeniture which results in the 'expropriation' of widows (SP 9), loses possession of the collection of antiques and the home she thought she owned.[66] Poole, however, rightly suggests that *The Spoils of Poynton* is not so much about the concept of property rights as an exploration of the ways in which identity is bound up in relationships with the material world.

Macleod, in her discussion of the female collector, has argued that there was a 'muted dialectic between women and their prized possessions [which] furthered their development as autonomous individuals and sparked a dynamic charge that propelled them out of their cloistered interiors into an engagement with public life'.[67] Adela Gereth may be an aggressive collector displaying many features in common with the New Woman, but she is nonetheless trapped in the past, her old-fashioned husband makes a will which does not allow her to take advantage of the reformed property laws, and she is disinclined to enter public life. The younger woman Mona, by contrast, is intent on her rights, a New Woman at home in *fin-de-siècle* culture. Set against these warrior women is Fleda Vetch, whose poverty, vulnerability and propensity for renunciation align her with the traditional Victorian heroine. While at first it appears that James validates a

---

[65] Mona Caird, 'Marriage' (1888), reprinted in Ledger and Luckhurst, pp. 77–80.

[66] See Poole, p. 91.

[67] Macleod, p. 3.

traditional feminine renunciation of property, the novel actually does a great deal to complicate the issue of human–object relations and to some extent valorizes the actions of the penetrating New Woman.

What makes *The Spoils of Poynton* unsettling, however, is that it sidelines the processes of patriarchy that lead to women's expropriation in order to focus on aggression between women. Whereas in *Portrait* and *The Aspern Papers* women are presented as sharing the same interests (even if Isabel and Madame Merle eventually part in hostility, both share a need to curb Osmond's power and, in the later text, Tina does carry out Juliana's plot to control the narrator), the battle between Mrs Gereth and Mona is just that, a crude battle for possession. The novel's plot is based on a 'squabble' between Mrs Gereth, temporarily placed as mistress of the beautiful Jacobean country house Poynton and its collection of *objets d'art*, and her son's fiancée, Mona Brigstock, who believes that the house and its treasures will be hers on her marriage (SP 67). Yet Poynton and its contents have hitherto belonged to men: first to Mrs Gereth's husband, and when he dies to her son Owen, whose very name suggests his status as the owner of the property. *The Spoils of Poynton* is unsettling firstly because James is reluctant to represent the conflict over property as a case of female dispossession brought about by a husband privileging his son at his wife's expense; and secondly, because the penniless heroine, Fleda Vetch, works tirelessly to help the propertied Owen retain possession of the things he legally, but by no means morally, owns. By doing this, Fleda helps to bring about the dispossession of her friend, whose life centres on the collection of antiques she created but never legally owned. The novel's conflict, then, is deflected from an exposé of women's exclusion from property ownership onto a battle between women for 'spoils', that is, Poynton and its antiques. The problem of primogeniture is elided. What follows is an attempt to account for this elision, which is not, I believe, a result of James's opposition to feminism (after all, he deplored the 'cruel system' of patriarchal custom), but his desire to turn the spotlight on women, to create a property drama where women take the centre stage and through which he can explore the human–object boundary as a sexually inflected one.

My allusions to the theatre are inspired by James's use of theatrical excess in the novel; the melodramatic potential of a widow legally 'robbed' of her cherished possessions by both her husband and son is matched by a comedy of errors based on the farcical shifting about the stage of the 'properties' as Mrs Gereth manoeuvres to retain possession of her collection. James even refers directly to the theatre when he describes a servant's arrival in the garden as the entrance of 'an actress in the drama', with Fleda watching Mrs Gereth 'across the footlights' (SP 55). He also uses stock melodramatic scenes, such as when Mrs Gereth falls on her knees before Fleda and asks her to 'save' her son (SP 86–7). The theatrical qualities of *The Spoils of Poynton* may owe something to Balzac's 1847 novel, *Le Cousin Pons*, which vacillates between farce and sentimental melodrama in its depiction of an obsessive collector's beloved possessions under threat.[68] However, many critics have linked the theatrical qualities of *Spoils* to James's ambitions to succeed as a playwright. The dramatic potential of a widow's dispossession and her subsequent fight to retain her cherished 'old things' has led Peter Brooks to argue that the novel 'stands at the inception of the line of James's most theatrical fiction, and its climactic scenes convey a sense of drawing-room melodrama at its best'.[69] This theatricality also serves to highlight the novel's experimental qualities, introducing the high level of ambiguity that came to characterize James's late fiction. Many have identified the period between 1890 and 1896 as a turning point in his career, a turn away from the novel to the theatre and, defeated, a turn back again. The period has variously been termed 'the treacherous years', the 'experimental period' and 'the most troubled decade in James's life'.[70] It also released a new quality in James: bawdy. As Michèle Mendelssohn has argued, 'The James we encounter in the mid-1890s is a noticeably freer and, at times, wittily bawdy man'.[71] *Spoils*, then, is not only melodramatic and farcical, morally ambiguous and linguistically playful, but also has its bawdy moments. Certainly Kenneth Graham identifies it as ushering in a 'new strangeness' in James's work and part of this 'strangeness' depends upon the novel's intensification of ambiguity.[72] A close reading of the novel suggests that Fleda and Adela have erotic relationships with *objets d'art*; however, James's equivocation means that we can never be sure if this is just our own dirty reading of an innocent pastime.

Another of this novel's 'strange' qualities is that the author's attack on the 'cruel' custom of primogeniture should result in the representation of a widow dispossessed by a husband who is described as 'sympathetic and generous' (SP 7) while she herself is 'despoiled' (SP 24). This demonization of the widow is surprising in relation to the 'germ' of the novel, which James describes in his 1908 Preface

---

[68]   Wendy Graham in 'A Narrative History of Class Consciousness', *boundary 2*, 15, (Autumn/Winter, 1986–87): 60 sees *The Spoils of Poynton* as the closest James comes to farce.

[69]   Peter Brooks, *The Melodramatic Imagination: Balzac, Henry James, Melodrama and the Mode of Excess* (New Haven and London: Yale University Press, 1976), p. 162. See also Joseph Litvak, *Caught in the Act: Theatricality in the Nineteenth-Century English Novel* (Berkeley: University of California Press, 1992) for a perceptive discussion of the role of theatricality in James's work.

[70]   See Leon Edel, *The Life of Henry James: The Treacherous Years* (Philadelphia: J.B. Lippincott, 1969); David Lodge, *Author, Author* (London: Faber, 2004); Jean Frantz Blackall, 'The Experimental Period' in Daniel Mark Fogel (ed.), *A Companion to Henry James Studies* (Westport & London: Greenwood Press, 1993), pp. 147–78; and Kenneth Graham, *Henry James: The Drama of Fulfilment: An Approach to the Novels* (Oxford: Clarendon Press, 1975).

[71]   Michèle Mendelssohn, *Henry James, Oscar Wilde and Aesthetic Culture* (Edinburgh: Edinburgh University Press, 2007), p. 206.

[72]   Kenneth Graham, *Henry James: A Literary Life* (Basingstoke: Macmillan, 1995), p. 104.

to the New York edition as (significantly) penetrating him like a 'virus' when he heard of a widow in Scotland who was prosecuted by her son when he inherited the family home because she retained possession of her collection of fine furniture and *objets d'art*.[73] Although this 'germ' leads ultimately to the representation of a legally helpless woman dispossessed by men, James refuses to condemn either husband or son, for Mr Gereth, despite bequeathing his property to Owen (and he is under no obligation to do so), remains blameless.[74] Even Mrs Gereth, inexplicably, never blames her husband for the dispossession he inflicted upon her; indeed she remembers him for his 'sympathy and generosity, his knowledge and love', seeing their marriage was one of 'perfect accord' (SP 7). However, her young friend Fleda is amazed by the way an 'amiable' man can so impoverish his wife (SP 9). Yet, despite Mr Gereth's knowledge of his wife's passion for Poynton and the antiques she shaped into a 'complete work of art' (SP 7), he based his will on the custom of primogeniture, assuming that his widow 'would settle questions with her son, and that he could depend on Owen's affection and Owen's fairness' (SP 9). Owen, however, is incapable of understanding his parents' love of beautiful things, and easily bullied by his fiancée, Mona Brigstock, who believes that she can wrest Poynton and its things from the formidable Adela Gereth to possess them for herself.

Yet Adela's desire for property is not based on a love of possession but is purely a matter of aesthetics and, unlike the New Woman, she does not attempt to make a political argument for her rights to Poynton and its treasures. Instead she condemns her son because 'he had never had the least imagination' about the collection (SP 32); for Owen only thinks it's 'awfully valuable' (SP 59). Mona makes it a condition of her marriage settlement that if she doesn't possess the spoils, she won't marry Owen. Yet Mrs Gereth transcends such materialism, caring 'nothing for mere possession. She thought solely and incorruptibly of what was best for the objects themselves' (SP 147). This privileging of art objects is problematized in the novel, however, because James continually emphasizes the link between aesthetic perfection and reification. Beauty seems to be dead; indeed there is something ominous in the fact that Mrs Gereth keeps her treasures within a 'museum' wrapped in 'linen shrouds' (SP 15), foreshadowing their doom when Poynton and its treasures are finally destroyed by fire.

James contrasts the aggressive, acquisitive New Woman, Mona, with that representative of traditional femininity, Fleda, who is ill prepared for survival in the modern world. As the heroine of the novel, it is from her point of view that we see the battle between Mrs Gereth and Mona played out, and her perception

---

[73]   See Peter Betjemann, 'Henry James' Shop Talk: *The Spoils of Poynton* and the Language of Artisanship', *American Literary Realism*, 40:3 (Spring 2008): 213 for a discussion of the novel's links with the objects in the Wallace collection.

[74]   Brown, in *A Sense of Things*, presumes that 'English law dictat[es] the ownership of the spoils' (p. 146); however, James makes it clear that Mr Gereth was free to dispose of his property as he wished.

of Owen as a victim in need of help is crucial in deflecting attention from his role as the property owner. Fleda's poverty, virtual orphanhood (her mother is dead and her father is a precursor of the irresponsible and dissolute Lionel Croy in *The Wings of the Dove*), her lack of aggression and self-assertion, along with her failure to make a career as an artist, align her with Tina in *The Aspern Papers*, for both resemble the dependent, vulnerable, heroines of nineteenth-century fiction who accept renunciation as women's lot in life. Fleda's keynote throughout the novel is failure: failure to make a career, failure to reconcile Mrs Gereth and her son, failure to marry Owen, failure to achieve happiness for herself, and even failure to possess the gift of the Maltese cross that Owen offers to her after his marriage to Mona. Although she seems to be an old-fashioned heroine in the age of the New Woman, Fleda does not even gain the eventual settlement which Dickens and Eliot confer on their impoverished heroines. She is often presented as 'little' (SP 44, 67, 69 and 72), a 'poor child' (SP 3), 'quiet as a mouse' and 'a lonely fly' (SP 98), physically shadowy and insubstantial in comparison to Mona, the 'massive maiden' who is 'a magnificent dead weight' (SP 137). Fleda, a passive onlooker in the battle for the 'spoils', is dominated by Mrs Gereth, who is imaged as a warrior engaged in a 'campaign' (SP 100) to retain her treasures, 'using such weapons as she could pick up' (SP 94).

As we have seen, James consistently represents property as necessitating violence. Yet in one of the novel's many contradictions the weakened, passive, objectified Owen, surrounded by female warriors battling for his *objets d'art*, is relegated to 'the one monstrosity of Poynton', a room decorated with 'an array of arms of aggression and castigation … eighteen rifles and forty whips' (SP 39). Although Owen on his father's death inherits a position as the new patriarch of Poynton, he is nevertheless rendered a passive object, on a par with the 'things' themselves, coerced into acting according to the instructions of Mona in arranging 'for settlements on his wife, he was doing things that would meet the views of the Brigstocks' (SP 39). Indeed, if James is determined that no blame be levelled against Owen or his father, he is equally determined to leave the parameters of women's property rights as vague as possible. Mona's demands for property are met because she is confident about entering upon 'the enjoyment of her rights' (SP 29); however, Mrs Gereth's property rights are extremely ill-defined: 'nothing at Poynton belonged to Mrs Gereth either more or less than anything else. She must either take everything or nothing' (SP 49). Like many of the representations of Victorian women discussed in this book, she simply refuses to recognize the legal system and its definitions of property ownership that control her relationship to the *objets d'art*. When Fleda informs her that Owen intends to resort to legal means to restore his property, Mrs Gereth says dismissively, 'Oh the lawyers!'; Fleda thinking that she 'never looked … so much in possession' (SP 75).

Yet possession is as much an erotic relationship as an issue of legal rights. Adela has a particularly intimate relationship with her collection and images of the fingering of surfaces abound in the novel, reinforcing the fetishistic functions of the objects, and suggesting an emotional or erotic investment in pleasurable contact. As Macleod has demonstrated, the touching of *objets d'art* offered a 'creative release' for female collectors who recorded their pleasure in 'touching, stroking and fantasizing over objects that had a special meaning for them'.[75] Adela also knows her antiques intimately: 'in the dark, with a brush of a finger, [she] could tell one from another' (SP 20). Fleda's initiation into the pleasures of her friend's collection takes the form of a series of sexualized encounters with the objects. When Fleda first visits Poynton, the effect of seeing the beautiful things is presented in terms of a sexual initiation:

> [T]he palpitating girl had the full revelation. "*Now* do you know how I feel?" Mrs Gereth asked when in the wondrous hall, three minutes after their arrival, her pretty associate dropped on a seat with a soft gasp and a roll of dilated eyes. The answer came clearly enough, and in the rapture of that first walk through the house Fleda took a prodigious span. She perfectly understood how Mrs Gereth felt – she had understood but meagrely before; and the two women embraced with tears over the tightening of their bond – tears which on the younger one's part were the natural and usual sign of her submission to perfect beauty … . Mrs Gereth left her guest to finger fondly the brasses that Louis Quinze might have thumbed, to sit with Venetian velvets just held in a loving palm … . To give it all up, to die to it – that thought ached in her breast. (SP 13–14)

Both women fall prey to the 'aura' of the antiques, identified by Walter Benjamin in his 1936 essay 'The Work of Art in the Age of Mechanical Reproduction' as the mystical, quasi-religious value conferred on original art objects in the industrial age.[76] The reference to Louis Quinze's thumbs suggests that Fleda and her patroness fetishize the objects by imagining that traces of the magical touch of the King's hand have somehow become part of the object itself. However, the narrator's qualification: 'might have thumbed', indicates that it is only through imagination that the things can possess the non-material qualities of holy relics. Indeed, Mrs Gereth even believes that her objects 'return the touch of [her] hand' (SP 20), suggesting that she enjoys the sort of reciprocal relationship that Madame Merle believes she has with her collection. Reciprocal property, as we have seen, can function on many levels. For the child, the doll or the toy can function as a substitute sister, mother or teacher. However, for James's women reciprocal property is almost invariably eroticized, functioning as a lover or autoerotically as a substitute for a body part (as in classic cases of fetishism). Fleda shares this belief in the agency of the objects when she thinks that they 'suffer like chopped limbs' on being transplanted to Adela's dower house, Ricks (SP 53). Fleda's actions on first encountering them, her 'soft gasp', rolling eyes and feelings of 'satiety' and 'dying' (the latter suggesting the metaphor for orgasm), suggest her 'fall' for she has now tasted 'the bitter tree of knowledge' (SP 98). However, although James

---

[75]   Macleod, p. 14.

[76]   Walter Benjamin, 'The Work of Art in the Age of Mechanical Reproduction' in *Illuminations*, Hannah Arendt (ed.) (London: Fontana, 1992), pp. 214–15.

reveals Fleda's relationship to the *objets d'art* as having its perversely erotic, even painful aspects, he also shows, in a language reminiscent of Wordsworth, how the memory of them lives within her imagination: 'they made a company with which solitude was warm' (SP 162).

Clearly, the antiques do not function simply as valuable portable property for either Fleda or Mrs Gereth. As Fotios Sarris has argued, the latter's 'valorization of Poynton' is 'fetishistic in the Marxian sense' because she is unaware of the human labour and social context that brought her 'spoils' into history.[77] The extent of Mrs Gereth's attachment to her 'spoils' is indicated by the levels of physical pain she would undergo to protect them from the 'contamination' of philistine owners. Fleda imagines the police trying to eject her friend from Poynton in terms of 'violence ... a tussle, dishevelment, pushes, scratches, shrieks ... of wounds inflicted and received' (SP 37). As we have seen in *The Portrait of a Lady*, there are distinct echoes of Dickens's representations of an anarchic material world in James's work, particularly the ways in which objects engender reversals in the human–object dyad and the violence that ensues. *The Spoils of Poynton* contains numerous references linking objects and violence, often foregrounding things as agents in the drama. Indeed, Graham considers the novel to mark a 'new zone of absurdist menace and bad dream' in James's work, where things and people uneasily blend into one another.[78]

Merle's likening of herself to an iron pot, 'shockingly chipped and cracked ... I've been cleverly mended; and I try to remain in the cupboard' (PL 214), is replicated in the later 'things' women of *The Spoils of Poynton*, where Mona has a voice 'like the squeeze of a doll's stomach' (SP 11); her eyes are 'blue beads' (SP 16), and her power over Owen is symbolized by her patent-leather shoes, which we are informed 'resembled a man's' (SP 19). However, when she is described as being 'apt at putting down her wonderful patent-leather foot' (SP 62), we find the material of the shoe actually *becomes* the foot itself and it is obvious that for James, Merle's question about the self – 'Where does it begin? Where does it end?' – has not been settled. 'Things' women in James's novels are always in danger of becoming things, feeling 'inappropriate' passions towards things or using things aggressively. James goes on to say of Mona's foot that she is 'prompt with her exercise of the member in question' (SP 62); her patent leather foot, resembling a man's, is a 'member' which serves as a form of phallus for Mona is associated with 'violation' (SP 10). Indeed Adela imagines having to live with her at Poynton as being like having to spend 'the remainder of her days with [the] creature's elbow half-way down her throat' (SP 12); she also fears that Mona's possessions, her 'cheap gimcracks', would be 'thrust in at one at every turn'(SP 21). It is as though portable property in this novel is likely to be used for violent or sexual purposes. Yet Adela herself does not lack a similar source of phallic power, for when Fleda

---

[77]   Fotios Sarris, 'Fetishism in *The Spoils of Poynton*', *Nineteenth-Century Literature*, 51:1 (1996): 56.

[78]   Graham, *Life of Henry James*, p. 126.

sees her boots peeping out from beneath her dress, she is instantly reminded of
Mona (SP 77). Indeed, Mona and Adela, despite the fact that one looks towards
the future and the other is focused on the past, in some ways function as doubles,
both possessing the traditional masculine qualities of aggression and self-assertion,
and each capable of extreme brutality (albeit in different forms). Fleda fears that
her friend is using her as an object to penetrate Owen, when, in another image of
violent oral penetration, she thinks Mrs Gereth is using her to 'thrust down the
fine open mouth' of her son, and is both 'scared and embarrassed' (SP 21) by her
attempts to reverse the sexual roles, feeling 'advertised and offered' when the older
woman alters her hair and dress to make her more attractive to Owen (SP 96). Fleda
also notes Adela's tendency to penetrate metaphorically with her 'strange, almost
maniacal disposition to thrust in everywhere the question of "things"' (SP 16).

Although Mona and Adela share this 'thrusting' tendency, the Brigstocks are
incapable of the sort of imaginative investment made by the novel's aesthetes.
Belonging to the ugly world James associates with commercialism, the Brigstocks's
'hideous home' (SP 12) is characterized by 'imbecilities of decoration' (SP 1);
however, as James indicates, they represent modernity, the inescapable world
of capitalism and industrialism. Although they prefer new things to old, buying
the newest fashions and acting as representatives of marketplace values, they are
aware of the monetary value, even the patina value, of the antiques. The basis
of Mrs Gereth's vulnerability in the face of the Brigstocks and of her ultimate
failure to retain possession of the spoils is her obsession with the past, her desire to
remove goods from circulation and arrest time. Poynton is her 'museum' (SP 147),
a temple devoted to the worship of the past, where no newly made object is
allowed entry. When Adela emerges from her museum she is 'condemned to
wince wherever she turned' for she 'could not leave her own house without peril
of exposure' (SP 7). Yet, as Theodor Adorno has remarked of objects in museums,
they 'are in the process of dying'.[79] Her complaint against Mona becoming the
mistress of Poynton is that she will destroy its dedication to the pre-industrial
past by bringing in 'the maddening relics of Waterbath, the little brackets and
pink vases, the sweepings of bazaars' (SP 12). James suggests that the stoppage
Mrs Gereth aims for is historically impossible.

James's linkage of violence and property ownership in this novel suggests
not only the competitive marketplace of circulating commodities indicative of
industrial capitalism, but also the ruthlessness of the collector. Yet the issue of
labour is also explored in terms of the social and psychological violence inflicted
on the labourer. The only form of property possessed by most people was their
own labour and clearly without other forms of capital James represents his
impoverished and dispossessed women as vulnerable to economic exploitation.
Like many Victorian critics of industrialism, he sees the worker as degraded by
the processes of industrial production. In his Preface he maintains that he intended
to throw 'a sharp light ... on that most modern of our current passions, the fierce

---

[79]   Quoted in Mignon Nixon, 'Dream Dust', *October*, 116 (Spring 2006): 65.

appetite for the upholsterer's and joiner's and brazier's work, the chairs and tables and cabinets and presses, the material odds and ends, of the more labouring ages' (SP xliii). Although James deflates the mysticism of the antiques by *emphasizing* the work that went into them, his reference to the origin of Adela's things in 'the more labouring ages' is revealing, suggesting a belief that people laboured 'more' in the past, as though factory production made labour 'easy'. He privileges the labour of the artist and craftsman above the labour of the factory worker, a view which accords with the values promoted by Ruskin and the Arts and Crafts movement which flourished in the late nineteenth century.[80] Yet he did not fail to be aware of how the exploited industrial worker maintained the rich in idleness and luxury. On a visit to the North of England James wrote to Grace Norton that:

> Yorkshire smoke-country is very ugly and depressing, both as regards the smirched and blackened landscape and the dense and dusky population, who form a not very attractive element in that grand total of labour and poverty on whose enormous base all the luxury and leisure of English country-houses are built up.[81]

In this respect James reveals his awareness of the alienation of workers under capitalism; as Marx states, the machinery of capitalist production is 'alien to [the worker] ... what is more, it seems to him that he has not contributed anything, or even that all this exists despite what he does'.[82] Clearly, Adela's labour in creating Poynton and its things into an aesthetic whole is devalued in the context of capitalist mass production, while the traditional English laws of property simply condone her dispossession. However, under natural law, based on the idea of labour, use and physical contact constituting possession, and in the context of ideas of traditional, pre-industrial working practices, Mrs Gereth (like Mrs Tulliver in *The Mill on the Floss*) is clearly the 'owner' of the products of her own labour. Poynton's collection of art objects is her own creation; she had 'waited for them, worked for them, picked them over, made them worthy of each other and the house, watched, loved them, lived with them' (SP 9). As Mrs Gereth informs Fleda, 'there are things in this house that we almost starved for!' (SP 20). Like another earlier 'things woman', Serena Merle, and Victorian wives before the passing of the Married Women's Property Acts, Adela finds she is not the owner of her own labour.

In a Marxist critique of *The Spoils of Poynton*, Wendy Graham sees the novel as 'a document of reification, a narrative which traces the process by which people lose their self-awareness, identity, through their association with objects and, indeed, come to think of themselves as objects'.[83] Yet the novel is more complicated

---

[80]   See Shearer West, 'The Visual Arts' in *The Cambridge Companion to the Fin de Siècle*, Gail Marshall (ed.) (Cambridge: Cambridge University Press, 2007), pp. 140–41.

[81]   4 January 1879, *Henry James Letters*, vol. 2, p. 209.

[82]   Marx, *Capital*, p. 391.

[83]   Graham, 'A Narrative History', p. 42.

than this suggests. As we have seen, women's objects in nineteenth-century novels tend to be presented as sources of comfort, cherished because they are placed outside the marketplace and its values, used as powerful fetishes and repositories of identity. For a woman such as Mrs Tulliver to acknowledge her daughter's value by referring to her as an item of furniture saved from the wreckage of her lost portable property (MF, 388), or Adela Gereth to see Fleda as 'a scrap of furniture', helping her face her 'abject' future in an empty 'nest' (SP 169–70), is not a loss of self-awareness or a denial of identity, but a way of interpreting human–object relations as fundamentally outside the marketplace and emphasizing the links between different manifestations of love.

Yet a Marxist reading is applicable to the novel in the sense that the labourers, the widow and the spinster, do most of the work and receive the fewest rewards. In this respect they resemble the exploited labourers discussed by Marx when he states: 'the means of production, the material conditions of labour, are not subject to the worker, but it is he who is subject to them: it is capital which employs labour. In this simple manner, this relationship enhances the personification of objects and the reification of people'.[84] Those with capital, the *nouveaux-riches* Brigstocks and the propertied Owen, members of the leisure class, living on capital based on the labour of others, extend their exploitative control over the labour of Mrs Gereth and Fleda. Everything about the Brigstocks speaks of leisure: Waterbath is described as 'a diurnal round of felicity' (SP 25) where the decoration of the home is presented as a leisure-time activity (SP 4). The inhabitants pass the time in sporting activities; Mona runs races and has 'the reflex actions of the custom of sport' (SP 19 and 23). She clearly conforms to the *Cornhill Magazine*'s definition of a New Woman as one who has the 'aggressive air of independence which finds its birth in the length of her stride'.[85] The main characteristic of the Brigstocks, like the Podsnaps, representatives of Victorian capital in Dickens's *Our Mutual Friend*, is their solidity. Mona is a 'massive' presence (SP 4) and 'image of successful immobility' (SP 137), while her fiancé, Owen, is also 'heavy' (SP 4) and has 'idle eyes' (SP 31). His 'business' in London (SP 13) is never explained, but seems to be centred on his club.

In contrast to these 'heavy' representatives of the property-owning class, Fleda and Adela Gereth are the disadvantaged labourers. Fleda is first introduced as having trained to be an artist, 'arming herself for the battle of life by a course with an impressionist painter. She was determined to work' (SP 8). Indeed, like Serena Merle and Henrietta Stackpole, her labour is her only property. While this suggests Fleda has something in common with the New Woman, she readily abandons her career as an artist to become a long-term guest with Adela and the *objets d'art* at Poynton: 'She had not indeed struggled with a brush since her visit to Waterbath .... Poynton, moreover, had been an impossible place for producing; no art more active than a Buddhistic contemplation could lift its head there' (SP 101). Fleda,

---

[84]   Marx, *Capital*, p. 390.
[85]   Cited in Ledger, p. 17.

then, works within a domestic context as her friend's ambassador and 'envoy' in the family feud over Poynton's spoils (SP 95), while the latter plans to 'employ' Fleda as the curator of Poynton on her marriage to Owen. At times in the novel, Fleda is represented as a very humble labourer, for she also works as a seamstress, embroidering a cloth as a wedding present and buying and sewing the materials for her sister Maggie's wedding clothes (SP 40–41). She even imagines herself descending the social scale when she gazes in shop windows like 'a servant-girl taking her "afternoon" … perhaps some day she would resemble such a person still more closely' (SP 101). At the end of the novel she does indeed become a sort of servant, a companion to Adela. Ultimately, Fleda has 'neither a home nor an outlook – nothing in all the wide world' (SP 99), as Owen tactlessly states: 'You don't – a – live anywhere in particular, do you?' (SP 67).

Mrs Gereth's work is managerial, she is an organizer who arranges 'a little army of workers' in transferring her treasures from Poynton to Ricks and back again (SP 50); however, she is also prepared to do manual labour, having 'lifted tons' herself (SP 51). In the battle for the spoils, she is like a New Woman, a military leader directing her campaign, at times she is a revolutionary (SP 55) or a martyr (SP 77). Her main work, however, is for her collection (SP 20), an artist creating a 'complete work of art' (SP 7) and, once it is complete, she works as the curator and cataloguer of her museum. Yet while Mrs Gereth first appears as 'one of those who impose' (SP 8), her confidence is based on her mistaken notion that she can retain control of the property. Fleda realizes that Mrs Gereth is made 'concrete and distinct' (SP 100) only in relation to Poynton and its antiques. Once she has lost her battle she becomes as insubstantial as Fleda herself, her face 'a dead grey mask. A tired old woman … with empty hands in her lap' (SP 164). For Mrs Gereth, the loss of her possessions equals the loss of her identity and she retreats to 'the empty house at Ricks' (SP 165). Fleda's failure is as complete as her friend's; she even fails to own the Maltese cross. The significance of this cross, the 'gem of the collection' (SP 179), is manifold. Owen's offer of this gift emphasizes the futility of the women's battle, for his continuous ownership of the spoils is asserted when he asks Fleda to take 'something of *mine*' (SP 178: emphasis added) from Poynton. He also emphasizes the value of portable property, suggesting that 'If it happens to be of such a sort that you can take immediate possession of it – carry it right away with you – so much the better' (SP 179). Fleda imagines herself returning home with this spoil, 'with her trophy under her cloak' (SP 181). Yet her drawn-out fantasies of possession ultimately jeopardize her ownership of the 'gem', for she hesitates for more than a month, enjoying the 'secret rapture' she feels, while becoming 'quite proudly erect' (SP 182) at the thought of her ownership, and here she almost joins the ranks of the novel's two 'phallic' New Women. Property, James suggests, functions as a sort of social phallus and it is significant that Mona is the only one of the three women who knows how to wield it successfully.

At the end of the novel there is nothing left for Fleda but to return empty-handed to her dependent life with Mrs Gereth. Indeed, the only 'spoil' Fleda retains from the conflict is the gift bought for her by Owen, a 'small pin-cushion costing sixpence, in which the letter F was marked out with pins' (SP 43), a reminder of her continual need to labour and another covert Victorian reference to pin money, with its connotation of female dependency.[86] Mrs Gereth's defeat is not ultimately complete, however, for she does retain at Ricks four pieces of her Poynton collection. She may even assert the ultimate right of the property owner as indicated by Hume: the right to 'move, alter or destroy it', for the destruction of Poynton and its treasures is foreshadowed earlier in the novel when Mrs Gereth tells Fleda, 'Rather than make them over to a woman ignorant and vulgar I think I'd deface them with my own hands' (SP 20).[87] In defiance of the English laws of property, and more than prepared to 'tussle' with the police (SP 37), Adela may have asserted her 'natural' rights as owner (although James is not, of course, explicit about this). Her propensity to take militant action also points towards those later militant women of the early twentieth century: the suffragettes.

After *The Mill on the Floss* George Eliot did not depict the destruction of life and property as an inevitable outcome for her heroines. They live on, and some of them even prosper. Yet, as we have seen, Henry James's fiction of the 1880s and 1890s resembles Dickens's, with property narratives culminating in the wholesale destruction of women's possessions. Just as Lady Dedlock dies bereft of property, Mrs Clennam's house falls down, and Miss Havisham's Satis House is dismantled, James also lingers on the destruction of the Aspern papers and the burning of the spoils of Poynton. Yet, while the violent crises of Dickens's novels are unequivocal, in the sense that the reader is allowed to witness scenes of destitution and property in fragments, James's endings are decidedly ambiguous. Tina says she has burned the love letters, but the reader has to take her word for this, and Mrs Gereth may have rescued her spoils before setting fire to Poynton. For James, the outcome of the Victorian property plot cannot be certain. His female owners are more than capable of stealing their own property, and, as this book has attempted to demonstrate, evasions of the law were not impossible for the determined woman faced with dispossession.

---

[86]   See Chapter 3 for a discussion of pin-money in relation to Dickens.

[87]   See Hume, p. 549.

Works Cited

Ackroyd, Peter, *Dickens* (London: Minerva, 1991).

Agnew, Jean-Christophe, 'The Consuming Vision of Henry James' in *The Culture of Consumption: Critical Essays in American History, 1880–1980*, Richard Wightman Fox and T. Jackson Lears (eds) (New York: Pantheon, 1983).

Appadurai, Arjun (ed.), *The Social Life of Things: Commodities in Cultural Perspective* (Cambridge: Cambridge University Press, 1986).

Apter, Emily, *Feminizing the Fetish: Psychoanalysis and Narrative Obsession in Turn-of-the-Century France* (Ithaca and London: Cornell University Press, 1991).

———, and William Pietz (eds), *Fetishism as Cultural Discourse* (Ithaca and London: Cornell University Press, 1993).

Arendt, Hannah, *The Human Condition* (Chicago: University of Chicago Press, 1969).

Arnold, Jean, 'Cameo Appearances: The Discourse of Jewelry in *Middlemarch*', *Victorian Literature and Culture* 30:1 (2002): 265–88.

Ashton, Rosemary, *George Eliot: A Life* (Harmondsworth: Penguin, 1996).

Austen, Jane, *Mansfield Park*, James Kinsley (ed.), Introduction by Jane Stabler (Oxford: Oxford University Press, 2003).

[Bagehot, Walter,] 'Charles Dickens', *National Review* (October 1858): reprinted in Philip Collins (ed.), *Charles Dickens: The Critical Heritage* (London: Routledge and Kegan Paul, 1986).

Baker, J.H., *An Introduction to English Legal History*, 4th ed. (Oxford: Oxford University Press, 2007).

Barthes, Roland, 'World as Object' in *Calligram*, Norman Bryson (ed.) (Cambridge: Cambridge University Press, 1988).

———, 'The Reality Effect', *The Rustle of Language*, Richard Howard (trans.) (Berkeley: University of California Press, 1989).

Bauer, Carol and Laurence Ritt (eds), *Free and Ennobled: Source Readings in the Development of Victorian Feminism* (Oxford and New York: Pergamon Press, 1979).

Beer, Gillian, *Arguing with the Past: Essays in Narrative Form from Woolf to Sydney* (London: Routledge, 1989).

———, *George Eliot* (Brighton: Harvester, 1986).

Bell, Millicent, *Meaning in Henry James* (Cambridge: Harvard University Press, 1991).

Benjamin, Walter, 'The Work of Art in the Age of Mechanical Reproduction' in *Illuminations*, Hannah Arendt (ed.) (London: Fontana, 1992).

Berg, Maxine, *Luxury and Pleasure in Eighteenth-Century Britain* (Oxford: Oxford University Press, 2005).

Berry, Christopher J. 'Property and Possession: Two Replies to Locke – Hume and Hegel', in J. Roland Pennock and John W. Chapman (eds), *Property* [NOMOS XXII] (New York: New York University Press, 1980).

Betjemann, Peter, 'Henry James' Shop Talk: *The Spoils of Poynton* and the Language of Artisanship', *American Literary Realism*, 40:3 (Spring 2008): 49–58 .

Blackall, Jean Frantz, 'The Experimental Period', Daniel Mark Fogel (ed.) *A Companion to Henry James Studies* (Westport and London: Greenwood Press, 1993).

Blackstone, William, *Blackstone's Commentaries on the Laws of England*, 2 vols, Wayne Morrison (ed.) (London and Sydney: Cavendish Publishing, 2001).

Boswell, James, *The Life of Johnson*, R.W. Chapman (ed.) (Oxford: Oxford University Press, 1998).

Bourdieu, Pierre, 'The Invention of the Artist's Life', trans. Erec R. Koch, *Yale French Studies*, 73 (1987): 75–103.

Bowen, John, *Other Dickens: From Pickwick to Chuzzlewit* (Oxford: Oxford University Press, 2000).

Bowlby, Rachel, *Just Looking: Consumer Culture in Dreiser, Gissing and Zola* (New York: Methuen, 1985).

Bradbury, Nicola, 'Introduction', Charles Dickens, *Bleak House*, Nicola Bradbury (ed.) (London: Penguin, 2003).

Braddon, M.E., *Lady Audley's Secret*, David Skilton (ed.) (Oxford: Oxford University Press, 1991).

Briggs, Asa, *Victorian People* (London: Penguin, 1965).

———, *Victorian Things* (London: B.T. Batsford, 1988).

Brooks, Peter, *The Melodramatic Imagination: Balzac, Henry James, Melodrama and the Mode of Excess* (New Haven and London: Yale University Press, 1976).

Brown, Bill, 'Thing Theory', *Critical Inquiry*, 28:1 (Autumn 2001): 1–22.

———, *A Sense of Things: The Object Matter of American Literature* (Chicago: University of Chicago Press, 2003).

Burke, Edmund, *Reflections on the Revolution in France and on the Proceedings in Certain Societies in London Relative to that Event. In a Letter to Have been Sent to a Gentleman in Paris* (London: J. Dodsley, 1790).

Cain, Lynn, *Dickens, Family, Authorship: Psychoanalytic Perspectives on Kinship and Creativity* (Aldershot: Ashgate, 2008).

Caird, Mona, 'Marriage' in Sally Ledger and Roger Luckhurst (eds), *The Fin de Siècle: A Reader in Cultural History* (Oxford: Oxford University Press, 2000).

Campbell, Colin, *The Romantic Ethic and the Spirit of Modern Consumerism* (Oxford: Blackwell, 1987).

Cannon, Kelly, *Henry James and Masculinity: The Man at the Margins* (New York: St Martin's Press, 1994).

Carrier, James, *Gifts and Commodities: Exchange and Western Capitalism Since 1700* (London: Routledge, 1995).

Certeau, Michel de, *The Practice of Everyday Life*, Steven Rendall (trans.) (Berkeley, Los Angeles and London: University of California Press, 1988).

Church, Joseph, 'Writing and the Dispossession of the Woman in *The Aspern Papers*', *American Imago*, 47:1 (Spring 1990): 23–42.

Collins, Philip (ed.), *Dickens: The Critical Heritage* (London: Routledge and Kegan Paul, 1986).

Conrad, Peter, *The Victorian Treasure-House* (London: Collins, 1973).

Coulson, Victoria, *Henry James, Women and Realism* (Cambridge: Cambridge University Press, 2007).

Cranston, Maurice, *John Locke: A Biography* (London: Longman, 1957).

Csikszentmihalyi, Mihaly and Eugene Rochberg-Halton, *The Meaning of Things: Domestic Symbols and the Self* (Cambridge: Cambridge University Press, 1981).

Davidoff, Leonore and Catherine Hall, *Family Fortunes: Men and Women of the English Middle Class, 1780–1850* (London: Hutchinson, 1987).

Dever, Carolyn, *Death and the Mother from Dickens to Freud: Victorian Fiction and the Anxiety of Origins* (Cambridge: Cambridge University Press, 1998).

Dickens, Charles, *The Mystery of Edwin Drood*, Margaret Cardwell (ed.) (Oxford: Oxford University Press, 1982).

———, *The Pilgrim Edition of the Letters of Charles Dickens*, 12 vols, Graham Storey (ed.) (Oxford: Clarendon Press, 1982).

———, *Little Dorrit*, John Holloway (ed.) (London: Penguin, 1987).

———, *Oliver Twist*, Kathleen Tillotson (ed.) (Clarendon: Oxford University Press, 1988).

———, *Our Mutual Friend*, Michael Cotsell (ed.) (Oxford: Oxford University Press, 1989).

———, *Great Expectations*, David Trotter and Charlotte Mitchell (eds) (London: Penguin, 1996).

———, *Bleak House*, Nicola Bradbury (ed.) (London: Penguin, 2003).

Dolin, Tim, *Mistress of the House: Women of Property in the Victorian Novel* (Aldershot: Ashgate, 1997).

Dowling, Linda, 'The Decadent and the New Woman', *Nineteenth-Century Fiction* 33:4 (1979): 434–53.

Edel, Leon, *The Life of Henry James: The Treacherous Years*, vol. 4, *The Life of Henry James* (Philadelphia: J.B. Lippincott, 1969).

———, *The Life of Henry James*, 2 vols, (London: Penguin, 1977).

——— (ed.), *Henry James Letters*, 4 vols, (Cambridge: Harvard University Press, 1975).

Eliot, George, *The George Eliot Letters*, Gordon S. Haight (ed.), 8 vols (London: Oxford University Press, 1956).

———, *The Mill on the Floss*, A.S. Byatt (ed.) (Harmondsworth: Penguin, 1985).

———, *Daniel Deronda*, Graham Handley (ed.) (Oxford: Oxford University Press, 1988)

———, *Romola*, Dorothea Barrett (ed.) (London: Penguin, 1996).

———, *The Journals of George Eliot*, Margaret Harris and Judith Johnston (eds), (Cambridge: Cambridge University Press, 1998).

———, *Middlemarch*, David Carroll (ed.) (Oxford: Oxford University Press, 1998).

Erikson, Amy Louise, *Women and Property in Early Modern England* (London: Routledge, 1993).

Finn, Margot, 'Women, Consumption and Coverture in England, c.1760–1860', *The Historical Journal*, 39:3 (Sept. 1996): 704–5.

———, *The Character of Credit: Personal Debt in English Culture, 1740–1914* (Cambridge: Cambridge University Press, 2003).

Flannery, Denis, *Henry James: A Certain Illusion* (Aldershot: Ashgate, 2000).

Flaubert, Gustave, *Madame Bovary*, Gerard Hopkins (trans.), Introduction by Anita Brookner (Oxford: Oxford University Press, 1999).

Flint, Kate, 'The Materiality of *Middlemarch*' in Karen Chase (ed.), *Middlemarch in the Twenty-First Century* (Oxford: Oxford University Press, 2006).

Foster, Dennis, *Sublime Enjoyment: On the Perverse Motive in American Literature* (Cambridge: Cambridge University Press, 1997).

Foster, Hal, 'The Art of Fetishism: Notes on Dutch Still Life' in Emily Apter and William Pietz (eds), *Fetishism as Cultural Discourse* (Ithaca and London: Cornell University Press, 1993).

Freedgood, Elaine, *The Ideas in Things: Fugitive Meaning in the Victorian Novel* (Chicago: University of Chicago Press, 2006).

Freud, Sigmund, 'Fetishism' in *On Sexuality*, Angela Richards (ed.), James Strachey (trans.), vol. 7, The Pelican Freud Library (London: Penguin, 1977).

———, 'The Uncanny' (1919), reprinted in Julie Rivkin and Michael Ryan (eds) *Literary Theory: An Anthology*, 2nd ed. (Oxford: Blackwell, 2004).

Gates, Sarah, '"A Difference of Native Language": Gender, Genre and Realism in *Daniel Deronda*', *ELH*, 68 (2001): 699–724.

Gordon, Lyndall, *A Private Life of Henry James: Two Women and his Art* (London: Chatto and Windus, 1998).

Graham, Kenneth, *Henry James: The Drama of Fulfilment: An Approach to the Novels* (Oxford: Clarendon Press, 1975).

———, *Henry James: A Literary Life* (Basingstoke: Macmillan, 1995).

Graham, Wendy, 'A Narrative History of Class Consciousness', *boundary 2*, 15 (Autumn/Winter 1986–87): 41–68.

———, *Henry James's Thwarted Love* (Stanford: Stanford University Press, 1999).

Griffin, Ben, 'Class, Gender, and Liberalism in Parliament, 1868–1882: The Case of the Married Women's Property Acts', *The Historical Journal*, 46:1 (2003): 59–87.

Grootenboer, Hanneke, *Rhetoric of Perspective: Realism and Illusionism in Seventeenth-Century Dutch Still-Life Painting* (Chicago and London: University of Chicago Press, 2005).

Habeggar, Alfred, *Henry James and the Woman Business* (Cambridge: Cambridge University Press, 1989).

Hadley, Tessa, *Henry James and the Imagination of Pleasure* (Cambridge: Cambridge University Press, 2002).

Hamilton, Susan, *Frances Power Cobbe and Victorian Feminism* (Basingstoke: Palgrave, 2006).

———— (ed.), *Criminals, Idiots, Women and Minors: Victorian Writing by Women on Women* (Ontario: Broadview Press, 1996).

Haralson, Eric, *Henry James and Queer Modernity* (Cambridge: Cambridge University Press, 2003).

Hart, Kevin, *Samuel Johnson and the Culture of Property* (Cambridge: Cambridge University Press, 1999).

Hegel, G.W.F., *Elements of the Philosophy of Right*, Allen W. Wood (ed.), H.B. Nisbet (trans.) (Cambridge: Cambridge University Press, 1991).

Helsinger, Elizabeth K., Robin L. Sheets and William Veeder (eds), *The Woman Question: Society and Literature in Britain and America, 1837–1883*, vol. 2 (Manchester: Manchester University Press, 1983).

Henry, Nancy, '"Ladies Do It?": Victorian Women Investors in Fact and Fiction', in Francis O'Gorman (ed.), *Victorian Literature and Finance* (Oxford: Oxford University Press, 2007).

Hepburn, Allan, 'Introduction', *Troubled Legacies: Narrative and Inheritance* Allan Hepburn (ed.) (Toronto and London: University of Toronto Press, 2007).

Hertz, Neil, *George Eliot's Pulse* (Stanford: Stanford University Press, 2003).

Hibbert, Christopher, *The House of Medici: Its Rise and Fall* (London: Allen Lane, Penguin, 1975).

Hicks, Michael A., *Richard III* (Stroud: Tempus, 2001).

Hinshelwood, R.D., *A Dictionary of Kleinian Thought* (London: Free Association Books, 1991).

Hobsbawm, Eric, *The Age of Capital, 1848–1875* (London: Abacus, 2004).

Holcombe, Lee, *Wives and Property: Reform of the Married Women's Property Law in Nineteenth-Century England* (Toronto and Buffalo: University of Toronto Press, 1983).

Horne, Philip (ed.), *Henry James: A Life in Letters* (London: Allen Lane, 1999).

Hoskins, Janet, 'Agency, Biography and Objects', in *Handbook of Material Culture*, Christopher Tilley et al. (eds) (London: Sage, 2006).

Howell, Martha C., 'Fixing Movables: Gifts by Testament in Late Medieval Douai', *Past and Present*, 150 (February 1996): 3–45.

Hume, David, *A Treatise of Human Nature*, Ernest C. Mosner (ed.) (London: Penguin, 1969).

Ingham, Patricia, *Dickens, Women and Language* (New York and London: Harvester Wheatsheaf, 1992).

Ingram, Jill Phillips, *Idioms of Self-Interest: Credit, Identity, and Property in English Renaissance Literature* (London: Routledge, 2006).

Izzo, Donatella, 'Nothing Personal: Women Characters, Gender Ideology, and Literary Representation' in *A Companion to Henry James*, Greg W. Zacharias (ed.) (Oxford: Blackwell, 2008): 343–59.

[James, Henry,] 'Modern Women', *The Nation* (October 22, 1868): 332–4.

————, 'The Future of the Novel: An Analysis and Forecast by Henry James', *New York Times*, 11 August 1900; reprinted at: http://query.nytimes.com/men/archive.

————, 'Paste' in *Fourteen Stories by Henry James*, David Garnett (ed.) (London: Rupert Hart-Davies, 1946).

————, *Henry James: Letters*, 4 vols, Leon Edel (ed.) (Cambridge: Harvard University Press 1975).

————, *The Notebooks of Henry James*, F.O. Mattiessen and Kenneth B. Murdock (eds) (Chicago and London: University of Chicago Press, 1981).

————, *The Spoils of Poynton*, Bernard Richards (ed.) (Oxford: Oxford University Press, 1982).

————, *The Turn of the Screw and The Aspern Papers*, Anthony Curtis (ed.) (London: Penguin, 1986).

————, *The Portrait of a Lady*, Nicola Bradbury (ed.) (Oxford: Oxford University Press, 1998).

Jameson, Frederic, *The Political Unconscious: Narrative as a Socially Symbolic Act* (London and New York: Routledge, 2007).

Jongh, E. de, *Questions of Meaning, Theme and Motif in Dutch Seventeenth-Century Painting* (Leiden: Primavera Pers, 2000).

Kaplan, Cora, *Victoriana: Histories, Fictions, Criticism* (Edinburgh: Edinburgh University Press, 2007).

Kent, Susan Kingsley, *Sex and Suffrage in Britain, 1860–1914* (Princeton: Princeton University Press, 1987).

Kopytoff, Igor, 'The Cultural Biography of Things: Commoditization as Process' in Arjun Appadurai (ed.), *The Social Life of Things: Commodities in Cultural Perspective* (Cambridge: Cambridge University Press, 1986).

Kreisel, Deanna, 'Superfluity and Suction: The Problem with Saving in *The Mill on the Floss*', *Novel*, 35:1 (Fall 2001): 69–103.

Langbauer, Laurie, *Women and Romance: The Consolations of Gender in the English Novel* (Ithaca and London: Cornell University Press, 1990).

Langland, Elizabeth, *Nobody's Angels: Middle-Class Women and Domestic Ideology in Victorian Culture* (Ithaca and London: Cornell University Press, 1995).

Lauretis, Teresa de, *Technologies of Gender: Essays on Theory, Film and Fiction* (Bloomington and Indianapolis: Indiana University Press, 1987).

Ledger, Sally, *The New Woman: Fiction and feminism at the fin de siècle* (Manchester: Manchester University Press, 1997).

————, and Roger Luckhurst (eds), *The Fin de Siècle: A Reader in Cultural History* (Oxford: Oxford University Press, 2000).

Levine, Philippa, *Victorian Feminism, 1850–1900* (London: Hutchinson, 1987).

Levy, Eric P., 'Property Morality in *The Mill on the Floss*', *Victorians Institute Journal*, 31 (2003): 173–86.

Lindner, Christoph, *Fictions of Commodity Culture: From the Victorian to the Postmodern* (Aldershot: Ashgate, 2003).

Litvak, Joseph, *Caught in the Act: Theatricality in the Nineteenth-Century English Novel* (Berkeley: University of California Press, 1992).

Locke, John, *Two Treatises of Government* in *Political Writings*, David Wootton (ed.) (London: Penguin, 1993).

Lodge, David, *Author, Author* (London: Faber, 2004).

Logan, Thad, *The Victorian Parlor* (Cambridge: Cambridge University Press, 2001).

McCracken, Grant, *Culture and Consumption: New Approaches to the Symbolic Character of Consumer Goods and Activities* (Bloomington and Indianapolis Indiana University Press, 1988).

McDonagh, Josephine, *George Eliot* (Plymouth: Northcote House, 1997).

Macleod, Dianne Sachko, *Enchanted Lives, Enchanted Objects: American Women Collectors and the Making of Culture, 1800–1940* (Berkeley and Los Angeles: University of California Press, 2008).

MacPherson, C.B., *The Political Theory of Possessive Individualism: Hobbes to Locke* (Oxford: Oxford University Press, 1962).

——— (ed.), *Property: Mainstream and Critical Opinions* (Toronto: University of Toronto Press, 1978).

Maine, Henry, *Ancient Law: Its Connection with the Early History of Society and its Relation to Modern Ideas* (London: John Murray, 1920).

Marcus, Sharon, *Between Women: Friendship, Desire and Marriage in Victorian England* (Princeton: Princeton University Press, 2007).

Marx, Karl, *The Economic and Philosophic Manuscripts of 1844*, Martin Milligan (trans.) (Moscow: Foreign Languages Publishing House, 1961).

———, *Capital*, David McLellan (ed.) (Oxford: Oxford University Press, 1999).

Maurer, Sara L., in 'The Nation's Wife: England's Vicarious Enjoyment in Anthony Trollope's The Palliser Novels' in *Troubled Legacies: Narrative and Inheritance*, Allan Hepburn (ed.) (Toronto and London: University of Toronto Press, 2007).

Mendelssohn, Michèle, *Henry James, Oscar Wilde and Aesthetic Culture* (Edinburgh: Edinburgh University Press, 2007).

Menon, Patricia, *Austen, Eliot, Charlotte Brontë and the Mentor-Lover* (Basingstoke: Palgrave, 2003).

Merish, Lori, *Sentimental Materialism: Gender, Commodity Culture and Nineteenth-Century American Literature* (Durham and London: Duke University Press, 2000).

Miller, Andrew H., *Novels Behind Glass: Commodity Culture and Victorian Narrative* (Cambridge: Cambridge University Press, 1995).

Miller, D.A., *Narrative and Its Discontents: Problems of Closure in the Traditional Novel* (Princeton: Princeton University Press, 1981).

———, *The Novel and the Police* (Berkeley: University of California Press, 1988).

Miller, J. Hillis, *Literature as Conduct: Speech Acts in Henry James* (New York: Fordham University Press, 2005).

Minogue, Kenneth R., 'The Concept of Property and Its Contemporary Significance' in J. Roland Pennock and John W. Chapman (eds), *Property* [NOMOS XXII] (New York: New York University Press, 1980).

Moers, Ellen, '*Bleak House*: The Agitating Women', *The Dickensian*, 69:1 (January 1973): 13–24.

Morris, Pam, *Imagining Inclusive Society in 19th-Century Novels: The Code of Sincerity in the Public Sphere* (Baltimore and London: The Johns Hopkins University Press, 2004).

Morris, R.J., *Men, Women and Property in England, 1780–1870* (Cambridge: Cambridge University Press, 2005).

Mulvey, Laura, *Fetishism and Curiosity* (London: British Film Institute, 1996).

Munt, Sally R., *Queer Attachments: The Cultural Politics of Shame* (Aldershot: Ashgate, 2007).

Nestor, Pauline, *George Eliot* (Basingstoke: Palgrave, 2002).

Nightingale, Florence, *Cassandra*, reprinted in M.H. Abrams (ed.), *The Norton Anthology of English Literature*, vol. 2 (New York and London: Norton, 2006).

Nixon, Mignon, 'Dream Dust', *October*, 116 (Spring 2006): 63–86.

Nunokawa, Jeff, *The Afterlife of Property: Domestic Security and the Victorian Novel* (Princeton: Princeton University Press, 1994).

Oliphant, Margaret, 'The Laws Concerning Women', *Blackwood's*, vol. 76 (1856): 379–87.

Olivecrona, Karl, 'Locke's Theory of Appropriation', *Philosophical Quarterly*, 24:96 (1974): 220–34.

Otten, Thomas J., '*The Spoils of Poynton* and the Properties of Touch', *American Literature*, 71:2 (June 1999): 263–90.

Parieu, M. Esquirou de, 'On Taxes Upon Enjoyments', *Journal of the Statistical Society of London*, 24:2 (June 1861): 167–97.

[Parkinson, J.C.,] 'Slaves of the Ring', *All The Year Round* (4 July 1868): 85–6.

Paxton, Nancy, *George Eliot and Herbert Spencer: Feminism, Evolutionism and the Reconstruction of Gender* (Princeton: Princeton University Press, 1991).

Pearce, Susan M., *On Collecting: An Investigation into Collecting in the European Tradition* (London: Routledge, 1995).

Pettitt, Clare, 'Monstrous Displacements: Anxieties of Exchange in *Great Expectations*', *Dickens Studies Annual*, 30 (2001): 243–62.

———, *Patent Inventions: Intellectual Property and the Victorian Novel* (Oxford: Oxford University Press, 2004).

———, 'On Stuff', *19: Interdisciplinary Studies in the Long Nineteenth Century*. http://www.19.bbk.ac.uk (Spring, 2008).

Pietz, William, 'Fetishism and Materialism: The Limits of Theory in Marx', in Emily Apter and William Pietz (eds), *Fetishism as Cultural Discourse* (Ithaca and London: Cornell University Press, 1993).

Pigeon, Elaine, *Queer Impressions: Henry James's Art of Fiction* (London and New York: Routledge, 2005).

Pinch, Adela, 'Stealing Happiness: Shoplifting in Early Nineteenth-Century England', in Patricia Spyer (ed.), *Border Fetishisms: Material Objects in Unstable Spaces* (New York and London: Routledge, 1998).

Plotz, John, *Portable Property: Victorian Culture on the Move* (Princeton: Princeton University Press, 2008).

Poole, Adrian, *Henry James* (Hemel Hempsted and London: Harvester Wheatsheaf, 1991).

Poovey, Mary, *Uneven Developments: The Ideological Work of Gender in Mid-Victorian England* (London: Virago, 1989).

———, *Genres of the Credit Economy: Mediating Value in Eighteenth- and Nineteenth-Century Britain* (Chicago and London: University of Chicago Press, 2008).

Psomiades, Kathy Alexis, 'Heterosexual Exchange and Other Victorian Fictions: *The Eustace Diamonds* and Victorian Anthropology', *Novel*, 33:1 (Autumn 1999): 93–118.

Pykett, Lyn, *The Improper Feminine: The Woman's Sensation Novel and the New Woman Writing* (London: Routledge, 1992).

———, *Charles Dickens* (Basingstoke: Palgrave, 2002).

Radin, Margaret Jane, *Reinterpreting Property* (Chicago and London: University of Chicago Press, 1993).

Redfern, Walter D., 'People and Things in Flaubert', *The French Review* (Winter 1971): 79–88.

Rignall, John (ed.), *Oxford Reader's Companion to George Eliot* (Oxford: Oxford University Press, 2000).

Riley, James C., 'A Widening Market in Consumer Goods' in Evan Cameron (ed.), *Early Modern Europe: An Oxford History* (Oxford: Oxford University Press, 2001).

Rosenman, Ellen Bayuk, 'More Stories About Clothing and Furniture: Realism and Bad Commodities', in Christine L. Krueger (ed.), *Functions of Victorian Culture at the Present Time* (Athens: Ohio State University Press, 2002).

Roth, Alan, 'He Thought He Was Right (But Wasn't): Property Law in Anthony Trollope's *The Eustace Diamonds*', *Stanford Law Review*, 44 (1992): 879–97.

Rowe, John Carlos, *The Theoretical Dimensions of Henry James* (London: Methuen, 1984).

Rubin, Gayle, 'The Traffic in Women: Notes on the "Political Economy" of Sex' in *Toward an Anthropology of Women*, Rayna R. Reiter (ed.) (New York: Monthly Review Press, 1975).

Sadoff, Dianne F., *Monsters of Affection: Dickens, Eliot and Brontë on Fatherhood* (Baltimore: The Johns Hopkins University Press, 1982).

Sadrin, Anny, *Parentage and Inheritance in the Novels of Charles Dickens* (Cambridge: Cambridge University Press, 1994).

Sarris, Fotios, 'Fetishism in *The Spoils of Poynton*', *Nineteenth-Century Literature*, 51:1 (1996): 53–83.

Schlicke, Paul (ed.), *Oxford Reader's Companion to Dickens* (Oxford: Oxford University Press, 1999).

Schmidgen, Wolfram, *Eighteenth-Century Fiction and the Law of Property* (Cambridge: Cambridge University Press, 2002).

Schor, Hilary M., *Dickens and the Daughter of the House* (Cambridge: Cambridge University Press, 1999).

Schwenger, Peter, *The Tears of Things: Melancholy and Physical Objects* (Minneapolis and London: University of Minnesota Press, 2006).

Scott, Joan W., 'Gender: A Useful Category of Historical Analysis', *The American Historical Review*, 91:5 (December 1986): 1053–75.

Sedgwick, Eve Kosofsky, *Touching Feeling: Affect, Pedagogy, Performativity* (Durham: Duke University Press, 2003).

Shanley, Mary Lyndon, *Feminism, Marriage and the Law in Victorian England, 1850–1895* (London: I.B. Tauris, 1989).

Shaw, Harry E., *Narrating Reality: Austen, Scott, Eliot* (Ithaca and London: Cornell University Press, 1999).

Showalter, Elaine, *Sexual Anarchy: Gender and Culture at the Fin de Siècle* (London: Bloomsbury, 1991).

Simmel, Georg, *The Philosophy of Money*, Tom Bottomore and Dan Frisby (trans.) (Boston: Routledge and Kegan Paul, 1978).

Slater, Michael, *Dickens and Women* (London: J.M. Dent, 1983).

Smith-Rosenberg, Carroll, *Disorderly Conduct: Visions of Gender in Victorian America* (New York: Alfred A. Knopf, 1985).

Snyder, Katherine V., *Bachelors, Manhood and the Novel, 1850–1925* (Cambridge: Cambridge University Press, 1999).

Stallybrass, Peter, 'Marx's Coat' in Spyer (ed.), *Border Fetishisms: Material Objects in Unstable Places* (New York and London: Routledge, 1998).

Stevens, Hugh, *Henry James and Sexuality* (Cambridge: Cambridge University Press, 1998).

Stewart, Susan, *On Longing: Narratives of the Miniature, the Gigantic, the Souvenir, the Collection* (Durham and London: Duke University Press, 1993).

Surridge, Lisa, 'Narrative Time, History and Feminism in Mona Caird's, *The Daughters of Danaus*', *Women's Writing*, 12:1 (March 2005): 127–41.

Tambling, Jeremy, *Henry James* (Basingstoke: Macmillan, 2000).

Tanner, Tony, *Adultery and the Novel: Contract and Transgression* (Baltimore and London: Johns Hopkins University Press, 1979).

Thomas, Paul, 'Property's Properties: From Hegel to Locke', *Representations*, 84 (Autumn 2003): 30–43.

Trentmann, Frank, 'Materiality in the Future of History: Things, Practices and Politics', *Journal of British Studies*, 48 (April 2009): 283–307.

Trollope, Anthony, *Framley Parsonage*, P.D. Edwards (ed.) (Oxford: Oxford University Press, 1988).

———, *The Eustace Diamonds*, W.J. McCormack (ed.) (Oxford: Oxford University Press, 1992).

Trotter, David, 'Household Clearances in Victorian Fiction', *19: Interdisciplinary Studies in the Long Nineteenth Century*, 6 (2008). http://www.19.bbk.ac.uk.

Uglow, Jennifer, *George Eliot* (London: Virago, 1987).

Van Ghent, Dorothy, 'The Dickens World: A View from Todgers's' in *Dickens: A Collection of Critical Essays*, Martin Price (ed.) (New Jersey: Prentice-Hall, 1987).

Vanden Bossche, Chris R., 'Class Discourse and Popular Agency in *Bleak House*', *Victorian Studies*, 47:1 (Autumn 2004): 7–31.

Veblen, Thorstein, *Theory of the Leisure Class* (London: Unwin, 1970).

Vries, Jan de, *The Industrious Revolution: Consumer Behavior and the Household Economy, 1650 to the Present* (Cambridge: Cambridge University Press, 2008).

Walsh, Susan, 'Bodies of Capital: *Great Expectations* and the Climacteric Economy', *Victorian Studies*, 37:1 (Autumn 1993): 73–98.

Weiner, Annette B., *Inalienable Possessions: The Paradox of Keeping-While-Giving* (Berkeley and Los Angeles: University of California Press, 1992).

Weisser, Susan Ostrov, 'Gwendolen's Hidden Wound: Sexual Possibilities and Impossibilities in *Daniel Deronda*', *Modern Language Studies*, 20:3 (Summer 1990): 3–13.

Welsh, Alexander, 'The Later Novels' in George Levine (ed.), *The Cambridge Companion to George Eliot* (Cambridge: Cambridge University Press, 2001).

West, Shearer, 'The Visual Arts' in *The Cambridge Companion to the Fin de Siècle*, Gail Marshall (ed.) (Cambridge: Cambridge University Press, 2007).

Whelan, Frederick G., 'Property as Artifice: Hume and Blackstone' in J. Roland Pennock and John W. Chapman (eds), *Property* [NOMOS XXII] (New York: New York University Press, 1980).

Wilde, Oscar, *The Importance of Being Earnest* in S. Greenblatt (ed.), *The Norton Anthology of English Literature*, 8th ed. (New York: Norton, 2006).

Willburn, Sarah A., *Possessed Victorians: Extra Spheres in Nineteenth-Century Mystical Writings* (Aldershot: Ashgate, 2006).

Wilt, Judith, '"He Would Come Back": The Fathers of Daughters in *Daniel Deronda*', *Nineteenth-Century Literature*, 42:3 (1987): 313–18.

Zimmerman, Bonnie S., '"Radiant as a Diamond": George Eliot, Jewelry and the Female Role', *Criticism*, 19:3 (Summer 1977): 212–22.

Index